T0338622

BASICS OF CONTEMPORARY CRYPTOGRAPHY FOR IT PRACTITIONERS

Series on Coding Theory and Cryptology

Editors: Harald Niederreiter *(National University of Singapore, Singapore)* and
San Ling *(Nanyang Technological University, Singapore)*

Published

Vol. 1   Basics of Contemporary Cryptography for IT Practitioners
         B. Ryabko and A. Fionov

Series on Coding Theory and Cryptology – Vol. 1

BASICS OF CONTEMPORARY CRYPTOGRAPHY FOR IT PRACTITIONERS

Boris Ryabko
Andrey Fionov

Siberian State University of Telecommunications
and Computer Science, Russia

 **World Scientific**

NEW JERSEY • LONDON • SINGAPORE • BEIJING • SHANGHAI • HONG KONG • TAIPEI • CHENNAI

Published by

World Scientific Publishing Co. Pte. Ltd.

5 Toh Tuck Link, Singapore 596224

USA office: 27 Warren Street, Suite 401-402, Hackensack, NJ 07601

UK office: 57 Shelton Street, Covent Garden, London WC2H 9HE

British Library Cataloguing-in-Publication Data
A catalogue record for this book is available from the British Library.

ISBN-13 978-981-256-405-4
ISBN-10 981-256-405-5

Printed in Singapore

Preface

For centuries, cryptography, as the science of ciphering or covering information from unauthorised use, had been employed mainly for protecting messages communicated between the military or governmental officials. Therefore, the circle of people employing cryptography was quite restricted and the very methods of this science secret. However, in the last decades, when the mankind has entered the information society stage, cryptographic methods of information protection become widely used, serving, in the first place, business needs. At that, not only inter-bank payments carried out over computer networks are meant or, say, electronic exchanges operating via the Internet, but also numerous transactions in which millions of "ordinary" people are involved every day, such as payments by credit cards, transferring wages onto bank accounts, ordering tickets and buying goods over the Internet, *etc.* It is a natural demand that all these transactions, as well as mobile phone conversations and electronic mail, be secured against dishonest or just overly inquisitive persons and organisations. Therefore nowadays many specialists working in the field of information technologies (IT) are engaged in designing and exploiting the systems of information protection. Since many of the methods used thereon are based on the results of contemporary cryptography, this subject is now studied in the universities preparing IT specialists.

The present book is to a great extent based on the courses taught by the authors at several universities in Russia, Germany, and Finland. The book describes the main techniques and facilities of contemporary cryptography. The topics covered include block ciphers, stream ciphers, public key encryption, digital signatures, cryptographic protocols, elliptic curve cryptography, theoretical security, and random numbers. The preference is given to the methods that become (part of) cryptographic standards.

As the book title suggests, the content of the book is intended to IT students and graduates. The aim of the authors was to provide a comprehensive introductory course of cryptography without resorting to complex mathematical constructions. All themes, even the elliptic curves and theoretical security, are conveyed so that only require the knowledge of secondary school mathematics. Some special facts of number and probability theories are considered when necessary, usually through examples rather than by giving strict and complex proofs. On the other hand, all cryptography results are proved. Thus the intended audience is very wide stretching from the IT specialists who wish to become qualified users of cryptographic algorithms to those who are looking for an elementary course to start a career of the developer of cryptosystems.

In conveying the matter, we tried to follow A. Einstein's principle: "everything should be made as simple as possible, but not simpler". All methods are described in sufficient details to enable their computer implementation. Justification for every method is always given, sometimes with reference to known results in number theory and other fields. When it is appropriate, algorithms written in pseudo-code are provided. All methods are supplied by numerical examples. In fact, for the sake of simplicity, all public-key algorithms are studied in the "integers modulo n" system. The higher algebraic terminology (rings, fields, *etc.*) is not used since it may be foreign to the majority of the intended readers. Nevertheless, all mathematical results (even in case of elliptic curves) are strict and consistent.

The contents of the first 5 chapters can be used as a basis for one-semester course. The other chapters can be read as specialisation courses. Our experience shows that successful learning is facilitated by practising exercises and problems and working in computer laboratories for implementing basic algorithms and systems. Therefore the book contains training problems supplied by the answers and themes for labs.

We hope that the present book will help the reader not only understand the main problems and methods of contemporary cryptography but also estimate the beauty and elegance of its ideas and results.

B. Ryabko
A. Fionov

Contents

Preface   v

1. Introduction   1

   Problems and Exercises   6

2. Public Key Cryptosystems   7

   2.1 Prehistory and Main Ideas   7
   2.2 The First Public Key System — Diffie–Hellman Key Agree-
        ment   12
   2.3 The Elements of Number Theory   15
   2.4 Shamir Cipher   22
   2.5 ElGamal Encryption   24
   2.6 RSA Encryption and Trapdoor Functions   27
   Problems and Exercises   30
   Themes for Labs   32

3. Solving Discrete Logarithm Problem   33

   3.1 Problem Setting   33
   3.2 The Baby-step Giant-step Algorithm   35
   3.3 Index Calculus Algorithm   37
   Problems and Exercises   42
   Themes for Labs   42

4. Digital Signatures   43

   4.1 RSA Digital Signature   43
   4.2 ElGamal Digital Signature   46

4.3 Digital Signature Standards   49
Problems and Exercises   52
Themes for Labs   53

5. Cryptographic Protocols   55

5.1 Mental Poker   55
5.2 Zero Knowledge Proofs   59
    5.2.1 Graph Colouring Problem   60
    5.2.2 Hamiltonian Cycle Problem   63
5.3 Digital Cash   70
5.4 Mutual Identification with Key Establishment   76
Problems and Exercises   81
Themes for Labs   82

6. Elliptic Curve Cryptosystems   83

6.1 Introduction   83
6.2 Mathematical Foundations   84
6.3 Choosing Curve Parameters   91
6.4 Constructing Cryptosystems   93
    6.4.1 Elliptic Curve ElGamal Encryption   94
    6.4.2 Elliptic Curve Digital Signature Algorithm   95
6.5 Efficient Implementation of Operations   95
6.6 Counting Points on Elliptic Curve   102
6.7 Using Standard Curves   110
Problems and Exercises   112
Themes for Labs   113

7. Theoretical Security of Cryptosystems   115

7.1 Introduction   115
7.2 Theory of Perfect Secrecy   116
7.3 Vernam Cipher   118
7.4 Elements of Information Theory   119
7.5 Unicity Distance for Secret Key Cipher   125
7.6 Ideal Cryptosystems   130
Problems and Exercises   136

8. Modern Secret Key Ciphers   137

8.1 Introduction   137

8.2 Block Ciphers 140

   8.2.1 The GOST 28147-89 Block Cipher 141

   8.2.2 The RC5 and RC6 Ciphers 144

   8.2.3 The Rijndael (AES) Cipher 148

8.3 Main Modes of Operation of Block Ciphers 158

   8.3.1 ECB Mode 159

   8.3.2 CBC Mode 159

8.4 Stream Ciphers 160

   8.4.1 The OFB Block Cipher Mode 162

   8.4.2 The CTR Block Cipher Mode 163

   8.4.3 The RC4 Algorithm 163

8.5 Cryptographic Hash Functions 165

9. Random Numbers in Cryptography   169

9.1 Introduction 169

9.2 Refining Physical Random Number Generators 170

9.3 Pseudo-Random Number Generators 173

9.4 Statistical Tests for Random and Pseudo-Random Number

   Generators 175

9.5 Statistical Attack to Block Ciphers 178

Answers to Problems and Exercises   185

Bibliography   189

Author Index   193

Subject Index   195

Chapter 1

Introduction

Let us begin the study of cryptography with the classical problem of transmitting secret messages from a sender A to a receiver B. Both the sender and the receiver may be persons, organisations, various technical systems. Sometimes one speaks of A and B as of subscribers of some network, users of some computer system, or, more formally, abstract "parties" or "entities" participating in information exchange. But it often occurs more convenient to identify the participants of exchange with some humans and use the names Alice and Bob instead of A and B.

It is assumed that messages are transmitted via an open communications channel which can potentially be accessed by a third party different from the sender and receiver. Such a situation arises in radio transmission (say, from a mobile phone) and is possible even in such "trusted" systems as wire telephone, telegraph, as well as in ordinary mail. The Internet, as a means of communication gaining the leading positions all over the world, offers a special interest of being extremely vulnerable for unauthorised access of third parties. In this environment, not only copying of data is easily implemented but also deletion and substitution.

It is generally assumed in cryptography that the person who sends and/or receives messages has an adversary or enemy E, which can be a competitor in business, a member of a criminal group, a foreign intelligence agent, or even an excessively jealous spouse, and that the adversary can read and analyse the messages transmitted. The adversary is often thought of as a person called Eve who has powerful computing facilities and is able to use cryptanalytic methods. Of course, Alice and Bob want their messages to be completely unclear to Eve, and, to achieve this, they use appropriate ciphers.

Before transmitting a message from A to B over an open communications channel, A encrypts (or enciphers) the message. In his turn, B, after having received the encrypted message (ciphertext), decrypts (or deciphers) it to recover the initial text (plaintext). It is important for the problem considered in this chapter that Alice and Bob can agree in advance about the cipher to be used (or rather about certain parameters thereof) *not via an open channel* but via a special "secure" channel which is inaccessible for Eva. Such a "secure channel" can be maintained with the aid of trusted messengers or couriers, or Alice and Bob can agree on the cipher during their private meeting, *etc.* It is necessary to take into account that, usually, maintaining the secure channel and transmitting messages over this channel is much more expensive compared with an open unsecured channel, and (or) the secure channel cannot be used at any time. For instance, courier post is far more expensive than the regular one, it transmits messages much slower than, say, electronic mail, and may be used not at any hour and not in any situation.

To be more concrete, consider an example of cipher. Since the problem of encryption has occurred long ago in centuries some ciphers are named after renowned historical persons. These ciphers are often used to introduce simple initial concepts and we shall follow that tradition. Let us start with a well-known cipher by Gajus Julius Caesar. In this cipher, each letter of a message is substituted by the other letter whose ordinal in the alphabet is increased by 3. For instance, the letter A is replaced by D, the letter B by E, and so on. The last 3 letters X, Y, Z are replaced by A, B, C, respectively. Thus the word SEQUENCE transforms to VHTXHQFH under the Caesar cipher.

Other Roman caesars have modified the cipher by using the shifts through 4, 5 and more letters in the alphabet. We can describe such ciphers in a general way if we enumerate (encode) the letters by their ordinal numbers (from 0 to 25). Then the rule of encryption will be

$$c = (m + k) \bmod 26 \,, \qquad (1.1)$$

where m and c are the ordinals of letters of plaintext and ciphertext, respectively, and k is an integer called the cipher key (in the Caesar cipher considered above, $k = 3$). (Here and after $a \bmod b$ denotes the remainder from division of integer a by integer b, the remainder being taken from the set $\{0, 1, \ldots, b - 1\}$. For instance, $13 \bmod 5 = 3$.)

To decrypt the ciphertext one should apply an "inverse" algorithm

$$m = (c - k) \bmod 26 \,. \qquad (1.2)$$

Let's imagine that the sender and receiver have agreed to use the cipher (1.1) but, to make the adversary's job more difficult, decided to occasionally change the cipher key. For that purpose, Alice somehow generates the number k, sends it to Bob over a secure channel, after which they communicate messages encrypted with that k. The key may be changed prior to each communication session or after transmitting a specified number of letters (say, encipher every ten letters using a different key) and so forth. In this situation, the key is said to be generated by a key source. A schematic view of the cryptosystem considered is shown in Fig. 1.1.

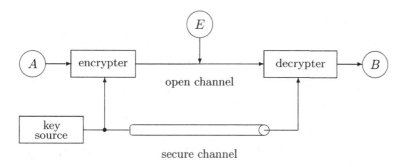

Fig. 1.1   Classical secret communications system.

Proceed now to the discussion about the actions of adversary who tries to recover the message and find the secret key, or, in other words, to break the cipher. Every attempt to break a cipher is called an *attack* to the cipher (or cryptosystem). It is generally assumed in cryptography that the adversary always has the ciphertext in her disposal and can learn everything about the encrypting algorithm used and the nature of data transmitted, but only does not know the secret key. These are the Kerckhoffs assumptions named after the scientist who was the first to formulate the main requirements to ciphers [Kerckhoffs (1883)]. Sometimes these assumptions may seem "overcautious" but such "overcautiousness" is by no means superfluous if, say, you send an order to transfer one million dollars from one account to another.

In our example, Eve knows that the plaintext was encrypted according to (1.1), the message was in English, and the ciphertext is VHTXHQFH. But the key is unknown to her.

The most obvious method to recover plaintext from ciphertext is to search through all possible keys (this is a so-called *brute-force attack* or *exhaustive key search*). Thus Eva tries successively all possible keys $k = 1, 2, \ldots$, applying them to decrypting algorithm and estimating the obtained results. Let us also try to use this method. The results of decrypting according to (1.2) under various keys and the ciphertext VHTXHQFH are shown in Table 1.1. In the majority of trials it was sufficient to decrypt only a few letters to reject the corresponding key due to the absence of the word in English that begins with these letters.

Table 1.1   Decrypting the word VHTXHQFH by exhaustive key search.

k	m	k	m	k	m	k	m
1	UGS	8	NZ	15	GS	22	ZL
2	TF	9	MYKOY	16	FRD	23	YK
3	SEQUENCE	10	LX	17	EQC	24	XJ
4	RD	11	KWI	18	DP	25	WIU
5	QC	12	JV	19	COAE	26	VHTXHQFH
6	PB	13	IU	20	BN		
7	OAM	14	HT	21	AMY		

We can see from Table 1.1 that the key $k = 3$ was used and hence the message SEQUENCE was enciphered. Moreover, when checking for the other values of key, it was not required to decrypt all 8 letters since the key might often be rejected after decrypting 2 or 3 initial letters. This example shows that the Caesar cipher is completely insecure: for breaking it, one needs to analyse several initial letters of the message after which the key is disclosed unambiguously and, consequently, the whole message may be deciphered.

What are the reasons of weakness of the considered cipher and how might its security be increased? Consider another example. Suppose that Alice hid some important documents in a safe with 5-digit combination lock. Now she would like to tell Bob the combination for opening the safe. She decided to use an analogue of the Caesar cipher adapted to the alphabet of decimal digits:

$$c = (m + k) \bmod 10. \tag{1.3}$$

Suppose she sent Bob the ciphertext 26047. Eve tries to decrypt it, as earlier, by searching through all possible keys. The results of her work are shown in Table 1.2.

We can see that all the variants are equivalent and Eve cannot decide on what combination is true. Based on the ciphertext only, she is unable to

Table 1.2 Decrypting the word
26047 by exhaustive key search.

k	m	k	m
1	15936	6	60481
2	04825	7	59370
3	93714	8	48269
4	82603	9	37158
5	71592	0	26047

find the secret key. Of course, before intercepting the encrypted message she had 10^5 possible lock combinations, and after that only 10. But it is important to note that in this particular example we have only 10 possible values of the key. Under such a key (one decimal digit) Alice and Bob could not count on better security.

The message in our first example is the text in natural language (English). So it obeys numerous rules, various letters and their combinations have different probabilities and, in particular, many combinations are forbidden (this property is referred to as redundancy of the text). And that is why the key was easily found and the message recovered, i.e. the redundancy had made it possible to break the cipher. But, in contrast, in our second example all combinations of digits are admissible. The "language" of combination lock does not possess any redundancy. Therefore even a simple cipher applied to messages in that language becomes unbreakable. In the classical work by C. Shannon [Shannon (1949)], a deep and elegant theory of secret key ciphers is constructed and, specifically, a "correct" measure of redundancy is suggested. We shall briefly touch upon these topics in Chap. 7, and in Chap. 8 some modern secret key ciphers will be described.

The attack to the cipher considered in the previous examples is said to be a *ciphertext-only attack*. But sometimes a so-called *known-plaintext attack* to the cipher may be maintained. This happens if Eve obtains in her disposal some plaintexts corresponding to previously transmitted ciphertexts. Eve tries to disclose the secret key by examining the pairs plaintext–ciphertext. If she succeeded, she would be able to decrypt all further messages from Alice to Bob.

One can imagine even a more "serious" attack, a so-called *chosen-plaintext attack*. In this attack, an adversary not only can access some plaintext–ciphertext pairs but is also able to create plaintexts on her own and encrypt them under the key she wants to disclose. For instance, during World War II, Americans, having bribed the guards, stole the cipher-machine in Japan Embassy for two days at weekend and had an opportunity to input various plaintext and obtain corresponding ciphertexts. They could not open the machine to directly determine the installed key because the damage would be detected and all the keys immediately changed (this and many other stories can be found in [Kahn (1967)]).

It may seem that the known- and chosen-plaintext attacks are rather artificial and hard to maintain. It is so to some extent. But the designers of modern cryptosystems strive to make them invulnerable even to those kinds of attacks and there are great achievements in this direction. It is customary to think that it is more reliable to use a cipher secure against chosen-plaintext attacks rather than organisationally ensure the impossibility of such attacks. Extremely cautious people do both things.

So, we have acquainted with the main characters of cryptography — Alice, Bob, and Eve, and with important notions of that science — a cipher, a key, an attack, open and secure channels. Note that an intriguing fact is connected with the last item: secure cryptosystems are possible to construct without any secure channel! In such cryptosystems Alice and Bob compute the secret key so that Eve cannot do that. This discovery was made in the seminal works ([Diffie and Hellman (1976); Mercle (1979)]) and has constituted a new epoch in modern cryptography. The main part of this book will be devoted to this kind of cryptosystems, referred to as *public-key* or *asymmetric-key* schemes.

Problems and Exercises

1.1 Find the keys of the Caesar cipher if the following plaintext–ciphertext pairs are known:

   (a) ORANGE – FIREXV
   (b) APRICOT – XMOFZLQ

1.2 Decrypt the following messages encrypted with the Caesar cipher and an unknown key k, $0 < k < 26$:

   (a) UNSJFUUQJ
   (b) GUHAI

Chapter 2

Public Key Cryptosystems

2.1 Prehistory and Main Ideas

Let's consider three problems whose solution will help us understand better the ideas and methods of public-key cryptography. All these problems are of great practical interest.

The first problem is storing passwords in a computer. We know that every user in a network has a confidential password. In order to log in to the network the user have to type in his/her login name (usually, publicly known) and password. The issue is the following: if the password is stored on a computer disk, then Eva can read it through (perhaps, temporarily dismounting the disk). Therefore it is necessary to store passwords in such a way that they could not be read (but could still be verified).

The second problem has occurred with the advent of radars and systems of air defence. When a plane is crossing the border, the radar system asks for a password. If the password is valid then the plane is admitted, otherwise the flight is denied. The problem here is that the password has to be transmitted over the public open channel (air) and can therefore be overheard by the enemy. After that, when the enemy plane is asked for a password, it simply replays the intercepted one and gets admittance.

The third problem is similar to the previous one. It arises in computer networks with remote access, e.g. in interactions between a bank and a client. In the beginning of a session the bank asks the client for the userid and password, but Eve can overhear the transmission since the communications line is public.

Nowadays all these problems are solved by applying cryptographic methods. The solution is based on an important notion of one-way function.

Definition 2.1   Let there be a function

$$y = f(x) \qquad (2.1)$$

defined on a finite set X ($x \in X$), for which the inverse function exists

$$x = f^{-1}(y). \qquad (2.2)$$

The function is said to be one-way if Eq. (2.1) is "easy" to compute for all x but for "essentially all" y the reverse computation (2.2) is "infeasible" (say, requires 10^6–10^{10} years on a supercomputer).

This definition is certainly informal. A rigorous definition of one-way function may be found in the literature (e.g. [Goldwasser and Bellare (2001); Menezes *et al.* (1996)]) but for our purposes the one given above will suffice.

As an example of one-way function, let us consider the following:

$$y = a^x \bmod p \qquad (2.3)$$

where p is a large prime number (i.e. an integer that is divisible only by 1 and itself) and a, x positive integers (some restrictions will apply in the sequel). The inverse function is denoted as

$$x = \log_a y \bmod p \qquad (2.4)$$

and is called the *discrete logarithm*.

To make computation of (2.4) really infeasible on all modern computers one have to use numbers of length more than 512 bits. In practice, other one-way functions are also used, e.g. so-called *hash functions* (considered in Chap. 8) that operate with shorter numbers of length 80–160 bits.

First we show that computation of (2.3), i.e. modular exponentiation, can be carried out fast. Begin with the example of computation of $a^{16} \bmod p$. We can write

$$a^{16} \bmod p = \left(\left(\left(a^2 \right)^2 \right)^2 \right)^2 \bmod p,$$

i.e. the value of this function is obtained for 4 modular multiplications instead of 15 in the "naive" variant $a \cdot a \cdot \ldots \cdot a$. This is the general algorithm based upon.

To describe the algorithm we introduce the quantity $t = \lfloor \log_2 x \rfloor$, i.e. the integer part of $\log_2 x$ (in what follows all logarithms are binary, so we shall not indicate the base 2 henceforth). Compute the series of numbers

$$a, \quad a^2, \quad a^4, \quad a^8, \quad \ldots, \quad a^{2^t} \quad (\bmod p). \qquad (2.5)$$

In Eq. (2.5) each number is obtained by squaring the preceding number modulo p. Write the exponent x in binary system:

$$x = (x_t x_{t-1} \ldots x_1 x_0)_2 \,.$$

Then the value $y = a^x \bmod p$ can be computed as

$$y = \prod_{i=0}^{t} a^{x_i \cdot 2^i} \bmod p \tag{2.6}$$

(all operations are modulo p).

Example 2.1 Let us compute $3^{74} \bmod 100$. We have $t = \lfloor \log 74 \rfloor = 6$. Compute the series of numbers (2.5):

$$
\begin{array}{ccccccc}
3 & 3^2 & 3^4 & 3^8 & 3^{16} & 3^{32} & 3^{64} \\
3 & 9 & 81 & 61 & 21 & 41 & 81 \,.
\end{array}
\tag{2.7}
$$

Write the exponent in binary system:

$$74 = (1001010)_2$$

and compute by (2.6):

$$
\begin{array}{ccc}
3^{64} & 3^8 & 3^2 \\
81 \cdot 1 \cdot 1 \cdot 61 \cdot 1 \cdot 9 \cdot 1 = 69 \,.
\end{array}
\tag{2.8}
$$

As few as 8 multiplications were required (6 for computation of (2.7) and 2 for (2.8)).

In general case, we have the following

Proposition 2.1 (complexity of exponentiation) *The number of multiplications to compute (2.3) using the described method does not exceed* $2 \log x$.

Proof. To compute the series (2.5) t multiplications (squarings) are required, to compute y by (2.6) we need at most t multiplications (see Example 2.1). So the total number of multiplications does not exceed $2t$. Since $t = \lfloor \log x \rfloor \leq \log x$ the correctness of the proposition is obvious. □

Remark It will be shown later that in exponentiation modulo p, it makes sense to use only exponents $x < p$. So we can say that the number of multiplications to compute (2.3) does not exceed $2 \log p$.

It is important to note that as effective algorithms for computing the inverse function (2.4) are unknown, one of the methods called "baby-step giant-step" algorithm will be described in detail in Sec. 3.2. This method requires on the order of $2\sqrt{p}$ operations. Let us show that under large p the function (2.3) is actually one-way if the "baby-step giant-step" algorithm is used. The results are given in Table 2.1.

Table 2.1   The number of multiplications for computing direct and inverse functions.

The number of decimal digits in p	Computation of (2.3) ($2\log p$ multiplications)	Computation of (2.4) ($2\sqrt{p}$ multiplications)
12	$2 \cdot 40 = 80$	$2 \cdot 10^6$
60	$2 \cdot 200 = 400$	$2 \cdot 10^{30}$
90	$2 \cdot 300 = 600$	$2 \cdot 10^{45}$

We can see that if the length of modulus is about 50–100 decimal digits then the direct function can be computed shortly but the inverse one is practically non-computable. Consider, for example, a supercomputer that multiplies two 90-digit numbers for 10^{-14} sec (for contemporary computers it is not achievable). To compute (2.3) such a computer will require

$$T_{\text{dir.}} = 600 \cdot 10^{-14} = 6 \cdot 10^{-12} \text{ sec}$$

but to compute (2.4)

$$T_{\text{inv.}} = 10^{45} \cdot 10^{-14} = 10^{31} \text{ sec,}$$

i.e. more than 10^{22} years. We see that computation of inverse functions is practically impossible if the length of numbers is about 90 decimal digits and the use of parallel and distributed systems does not essentially affect the situation. In the example considered, we assumed that the inverse function was computed for $2\sqrt{p}$ operations. At present time "faster" methods for computing discrete logarithms are known but the pattern is the same: the number of required operations is far greater than $2\log p$. So, we can conclude that the function (2.3) is indeed one-way with the only one reservation: nobody has strictly proved that the inverse function (2.4) cannot in principle be computed as fast as the direct function.

Now we shall use the one-way function (2.3) for solving all three problems stated in the beginning of the section, though taking into account that any other one-way function may be used instead.

Begin with storing passwords in a computer. The solution of the problem is based on the idea that passwords are not stored at all! To log in to the computer the user types in his/her login name and password. Let, for instance, the login name be "fruit" and the password "apricot". The computer treats the word "apricot" as the binary record of the number x and computes (2.3), where a and p are two non-secret numbers, perhaps, publicly known. After that the computer creates and stores the pair (login name, y), where y is obtained from (2.3) under x = password. Upon the user's login, after entering the pair ("fruit", "apricot"), the computer finds by (2.3) a new value y_{new} under x = "apricot" and compares it with the y already stored in the memory. If y_{new} is the same as the y corresponding to the specified login name the user is admitted to the system. Otherwise, the access is denied.

Eve might try to find x if she somehow learned y. However we have seen that even with 90-digit numbers it would require more than 10^{22} years. In that way, the presented scheme of storing passwords is reliable and used in many operating systems.

Let us discuss a solution of the second problem (a plane and air defence). One can use the following method. Each "legitimate" plane is assigned a secret name (i.e. password) which is known only to the air defence system and to the pilot (or, more precisely, to the on-board computer). Let, for instance, one of the planes be assigned the secret name FALCON and the plane is approaching the border on February 1, 2005 at 12:45. Then the on-board computer constructs the word

FALCON	05	02	01	12	45
(name	year	month	day	hours	minutes).

In other words, the on-board computer, as well as the radar system, append the timestamp to the name. Now they treat the word obtained as the number x and compute $y = a^x \bmod p$, where a and p are non-secret. After that the plane communicate the number y to the radar system. The latter compares its own y to the received value. If both values are equal the plane is admitted as legitimate.

The enemy cannot break this system. Indeed, on the one hand, she does not know the secret name FALCON and cannot recover it from y, since finding x given y requires, say, 10^{22} years. On the other hand, she cannot replay the same y in the future as the response to the radar system since the time of crossing border will never be the same and the subsequent values of y will differ from the one stored by the enemy.

This way of solution of the "air defence" problem requires precise synchronisation of the clocks on the plane and in the radar system. The issue can be easily settled. For instance, the navigation control service periodically transmits timestamps and all radars and planes use these to synchronise their clocks. But there are more delicate issues. A timestamp is appended to the word x in order to make all computed values of y different and to preclude replaying by the enemy. However the enemy may try to replay y immediately within the current minute. How to prevent this opportunity? This is the first question. The other difficulty arises in a situation when the plane sends the number y in the end of 45-th minute, and the radar receives it in the beginning of 46-th. We give the reader an opportunity independently to offer a variant of the solution to these issues.

The other way of solution of the "air defence" problem is possible if we use an extra communications channel for transmitting data from the radar system to the plane. As before, each "legitimate" plane is assigned a secret name such as FALCON which is also known to the radar. Having located a target, the radar sends a randomly generated number a ("challenge"). The plane computes $y = a^x \bmod p$, where x is the secret word (FALCON) and communicates y ("response") to the radar. The radar performs the same computations and compares the received and computed values of y. In this scheme, synchronising clocks is not needed but, as earlier, the enemy cannot replay y since the radar sends a different challenge (a) each time. It is interesting, that this problem, apparently, was historically the first to be solved with the aid of one-way functions.

The third problem is solved absolutely similarly and both methods of transmitting passwords are applicable and used in practical network protocols.

2.2   The First Public Key System — Diffie–Hellman Key Agreement

This cryptosystem was discovered in the middle 70-s by Whitfield Diffie and Martin Hellman [Diffie and Hellman (1976)] and caused a revolution in cryptography and its applications. It was the first system that allowed to protect information without using secret keys transmitted over secure channels. To show one of application schemes of such a system, consider a communications network with N users, where N is large. Suppose we are to organise secret communications for each pair of users. If we use an ordinary key distribution scheme, then each pair of users must be supplied with its own secret key which results in the total number of keys $\binom{N}{2} = \frac{N(N-1)}{2} \approx \frac{N^2}{2}$.

So if we have 100 users then 5000 keys are required, if we ever have 10^4 users then as many as $5 \cdot 10^7$ keys must be supplied. We can see that under the large number of users the system of supplying secret keys becomes very bulky and expensive.

Diffie and Hellman have solved this problem by means of public distribution and computation of keys. Proceed to description of the system suggested.

Denote the users of a network by $A, B, C, \ldots$. For all the users the following common parameters are chosen: a large prime number p and an integer g, $1 < g < p-1$, such that all numbers from the set $\{1, 2, \ldots, p-1\}$ might be represented as powers of g modulo p (i.e. g^1, g^2, $\ldots$, g^{p-1} (mod p) be different numbers; such a g is called a *generator* and various approaches are known for finding generators, one of which will be presented below). The numbers p and g are assumed to be non-secret and known to all the users.

The users choose large numbers X_A, X_B, X_C, $\ldots$, which are kept in secret and called their *private keys* (it is usually recommended to make the choice randomly with the aid of random number generators). Then every user computes a corresponding number Y and sends it to the other users in cleartext,

$$\begin{aligned}
Y_A &= g^{X_A} \bmod p, \\
Y_B &= g^{X_B} \bmod p, \\
Y_C &= g^{X_C} \bmod p.
\end{aligned} \tag{2.9}$$

The numbers Y_A, Y_B, Y_C, $\ldots$ are called the *public keys* of the users. All users' information is collected in Table 2.2.

Table 2.2   User keys in Diffie–Hellman system.

User	Private key	Public key
A	X_A	Y_A
B	X_B	Y_B
C	X_C	Y_C

Suppose user A wants to securely communicate with user B and they both have the public information from Table 2.2. User A asks B over an open channel to start a communication session. Then A computes

$$Z_{AB} = (Y_B)^{X_A} \bmod p \tag{2.10}$$

(nobody else can do that since X_A is kept secret). Concurrently user B computes

$$Z_{BA} = (Y_A)^{X_B} \bmod p. \qquad (2.11)$$

Proposition 2.2 $Z_{AB} = Z_{BA}$.

Proof.   Indeed,

$$Z_{AB} = (Y_B)^{X_A} \bmod p = (g^{X_B})^{X_A} \bmod p$$
$$= g^{X_A X_B} \bmod p = (Y_A)^{X_B} \bmod p = Z_{BA}.$$

(Here the first equality follows from (2.10), the second and fourth from (2.9), and the last from (2.11).)   □

Review the main properties of the system:

(1) users A and B have obtained the same number $Z = Z_{AB} = Z_{BA}$ that was not transmitted over the open channel;
(2) Eve cannot compute Z_{AB} since she does not know the secret numbers X_A and X_B (strictly speaking, she might try to find secret X_A from Y_A (see (2.9)), however under large p, this is practically impossible (requires millions years)).

Now users A and B can utilise Z_{AB} as a secret key for encryption and decryption of their data. Similarly, each pair of users can compute a key which will be known only to that pair.

Let's now discuss briefly the above mentioned problem of selecting the generator g. The general method known so far relies on factorisation of $p-1$. But, on the one hand, if p is randomly chosen then, with high probability, $p - 1$ will have a large prime divisor which is very difficult to determine. On the other hand, in the system considered, the number $p - 1$ have to have a large prime divisor since otherwise the Pohlig–Hellman algorithm ([Pohlig and Hellman (1978)]; see also [Menezes *et al.* (1996)]) would be able to compute the discrete logarithm fast. So, under arbitrary chosen p, finding g is hard. Therefore it is often recommended to use the following approach. The prime number p is chosen so that

$$p = 2q + 1$$

where q is also prime. Then g may be any number for which the following inequalities are satisfied:

$$1 < g < p - 1 \quad \text{and} \quad g^q \bmod p \neq 1.$$

Example 2.2   Let $p = 23 = 2 \cdot 11 + 1$ ($q = 11$). Now select g. Let's try $g = 3$. Check it: $3^{11} \bmod 23 = 1$, which means that this value is irrelevant. Take $g = 5$. Check it: $5^{11} \bmod 23 = 22 \neq 1$, that's OK. So we have chosen the parameters for the Diffie–Hellman system: $p = 23$, $g = 5$. Now each user chooses a secret number and computes a corresponding public number. Let $X_A = 7$, $X_B = 13$. Compute $Y_A = 5^7 \bmod 23 = 17$, $Y_B = 5^{13} \bmod 23 = 21$. Let A and B decided to establish a common secret key. For that purpose A computes $Z_{AB} = 21^7 \bmod 23 = 10$ and B computes $Z_{BA} = 17^{13} \bmod 23 = 10$. They have now the common key, 10, which has never been transmitted over communications channel.

2.3   The Elements of Number Theory

Many cryptographic algorithms are based on the results of classical theory of numbers. We shall consider the necessary minimum from the whole theory. The classical theorems due to Fermat, Euler and a number of other number-theoretic results will be given without proofs since they may be found in almost any textbook on number theory, e.g. [Rosen (1992)]. The readers familiar with number theory may wish to proceed immediately to Sec. 2.4.

Definition 2.2   A positive integer p is *prime* if it has no divisors but 1 and itself.

Example 2.3   The numbers 11, 23 are prime, the numbers 27, 33 are composite (27 can be divided by 3 and by 9, 33 has divisors 3 and 11).

Theorem 2.1 (fundamental theorem of arithmetic)   *Any positive integer can be represented as a product of prime numbers, this representation being unique.*

Example 2.4 $27 = 3 \cdot 3 \cdot 3$, $33 = 3 \cdot 11$.

Definition 2.3   Two numbers are said to be *coprime* (or *relatively prime*) if they have no common divisors but 1.

Example 2.5   The numbers 27 and 28 are coprime (the have no common divisors except 1), the numbers 27 and 33 are not (they have common divisor 3).

Definition 2.4 (Euler (totient) function) Let there be given an integer $N \geq 1$. *Euler function* $\varphi(N)$ is the quantity of numbers among $1, 2, 3, \ldots, N - 1$ that are coprime to N.

Example 2.6

$$\varphi(10) =? \qquad\qquad\qquad \varphi(12) =?$$
$$1, \not{2}, 3, \not{4}, \not{5}, \not{6}, 7, \not{8}, 9, \qquad 1, \not{2}, \not{3}, \not{4}, 5, \not{6}, 7, \not{8}, \not{9}, \not{10}, 11$$
$$\varphi(10) = 4 \qquad\qquad\qquad \varphi(12) = 4$$

(struck out are the numbers not coprime to the argument).

Proposition 2.3 *If p is prime then $\varphi(p) = p - 1$.*

Proof. In the series $1, 2, 3, \ldots, p - 1$ all numbers are coprime to p since p is prime and, by definition, is not divisible by any other number. $\square$

Proposition 2.4 *Let p and q be distinct primes ($p \neq q$). Then $\varphi(pq) = (p - 1)(q - 1)$.*

Proof. In the series $1, 2, \ldots, pq - 1$ the numbers *not* relatively prime to pq are $p, 2p, 3p, \ldots, (q - 1)p$ and $q, 2q, 3q, \ldots, (p - 1)q$. The total of such numbers is $(q - 1) + (p - 1)$. Hence, the number of coprimes to pq is $pq - 1 - (p - 1) - (q - 1) = pq - q - p + 1 = (p - 1)(q - 1)$. $\square$

Theorem 2.2 (Fermat) *Let p be prime and $0 < a < p$. Then*

$$a^{p-1} \bmod p = 1.$$

Example 2.7 $p = 13, a = 2$;

$$2^{12} \bmod 13 = \left(2^2\right)^2 \cdot \left(\left(2^2\right)^2\right)^2 \bmod 13 = 3 \cdot 9 \bmod 13 = 1,$$
$$10^{10} \bmod 11 = 10^2 \cdot \left(\left(10^2\right)^2\right)^2 \bmod 11 = 1 \cdot 1 = 1.$$

Theorem 2.3 (Euler) *Let a and b be coprime. Then*

$$a^{\varphi(b)} \bmod b = 1.$$

The Fermat theorem is a special case of the Euler theorem when b is prime.

Example 2.8

$$\varphi(12) = 4,$$
$$5^4 \bmod 12 = \left(5^2\right)^2 \bmod 12 = \left(1^2\right)^2 \bmod 12 = 1.$$
$$\varphi(21) = 2 \cdot 6 = 12,$$
$$2^{12} \bmod 21 = 2^4 \cdot \left(2^4\right)^2 \bmod 21 = 16 \cdot 4 \bmod 21 = 1.$$

We shall need another theorem close to Euler's.

Theorem 2.4   *If p and q are distinct primes, $p \neq q$, and k is an arbitrary integer then*

$$a^{k\varphi(pq)+1} \bmod (pq) = a. \qquad (2.12)$$

Example 2.9   Let's take $p = 5$, $q = 7$. Then $pq = 35$ and the Euler function $\varphi(35) = 4 \cdot 6 = 24$. Consider the case of $k = 2$, i.e. we shall raise numbers to the power $2 \cdot 24 + 1 = 49$. We obtain

$$9^{49} \bmod 35 = 9, \quad 23^{49} \bmod 35 = 23.$$

This is not surprise because each of the numbers 9 and 23 is coprime to the modulus 35 and by the Euler theorem $9^{24} \bmod 35 = 1$, $23^{24} \bmod 35 = 1$. However, Theorem 2.4 remains right even for the following numbers:

$$10^{49} \bmod 35 = 10, \quad 28^{49} \bmod 35 = 28,$$

whereas the Euler theorem cannot be applied to these numbers (the numbers 10 and 28 are not coprime to the modulus 35 and $10^{24} \bmod 35 = 15$, $28^{24} \bmod 35 = 21$).

Definition 2.5   Let a and b be two positive integers. The *greatest common divisor* of a and b, denoted $\gcd(a,b)$, is the biggest number c which divides both a and b:

$$c = \gcd(a,b).$$

Example 2.10 $\gcd(10, 15) = 5$; $\gcd(8, 28) = 4$.

To find the greatest common divisor one may use the following algorithm which is known as the Euclidean algorithm.

Algorithm 2.1   EUCLIDEAN ALGORITHM.

INPUT: Positive integers a, b, $a \geq b$.
OUTPUT: The greatest common divisor $\gcd(a,b)$.
1.   WHILE $b \neq 0$ DO
2. $r \leftarrow a \bmod b$, $a \leftarrow b$, $b \leftarrow r$.
3.   RETURN a.

Example 2.11 Let's show how the Euclidean algorithm is used to compute $\gcd(28, 8)$:

$$a : 28 \ 8 \ 4$$
$$b : \ \ 8 \ 4 \ 0$$
$$r : \ \ 4 \ 0$$

Here each column represents one iteration of the algorithm. The process continues until b turns to zero. Then the value of a holds the result (4).

For many cryptographic systems to be considered in the book the so-called *extended Euclidean algorithm* is important to which the following theorem is associated.

Theorem 2.5 *Let a and b be positive integers. Then the integer (not necessarily positive) numbers x and y exist such that*

$$ax + by = \gcd(a, b). \tag{2.13}$$

The extended Euclidean algorithm serves for finding $\gcd(a, b)$ and x, y satisfying (2.13). Introduce three vectors $U = (u_1, u_2, u_3)$, $V = (v_1, v_2, v_3)$, and $T = (t_1, t_2, t_3)$. The algorithm is written as follows.

Algorithm 2.2 EXTENDED EUCLIDEAN ALGORITHM.

INPUT: Positive integers a, b, $a \geq b$.
OUTPUT: $\gcd(a, b)$, x and y satisfying (2.13).
1. $U \leftarrow (a, 1, 0)$, $V \leftarrow (b, 0, 1)$.
2.   WHILE $v_1 \neq 0$ DO
3. $q \leftarrow u_1$ div v_1;
4. $T \leftarrow (u_1 \bmod v_1, u_2 - qv_2, u_3 - qv_3)$;
5. $U \leftarrow V, V \leftarrow T$.
6.   RETURN $U = (\gcd(a, b), x, y)$.

Vector U contains the result.
Operation div in the algorithm is integer division

$$a \text{ div } b = \lfloor a/b \rfloor.$$

The proof of correctness of Algorithm 2.2 may be found in [Aho *et al.* (1976); Knuth (1981)].

Example 2.12 Let $a = 28$, $b = 19$. Find x and y satisfying (2.13).

$$
\begin{array}{lrrrl}
U & 28 & 1 & 0 & \\
V\, U & 19 & 0 & 1 & \\
T\, V\, U & 9 & 1 & -1 & q = 1 \\
T\, V\, U & 1 & -2 & 3 & q = 2 \\
T\, V & 0 & 19 & -28 & q = 9
\end{array}
$$

Let us comment the presented schema. First, vector U is filled with numbers $(28,1,0)$ and vector V with $(19,0,1)$ (these are the first two rows in the schema). Vector T is computed (3rd row). After that the 2nd row becomes vector U, the 3rd row becomes vector V, and again vector T is computed (4th row). The process continues until the first element of V turns to 0. Then the next to last row holds the result. In our case $\gcd(28, 19) = 1$, $x = -2$, $y = 3$. Check up the result: $28 \cdot (-2) + 19 \cdot 3 = 1$.

Consider one important application of extended Euclidean algorithm. In many cryptographic schemes, it is required to find for specified numbers c, m a number $d < m$ such that

$$cd \bmod m = 1 \,. \tag{2.14}$$

Notice that such d exists if and only if c and m are coprime.

Definition 2.6 A number d satisfying (2.14) is called the *inverse* of c modulo m and often denoted $c^{-1} \bmod m$.

The above notation for the inverse is quite natural since we can now rewrite (2.14) as

$$cc^{-1} \bmod m = 1 \,.$$

Multiplication by c^{-1} corresponds to division by c when operating modulo m. By analogy, arbitrary negative powers modulo m can be introduced:

$$c^{-e} = (c^e)^{-1} = (c^{-1})^e \pmod{m} \,.$$

Example 2.13 $3 \cdot 4 \bmod 11 = 1$, therefore 4 is the inverse of 3 modulo 11. We can write $3^{-1} \bmod 11 = 4$. The number $5^{-2} \bmod 11$ can be found in two ways:

$$5^{-2} \bmod 11 = (5^2 \bmod 11)^{-1} \bmod 11 = 3^{-1} \bmod 11 = 4 \,,$$

$$5^{-2} \bmod 11 = (5^{-1} \bmod 11)^2 \bmod 11 = 9^2 \bmod 11 = 4 \,.$$

In the second variant, we used the equality $5^{-1} \bmod 11 = 9$. Indeed, $5 \cdot 9 \bmod 11 = 45 \bmod 11 = 1$.

Let us show how one computes the inverse by use of extended Euclidean algorithm. The equality (2.14) means that for some integer k

$$cd - km = 1 .\tag{2.15}$$

Taking into account that c and m are relatively prime rewrite (2.15) as

$$m(-k) + cd = \gcd(m, c) ,\tag{2.16}$$

which agrees with (2.13) up to the names of variables. Therefore to compute $c^{-1} \bmod m$, i.e. to find d, one can use the extended Euclidean algorithm for solving Eq. (2.16). Notice that the value of k is not interesting for us, so it makes sense not to compute the second element of vectors U, V, T. Besides, if the value of d occurs negative, we must add to it the modulus m because, by definition, $a \bmod m$ belongs to the set $\{0, 1, \ldots, m - 1\}$.

Example 2.14   Compute $7^{-1} \bmod 11$. We use the same form of presentation as in Example 2.12.

$$
\begin{array}{rrl}
11 & 0 & \\
7 & 1 & \\
4 & -1 & q = 1 \\
3 & 2 & q = 1 \\
1 & -3 & q = 1 \\
0 & 11 & q = 3 .
\end{array}
$$

We obtain $d = -3$ and since it is negative we add the modulus: $-3 + 11 = 8$, i.e. $7^{-1} \bmod 11 = 8$. Check the result: $7 \cdot 8 \bmod 11 = 56 \bmod 11 = 1$.

One of the main operations in public-key cryptography is modular exponentiation. The idea of efficient algorithmic construction for exponentiation has already been shown in Eqs. (2.5) and (2.6). It is possible to implement this algorithm without storing in memory the series of numbers (2.5). Now we give the description of the algorithm in a form suitable for its immediate computer implementation. The name of the algorithm reflects the fact that the bits of exponent are examined from right to left, i.e. from the least-significant bit to the most-significant.

Algorithm 2.3 MODULAR EXPONENTIATION (FROM RIGHT TO LEFT).

INPUT: Integer numbers a, $x = (x_t x_{t-1} \ldots x_0)_2$, p.
OUTPUT: The number $y = a^x \bmod p$.
1. $y \leftarrow 1$, $s \leftarrow a$.
2.   FOR $i = 0, 1, \ldots, t$ DO
3.   IF $x_i = 1$ THEN $y \leftarrow y \cdot s \bmod p$;
4. $s \leftarrow s \cdot s \bmod p$.
5.   RETURN y.

To show how the algorithm works, trace the powers after each iteration. Let $x = 74 = (1001010)_2$ as in Example 2.1.

i:	0	1	2	3	4	5	6
x_i:	0	1	0	1	0	0	1
y:	1	a^2	a^2	a^{10}	a^{10}	a^{10}	a^{74}
s:	a^2	a^4	a^8	a^{16}	a^{32}	a^{64}	a^{128}.

There are situations where the following algorithm is more effective. It differs from the previous algorithm in that the bits of exponent are examined from left to right, i.e. from the most-significant bit to the least-significant.

Algorithm 2.4 MODULAR EXPONENTIATION (FROM LEFT TO RIGHT).

INPUT: Integer numbers a, $x = (x_t x_{t-1} \ldots x_0)_2$, p.
OUTPUT: The number $y = a^x \bmod p$.
1. $y \leftarrow 1$.
2.   FOR $i = t, t - 1, \ldots, 0$ DO
3. $y \leftarrow y \cdot y \bmod p$;
4.   IF $x_i = 1$ THEN $y \leftarrow y \cdot a \bmod p$.
5.   RETURN y.

To assure oneself that Algorithm 2.4 computes exactly the same value as Algorithm 2.3, trace again the powers after each iteration for $x = 73$.

i:	6	5	4	3	2	1	0
x_i:	1	0	0	1	0	1	0
y:	a	a^2	a^4	a^9	a^{18}	a^{37}	a^{74}

In fact, the number-theoretic results provided in this section will be enough for the description of basic cryptographic algorithms and methods in the rest of the book.

2.4   Shamir Cipher

This cipher attributed to Adi Shamir (see [Menezes *et al.* (1996)]) was one of the first public-key systems that allowed two parties to securely exchange messages over an open channel provided these parties had neither secure channels nor secret keys and, perhaps, had never seen each other. (Recall that Diffie–Hellman key-agreement scheme allows for creating only a secret key but for secure message transmission a cipher is needed where this key can be used.)

Proceed to description of the system. Let there be two users A and B connected by an open communications line. User A wants to send a message m to user B so that nobody but B could be able to learn its contents. A randomly chooses a large prime number p and sends it to B. Then A selects two numbers c_A and d_A such that

$$c_A d_A \bmod (p-1) = 1 \,. \qquad (2.17)$$

A keeps these numbers secret, they will not be transmitted. B, similarly, selects two numbers c_B and d_B such that

$$c_B d_B \bmod (p-1) = 1 \,, \qquad (2.18)$$

and also keeps them secret.

After that A transmits her message m using the three-step protocol described below. If $m < p$ (m is viewed as a number) then m is transmitted at once. If $m \geq p$ then the message is represented as a sequence of blocks $m_1, m_2, \ldots, m_t$, where all $m_i < p$, and these blocks are transmitted by turn. For secure transmission of each m_i, it is better to randomly select new pairs (c_A, d_A) and (c_B, d_B), otherwise the security of the system decays. In present time such a cipher is commonly used as a transport for secret keys whose values are less than p. So we shall focus on the case $m < p$. The protocol is as follows.

Step 1 A computes

$$x_1 = m^{c_A} \bmod p \tag{2.19}$$

and sends x_1 to B.

Step 2 B, upon the receipt of x_1, computes

$$x_2 = x_1^{c_B} \bmod p \tag{2.20}$$

and sends x_2 back to A.

Step 3 A computes

$$x_3 = x_2^{d_A} \bmod p \tag{2.21}$$

and sends it to B.

Step 4 B, upon the receipt of x_3, computes

$$x_4 = x_3^{d_B} \bmod p. \tag{2.22}$$

Proposition 2.5 (properties of Shamir protocol)

(1) $x_4 = m$, *i.e. realisation of the protocol succeeds in transmitting the message m from A to B;*

(2) *adversary cannot figure out what a message was transmitted (if p is large).*

Proof. Notice first that any integer $e \geq 0$ can be represented as $e = k(p-1) + r$ where $r = e \bmod (p-1)$. Therefore, by Fermat's theorem

$$x^e \bmod p = x^{k(p-1)+r} \bmod p = \left(x^{p-1}\right)^k \cdot x^r \bmod p$$
$$= (1^k \cdot x^r) \bmod p = x^{e \bmod (p-1)} \bmod p. \tag{2.23}$$

By the protocol construction

$$x_4 = x_3^{d_B} \bmod p = (x_2^{d_A})^{d_B} \bmod p = (x_1^{c_B})^{d_A d_B} \bmod p$$
$$= (m^{c_A})^{c_B d_A d_B} \bmod p = m^{c_A d_A c_B d_B} \bmod p.$$

Taking into account Eq. (2.23) and then Eqs. (2.17) and (2.18)) we may continue

$$x_4 = m^{(c_A d_A c_B d_B) \bmod (p-1)} \bmod p$$
$$= m^{(c_A d_A \bmod (p-1))(c_B d_B \bmod (p-1))} \bmod p = m^{1 \cdot 1} \bmod p = m$$

which proves the first statement of the proposition.

The proof of the second statement is based on the assumption that for an adversary trying to recover m, there is no strategy more effective than the following. She computes c_B from (2.20), then finds d_B and computes $x_4 = m$ by (2.22). But to implement this strategy the adversary has to solve discrete logarithm problem which is impossible if p is large.   □

Let us discuss a method of selecting pairs c_A, d_A and c_B, d_B satisfying (2.17) and (2.18). It suffices only to consider the actions of user A because user B acts the same way. The number c_A is chosen randomly but must be coprime to $p - 1$ (by searching through odd numbers since $p - 1$ is even). Then d_A may be computed by use of extended Euclidean algorithm as was explained in Sec. 2.3.

Example 2.15   If A wants to send B the message $m = 10$, A chooses $p = 23$ and sends it to B. Then A selects $c_A = 7$ ($\gcd(7, 22) = 1$) and computes $d_A = 19$. Similarly, B selects $c_B = 5$ (coprime to 22) and computes $d_B = 9$. The Shamir protocol begins.

(Step 1) $A \longrightarrow B :$ $x_1 = 10^7 \bmod 23 = 14$.
(Step 2) $A \longleftarrow B :$ $x_2 = 14^5 \bmod 23 = 15$.
(Step 3) $A \longrightarrow B :$ $x_3 = 15^{19} \bmod 23 = 19$.
(Step 4) B computes $x_4 = 19^9 \bmod 23 = 10$.

We can see that B has received the message $m = 10$.

2.5   ElGamal Encryption

Let there be users A, B, C, ..., who wish to communicate each other secret messages but have no secure communications channels. In this section, we consider a cipher suggested by Taher ElGamal [ElGamal (1985)] which solves the problem and uses only one message pass in contrast to three-pass protocol by Shamir. In fact, the ElGamal scheme is based on Diffie–Hellman key-agreement protocol which is used for a pair of users to obtain a common secret key. The message is then encrypted by multiplication with that key. For any subsequent messages the secret key is computed anew. Proceed to the details of the method.

For the whole group of users a large prime p and integer g are chosen so that distinct powers of g be distinct numbers modulo p (cf. Sec. 2.2). Numbers p and g are transmitted to users in clear and may be used by all users of a network.

Then every user selects his/her own secret number c_i (private key), $1 < c_i < p - 1$, and computes the corresponding public number d_i (public key),

$$d_i = g^{c_i} \bmod p. \tag{2.24}$$

This results in Table 2.3.

Table 2.3   User keys in ElGamal system.

User	Private key	Public key
A	c_A	d_A
B	c_B	d_B
C	c_C	d_C

Let's show now how A transmits a message m to B. We shall assume, as in the case of Shamir cipher, that the message is represented as a number $m < p$.

Step 1 A generates a random number k, $1 \le k \le p - 2$, computes

$$r = g^k \bmod p, \tag{2.25}$$

$$e = m \cdot d_B{}^k \bmod p \tag{2.26}$$

and transmits the pair of numbers (r, e) to user B.

Step 2 B, upon the receipt of (r, e), computes

$$m' = e \cdot r^{p-1-c_B} \bmod p. \tag{2.27}$$

Proposition 2.6 (properties of ElGamal cipher)

(1) *User B has received the message, i.e. $m' = m$;*
(2) *An adversary who knows p, g, d_B, r, and e, cannot compute m.*

Proof. Substitute the value of e from (2.26) into (2.27):

$$m' = m \cdot d_B{}^k \cdot r^{p-1-c_B} \bmod p.$$

Now substitute (2.25) in place of r and (2.24) in place of d_B:

$$m' = m \cdot (g^{c_B})^k \cdot (g^k)^{p-1-c_B} \bmod p$$
$$= m \cdot g^{c_B k + k(p-1) - k c_B} \bmod p = m \cdot g^{k(p-1)} \bmod p. \tag{2.28}$$

By Fermat's theorem

$$g^{k(p-1)} \bmod p = 1^k \bmod p = 1$$

and thus we obtain the first statement of the proposition.

To prove the second statement notice that the adversary cannot compute k in (2.25) since it is the discrete logarithm problem. Hence, she cannot compute m in (2.26) since m was multiplied by an unknown factor. The adversary also cannot reproduce the actions of the legitimate receiver (user B) because she does not know the secret number c_B (computation of c_B based on (2.24) is again the discrete logarithm problem). $\square$

Example 2.16 Transmit the message $m = 15$ from A to B. Choose the parameters in the same way as in Example 2.2 on page 15. Let $p = 23$, $g = 5$. Let user B choose his secret number $c_B = 13$ and compute by (2.24)

$$d_B = 5^{13} \bmod 23 = 21 \,.$$

User A generates random number k, say $k = 7$, and computes by (2.25), (2.26):

$$r = 5^7 \bmod 23 = 17, \quad e = 15 \cdot 21^7 \bmod 23 = 15 \cdot 10 \bmod 23 = 12 \,.$$

Then A sends B the encrypted message as a pair of numbers $(17, 12)$. B computes by (2.27)

$$m' = 12 \cdot 17^{23-1-13} \bmod 23 = 12 \cdot 17^9 \bmod 23 = 12 \cdot 7 \bmod 23 = 15 \,.$$

We can see that B has been able to decrypt the message transmitted.

It is clear that the same scheme may be used by all the users in a network. Note that any user who knows the public key of user B (d_B) can send B messages encrypted using d_B. But it is only user B, and nobody else, who is able to decrypt those messages since decryption is done by utilising the private key c_B which is known only to B. Note also that the length of the ciphertext is twice the length of the plaintext but only one pass in needed (provided the table with public keys was delivered to all users in advance).

2.6 RSA Encryption and Trapdoor Functions

Named after its developers Ron Rivest, Adi Shamir, and Leonard Adleman, this cipher proposed in [Rivest *et al.* (1978)] is so far one of most widely used.

We have seen that Shamir's cipher completely solves the problem of secure message exchange in the case when only open channels are available. But as a disadvantage, the message is passed three times from one user to another. The ElGamal cipher allows to solve the same problem in only one pass, but also has a disadvantage of expanding the message: the ciphertext is twice as long as the plaintext. The RSA encryption is free of such disadvantages. It is interesting that this system is based on other one-way function different from discrete logarithm. Moreover, we meet here one more invention of contemporary cryptography — *trapdoor function*.

The RSA system is based on the following two facts from number theory:

Fact 1 testing numbers for primality (and finding primes) is relatively easy (see, e.g. [Menezes *et al.* (1996)]);

Fact 2 the problem of factoring numbers of the form $n = pq$, where p and q are primes of roughly the same size, i.e. finding p and q given n, is very hard (or computationally infeasible) when p and q are sufficiently large (see also [Menezes *et al.* (1996)]).

Let again there be users A, B, C, ... Each user chooses randomly two large primes P and Q and computes

$$N = PQ. \tag{2.29}$$

Then the user computes the number $\phi = (P-1)(Q-1)$ and selects a number $d < \phi$ relatively prime to ϕ after which finds using the extended Euclidean algorithm a number c such that

$$cd \bmod \phi = 1. \tag{2.30}$$

The user keeps secret the number c (as well as P, Q, and ϕ, but these will not be needed any more) and publishes the numbers N and d. The number c is the private key of the user and the pair of numbers N, d is the corresponding public key. All information associated with the users is shown in Table 2.4.

Proceed to the description of RSA protocol. If Alice wants to send a message m to Bob, she will treat the message m as a number satisfying the

Table 2.4   User keys in RSA system.

User	Private key	Public key
A	c_A	d_A, N_A
B	c_B	d_B, N_B
C	c_C	d_C, N_C

inequality $m < N_B$ (further on subscript B indicates that the corresponding parameters belong to Bob).

Step 1 Alice encrypts the message as follows

$$e = m^{d_B} \bmod N_B \tag{2.31}$$

using Bob's public keys and transmits e over an open channel.

Step 2 Bob, having received the encrypted message, computes

$$m' = e^{c_B} \bmod N_B. \tag{2.32}$$

Proposition 2.7   *For the described protocol, $m' = m$, i.e. user B receives the message sent by A.*

Proof.   By the protocol construction

$$m' = e^{c_B} \bmod N_B = m^{d_B c_B} \bmod N_B.$$

Equation (2.30) means that for some k

$$c_B d_B = k\phi_B + 1.$$

By Proposition 2.4

$$\phi_B = (P_B - 1)(Q_B - 1) = \varphi(N_B)$$

where $\varphi(\cdot)$ is the Euler function. Hence by Theorem 2.4

$$m' = m^{k\varphi(N_B)+1} \bmod N_B = m. \qquad \square$$

Proposition 2.8   (properties of RSA protocol)

(1) *The protocol encrypts and decrypts data correctly;*
(2) *An adversary who overhears all transmitted messages and knows all public information cannot recover the plaintext message if P and Q are large.*

Proof. The first property follows from Proposition 2.7. To prove the second property notice that the adversary knows only public parameters N and d. In order to find c she must know the value $\phi = (P-1)(Q-1)$ for which, in turn, P and Q must be known. Generally speaking, P and Q can be found by factoring N but it is a hard problem (Fact 2). Note, however, that the choice of large random primes P and Q can be done in acceptable time (Fact 1). $\square$

The one-way function $y = x^d \bmod N$ employed in RSA has a so-called "trapdoor" which allows for easy computation of the inverse function $x = \sqrt[d]{y} \bmod N$ if the factorisation of N is known. (Indeed, it is easy to compute $\phi = (P-1)(Q-1)$ and then $c = d^{-1} \bmod \phi$.) If P and Q are unknown then to compute the inverse function is practically impossible because to find P and Q given N is very hard (Fact 2), i.e. the knowledge of P and Q is a "trapdoor". The trapdoor functions are employed in other branches of cryptography, as well.

Notice that it is important for the RSA system that each user chooses his own pair of primes P and Q, i.e. that all moduli N_A, N_B, N_C, ... be different (otherwise one user would be able to read encrypted messages destined to another user). But it is not required for the second public parameter d. The parameter d can be the same for all users. It is often recommended to choose $d = 3$ (for correspondingly chosen P and Q), see e.g. [Menezes *et al.* (1996)]. In this case encryption is maximally fast (it requires only 2 modular multiplications).

Example 2.17 Suppose Alice wants to send Bob the message $m = 15$. Let Bob's parameters be

$$P_B = 3,\ Q_B = 11,\ N_B = 33,\ d_B = 3$$

(3 is coprime to $\varphi(33) = 20$). Find c_B using the extended Euclidean algorithm: $c_B = 7$ (check it: $3 \cdot 7 \bmod 20 = 1$). Encrypt m using Eq. (2.31):

$$e = 15^3 \bmod 33 = 15^2 \cdot 15 \bmod 33 = 27 \cdot 15 \bmod 33 = 9\,.$$

Alice sends the number 9 to Bob over an open channel. Only Bob knows $c_B = 7$ so he decrypts by (2.32):

$$m' = 9^7 \bmod 33 = \left(9^2\right)^2 \cdot 9^2 \cdot 9 \bmod 33 = 15^2 \cdot 15 \cdot 9 \bmod 33 = 15\,.$$

We can see that Bob has deciphered the message.

The considered system is unbreakable if P and Q are large but has the following imperfection: A sends a message to B by utilising B's public information (the numbers N_B and d_B). Adversary E cannot read the messages destined for B but she is able to send a message to B on behalf of A, i.e. E can impersonate A. Surely, we need more complex protocols to avoid this. It is interesting that one of the possible solutions may be based entirely on the RSA scheme, as the following.

A wants to send B message m. First A computes the number $e = m^{c_A} \bmod N_A$. E cannot do that since c_A is secret. Then A computes the number $f = e^{d_B} \bmod N_B$ and sends f to B. B receives f and computes sequentially $u = f^{c_B} \bmod N_B$ and $w = u^{d_A} \bmod N_A$.

As a result, B obtains the message $w = m$. As in the conventional RSA system, E cannot recover the message but, in contrast to RSA, she also cannot send a message on behalf of A (because she does not know the secret c_A).

Here we meet a new situation. B knows that the message was originated by A as if it were signed by A. A virtually signs the message by encrypting it with the use of her secret parameter c_A. This is an example of the so-called *digital signature*. The digital signature is one of the widely used inventions of modern cryptography. It will be systematically studied in Chap. 4.

Problems and Exercises

2.1 Reduce the results of expressions 5, 16, 27, -4, -13, $3 + 8$, $3 - 8$, $3 \cdot 8$, $3 \cdot 8 \cdot 5$

   (a) modulo 10,
   (b) modulo 11.

2.2 Compute using fast modular exponentiation algorithms $2^8 \bmod 10$, $3^7 \bmod 10$, $7^{19} \bmod 100$, $7^{57} \bmod 100$.

2.3 Factor numbers 108, 77, 65, 30, 159.

2.4 Determine what pairs of numbers $(25, 12)$, $(25, 15)$, $(13, 39)$, $(40, 27)$ are relatively prime.

2.5 Find values of Euler function $\varphi(14)$, $\varphi(20)$.

2.6 Compute using the properties of Euler function $\varphi(53)$, $\varphi(21)$, $\varphi(159)$.

2.7 Compute the quantities $3^{13} \bmod 13$, $5^{24} \bmod 11$, $3^{17} \bmod 5$ using the Fermat theorem.

2.8 Compute the quantities $3^9 \bmod 20$, $2^{14} \bmod 21$, $2^{107} \bmod 159$ using the Euler theorem.

2.9 Find using the Euclidean algorithm $\gcd(21, 12)$, $\gcd(30, 12)$, $\gcd(24, 40)$, $\gcd(33, 16)$.

2.10 Using the extended Euclidean algorithm, find x and y in equations

(a) $21x + 12y = \gcd(21, 12)$,
(b) $30x + 12y = \gcd(30, 12)$,
(c) $24x + 40y = \gcd(24, 40)$,
(d) $33x + 16y = \gcd(33, 16)$.

2.11 Compute $3^{-1} \bmod 7$, $5^{-1} \bmod 8$, $3^{-1} \bmod 53$, $10^{-1} \bmod 53$.

2.12 Write out all primes less than 100. Which of them are of the form $p = 2q + 1$, where q is also prime?

2.13 Find all relevant values for the parameter g in the Diffie–Hellman system with $p = 11$.

2.14 Compute secret keys Y_A, Y_B and a corresponding common key Z_{AB} in the Diffie–Hellman system with parameters

(a) $p = 23$, $g = 5$, $X_A = 5$, $X_B = 7$;
(b) $p = 19$, $g = 2$, $X_A = 5$, $X_B = 7$;
(c) $p = 23$, $g = 7$, $X_A = 3$, $X_B = 4$;
(d) $p = 17$, $g = 3$, $X_A = 10$, $X_B = 5$;
(e) $p = 19$, $g = 10$, $X_A = 4$, $X_B = 8$.

2.15 For Shamir's cipher with specified parameters p, c_A, c_B find missing parameters and describe the process of transmitting message m from A to B

(a) $p = 19$, $c_A = 5$, $c_B = 7$, $m = 4$;
(b) $p = 23$, $c_A = 15$, $c_B = 7$, $m = 6$;
(c) $p = 19$, $c_A = 11$, $c_B = 5$, $m = 10$;
(d) $p = 23$, $c_A = 9$, $c_B = 3$, $m = 17$;
(e) $p = 17$, $c_A = 3$, $c_B = 13$, $m = 9$.

2.16 For ElGamal's cipher with specified parameters p, g, c_B, k find missing parameters and describe the process of transmitting message m to user B

(a) $p = 19$, $g = 2$, $c_B = 5$, $k = 7$, $m = 5$;
(b) $p = 23$, $g = 5$, $c_B = 8$, $k = 10$, $m = 10$;
(c) $p = 19$, $g = 2$, $c_B = 11$, $k = 4$, $m = 10$;
(d) $p = 23$, $g = 7$, $c_B = 3$, $k = 15$, $m = 5$;
(e) $p = 17$, $g = 3$, $c_B = 10$, $k = 5$, $m = 10$.

2.17 For the RSA system with specified parameters P_A, Q_A, d_A find missing parameters and describe the process of transmitting message m

to user A

(a) $P_A = 5$, $Q_A = 11$, $d_A = 3$, $m = 12$;
(b) $P_A = 5$, $Q_A = 13$, $d_A = 5$, $m = 20$;
(c) $P_A = 7$, $Q_A = 11$, $d_A = 7$, $m = 17$;
(d) $P_A = 7$, $Q_A = 13$, $d_A = 5$, $m = 30$;
(e) $P_A = 3$, $Q_A = 11$, $d_A = 3$, $m = 15$.

2.18 The encrypted message $e = 100$ is sent to the RSA user with parameters $N = 187$, $d = 3$. Decrypt the message by breaking the RSA system of the user.

Themes for Labs

2.19 Write and debug the set of program functions implementing the basic algorithms used in the cryptosystems studied: modular exponentiation ($a^x \bmod m$), greatest common divisor ($\gcd(a, b)$), inversion ($x^{-1} \bmod m$).

2.20 Write a program implementing the Diffie–Hellman key agreement. The following parameter values are recommended: $p = 30803$, $g = 2$. Secret keys are to be randomly generated.

2.21 Write a program implementing the Shamir cipher. The number $p = 30803$ may be taken as a prime modulus. The other parameters are to be randomly generated.

2.22 Write a program implementing the ElGamal cipher. The following parameter values are recommended: $p = 30803$, $g = 2$. Private keys and the other parameters are to be randomly generated.

2.23 Write a program implementing the RSA cipher for transmitting messages to users A or B. The following parameter values are recommended: $P_A = 131$, $Q_A = 227$, $P_B = 113$, $Q_B = 281$, $d_A = d_B = 3$.

Chapter 3

Solving Discrete Logarithm Problem

3.1 Problem Setting

In order to construct a reliable cryptosystem one should take into account the methods of disclosure the adversary can employ. This allows one to choose cryptosystem parameters (e.g. the length of numbers) so that the adversary's methods become infeasible. In the present section, we shall consider two such methods to give the reader some insight into this "mysterious" field.

We have seen that many of the public-key ciphers are based on the one-way function

$$y = a^x \bmod p \tag{3.1}$$

and we know that given a and x the value of y can be computed with not more than $2 \log x$ operations (Proposition 2.1) But finding x given a and y, i.e. computing the discrete logarithm, is assumed to be a much more complex problem.

As it was shown in the justification of Shamir cipher (see (2.23)), by Fermat's theorem, when exponentiating modulo a prime p exponents are reduced modulo $p-1$. Therefore it suffices to deal with only the exponents x satisfying the inequality $0 \leq x \leq p-1$.

Denote by t_y the number of multiplications needed for computation of y in (3.1) given a and x and, for brevity, we shall call t_y time of computation. Time of exponentiation with the algorithms of Sec. 2.1 is not more than $2 \log x$ and $x < p$. Hence

$$t_y \leq 2 \log p \tag{3.2}$$

for any exponent x.

Now proceed to the problem of finding x in (3.1) given a and y. First estimate the complexity of the exhaustive search. In the exhaustive search, we begin with a^1 and check whether $a^1 = y$. If it is not the case, check whether $a^2 = y$, $a^3 = y$, and so on until $a^i = y$ is found (then $x = i$). On average, it will require to multiply by a and check for equality $(p-1)/2$ times. So the time of exhaustive search

$$t_{\text{e.s.}} \approx p/2.$$

With the "baby-step giant-step" algorithm described below the time of finding x is noticeably smaller:

$$t_{\text{b.s.g.s.}} \approx 2 \cdot \sqrt{p},$$

and with the index calculus algorithm also described below this time is even substantially smaller:

$$t_{\text{i.c.}} \approx c_1 \cdot 2^{c_2 \sqrt{\log p \log \log p}}$$

where c_1, c_2 are some positive constants.

To make the comparison more illustrative, express the time of computation through the bitlength of the numbers in (3.1). Denote the bitlength of p by n. When making computations modulo p we have $n \approx \log p$. Therefore the order of complexity (time of computation) for the above mentioned algorithms will be the following:

$$t_y \approx n,$$
$$t_{\text{e.s.}} \approx 2^{n-1},$$
$$t_{\text{b.s.g.s.}} \approx 2^{n/2},$$
$$t_{\text{i.c.}} \approx 2^{c_2 \sqrt{n \log n}},$$

where $\approx$ loosely denotes "proportional".

We can see that the time of exponentiation grows linearly as the length of numbers (n) increases but the time of solving the inverse problem grows exponentially or (for the index calculus algorithm) subexponentially. The issue of the existence of faster algorithms for computing discrete logarithms, as well as for solving other inverse problems in cryptography, remains an open question.

3.2   The Baby-step Giant-step Algorithm

In the unclassified literature this method was first described by Daniel Shanks (see [Knuth (1973)]); references thereto have been known since 1973. It was one of the first methods to show that the discrete logarithm problem can be solved much faster than by the exhaustive search. The algorithm is as follows.

Step 1 Take two integers m and k such that

$$mk > p.$$ (3.3)

Step 2 Compute two number series

$$y, \quad ay, \quad a^2 y, \quad \ldots, \quad a^{m-1} y \pmod{p};$$ (3.4)

$$a^m, \quad a^{2m}, \quad \ldots, \quad a^{km} \pmod{p}$$ (3.5)

(all computations are carried out modulo p).

Step 3 Find such i and j that

$$a^{im} = a^j y.$$ (3.6)

Proposition 3.1   *A number*

$$x = im - j$$ (3.7)

is the solution of Eq. (3.1). Besides, the integers i, j satisfying (3.6) exist.

Proof.   The correctness of (3.7) follows from the chain of equalities below, where all computations are modulo p and division corresponds to multiplication by an inverse number:

$$a^x = a^{im-j} = \frac{a^{im}}{a^j} = \frac{a^{im} y}{a^j y} = \frac{a^{im} y}{a^{im}} = y$$

(here the next to last equality follows from (3.6)). Next, show that the numbers i and j satisfying (3.6) exist. For that purpose place all numbers of the form (3.7) into the table (Table 3.1).

We can see that all numbers from 1 to km are contained in the table. It means by (3.3) that the table contains all numbers from 1 to p. So any exponent $x < p$ is present in the table, i.e. the number x satisfying (3.1) can be represented in the form (3.7), and (3.6) always has a solution. $\square$

Table 3.1   Numbers of the form $im - j$.

$i \downarrow$ $j \rightarrow$	0	1	2	...	$m - 1$
1	m	$m - 1$	$m - 2$	...	1
2	$2m$	$2m - 1$	$2m - 2$	...	$m + 1$
...	...	...	...	...	...
k	km	$km - 1$	$km - 2$	...	$(k-1)m + 1$

Example 3.1   Find the solution of the equation $2^x \bmod 23 = 9$ with the aid of baby-step giant-step algorithm.

Choose m and k. Let $m = 6$, $k = 4$. We can see that (3.3) is fulfilled. Compute the series (3.4), (3.5):

$$(3.4): \; 9, 18, 13, 3, 6, 12\,;$$

$$(3.5): \; 18\,.$$

Here we stop computations since there are equal numbers in (3.4) and (3.5) under $i = 1$, $j = 1$. By (3.7) we obtain

$$x = 1 \cdot 6 - 1 = 5\,.$$

Check it: $2^5 \bmod 23 = 9$. Indeed, $x = 5$ is the solution.

Let us explain the name of the algorithm considered. We know that in cryptography, p is a large number, hence m and k are also large. In the series (3.4), the exponent is increased by 1 (baby step), and in the series (3.5), the exponent is increased by m (giant step).

Let's now estimate the complexity of the method.

Proposition 3.2   *With the given method and for large p, computation time satisfies the inequality*

$$t_{b.s.g.s.} \leq \text{const} \cdot \sqrt{p} \log^2 p\,. \tag{3.8}$$

(Here we speak of the total time rather than of the number of multiplications.)

Proof.   We can take

$$k = m = \lfloor \sqrt{p} \rfloor + 1 \tag{3.9}$$

which, obviously, satisfies (3.3). Then no more than $2\sqrt{p}$ multiplications are required for computation of (3.4) and (3.5). We know that for "usual" ("secondary school") methods of multiplication and division, the time of computation with r-digit operands is proportional to r^2. We have all the numbers taken from the set $\{1, \ldots, p\}$, so $r \leq \log p$ and computation time is proportional to $\log^2 p$. Hence we immediately obtain the time needed for computation of the series (3.4) and (3.5). However we have not considered all stages of the algorithm. Namely, we have not considered the time required for the search of equal numbers between the two series. Under large k and m this is far from being simple. The problem can be solved in the following way: first ascribe to each number in a series the corresponding value of i or j and one extra bit indicating the series (3.4) or (3.5). Then join both series in one and sort with respect to the values of numbers. The length of the joint series is $k + m \approx 2\sqrt{p}$. For the best sorting methods, $S \log S$ comparisons are required, where S is the number of elements to sort (see e.g. [Aho *et al.* (1976)]). In our case $S = 2\sqrt{p}$ and consequently $2\sqrt{p} \log \left(2\sqrt{p}\right) \approx \sqrt{p} \log p$ comparisons with words of length $\log p$ bits are required, which totals to about $\sqrt{p} \log^2 p$ bit operations. After having sorted the joint series we look it through and find two equal numbers from different initial series (using the bit flag). Finally, summing up the times on all stages of the algorithm we obtain the estimate (3.8). $\qquad\square$

3.3 Index Calculus Algorithm

The main ideas behind the *index calculus algorithm* had been known in number theory since 1920s. But only in 1979 Adleman, one of the inventors of RSA, pointed out this algorithm as a means for solving Eq. (3.1) and investigated its complexity [Adleman (1979)]. At present time, the index calculus algorithm and its enhanced variants offer the fastest methods for computation of discrete logarithms in equations like (3.1).

Before describing the algorithm we introduce the following notion.

Definition 3.1 A number n is said to be *p-smooth* if all its prime factors are less than or equal to p.

Example 3.2 The numbers 15, 36, 45, 270, 2025 are 5-smooth (their factorisation includes only the prime factors 2, 3, and 5).

Proceed to the description of the algorithm.

Step 1 Select a factor base

$$S = \{p_1, p_2, \ldots, p_t\}$$

which consists of the first t primes (2, 3, 5, ..., a remark concerning the choice of t will be given below).

Step 2 By randomly selecting k find $t+\epsilon$ (ϵ is a small integer, see below) p_t-smooth numbers of the form $a^k \bmod p$. That is, for each k, we compute the number $a^k \bmod p$ and check its smoothness by trial division over the elements of S. If the number is p_t-smooth then we pick it for further use, else discard it and proceed with the next k. Write each p_t-smooth number found as a product of elements in S:

$$a^k \bmod p = \prod_{i=1}^{t} p_i^{c_i}, \quad c_i \geq 0 \tag{3.10}$$

(for each value of k we obtain the corresponding set of numbers c_i).

Step 3 Take logarithms on both sides of (3.10):

$$k = \sum_{i=1}^{t} c_i \log_a p_i \tag{3.11}$$

for each p_t-smooth number found at Step 2. We obtain a system of $t + \epsilon$ linear equations of the form (3.11) with t unknowns ($\log_a p_i$). We know that, in principle, t equations are enough for finding t unknowns. However, it may happen that some of the equations will be linearly dependent. That is why the number of equations is greater by ϵ than the number of unknowns. This increases the probability of obtaining a unique solution should some relations be linearly dependent. Now we solve the system using linear algebra methods with all calculations carried out modulo $p-1$ (recall that exponents and hence logarithms are reduced modulo $p-1$). As a result, we obtain the values of logarithms of elements from S: $\log_a p_1, \log_a p_2, \ldots, \log_a p_t$.

Step 4 By randomly selecting r find p_t-smooth number of the form $y \cdot a^r \bmod p$:

$$y \cdot a^r \bmod p = \prod_{i=1}^{t} p_i^{e_i}, \quad e_i \geq 0. \tag{3.12}$$

That is, similar to Step 2, compute the number $y \cdot a^r \bmod p$ and check whether it is p_t-smooth. If not, try the next r.

Step 5 Taking logarithms on both sides of (3.12) obtain the final result

$$x = \log_a y = \left(\sum_{i=1}^{t} e_i \log_a p_i \quad - r \right) \bmod (p-1). \tag{3.13}$$

The correctness of the described algorithm is quite obvious and its effectiveness is connected with the following observation. If we select randomly a number from the infinite set of integers then with probability $1/2$ it is divisible by 2, with probability $1/3$ divisible by 3, with probability $1/5$ divisible by 5, and so on. So we may expect that in the interval from 1 to $p-1$ there are sufficiently many numbers whose prime factors are only the elements of our factor base S. Exactly such numbers are being sought at steps 2 and 4 of the algorithm.

As we have mentioned above, the parameter ϵ must ensure a unique solution at Step 3. It is believed that given a large p the value of ϵ about 10 guarantees the uniqueness of solution with high probability (see [Menezes *et al.* (1996)]). If it is not the case then it is necessary to revert to Step 2 and use other values of k.

Now let's discuss the complexity issues. The running time of the algorithm depends on the choice of t. The more is t, i.e. the number of prime factors in S, the less fails we meet when searching smooth numbers at steps 2 and 4 (it is easy to see that complexity of Step 2 is $t + \epsilon$ times greater than that of Step 4). But with large t the complexity of Step 3 drastically increases since we have to solve the system with $t + \epsilon$ equations. Finding an optimum t which minimises the overall time may usually be done by numerical methods. Adleman [Adleman (1979)] showed that under an optimal choice of t the complexity of the algorithm is estimated as

$$t_{\text{i.c.}} < c_1 2^{(c_2 + o(1))\sqrt{\log p \log \log p}}$$

where c_1, c_2 are some positive constants.

Example 3.3 Apply the index calculus algorithm to solve the equation

$$37 = 10^x \bmod 47. \tag{3.14}$$

We have $y = 37$, $a = 10$, $p = 47$. Take as a factor base $S = \{2, 3, 5\}$, $t = 3$, and assume $\epsilon = 1$, i.e. we shall construct a system of 4 equations. We completed the first step of the algorithm and proceed to the second.

Let's find four 5-smooth numbers (taking $k = 1, 2, 3, \ldots$):

$$
\begin{aligned}
10^1 \bmod 47 &= 10 = 2 \cdot 5 && \checkmark \\
10^2 \bmod 47 &= 6 \;\; = 2 \cdot 3 && \checkmark \\
10^3 \bmod 47 &= 13 = 13 \\
10^4 \bmod 47 &= 36 = 2 \cdot 2 \cdot 3 \cdot 3 && \checkmark \\
10^5 \bmod 47 &= 31 = 31 \\
10^6 \bmod 47 &= 28 = 2 \cdot 2 \cdot 7 \\
10^7 \bmod 47 &= 45 = 3 \cdot 3 \cdot 5 && \checkmark
\end{aligned}
$$

We have found four 5-smooth numbers (marked with a $\checkmark$) corresponding to the exponents 1, 2, 4, and 7.

Begin the third step of the algorithm. For ease of exposition, denote the logarithms of the numbers p_1, p_2, p_3 from S by u_1, u_2, u_3, respectively, e.g. $u_3 = \log_{10} 5 \bmod 47$. For the equations checked with a $\checkmark$ at the previous step, turn to the logarithms and construct a system

$$1 = u_1 + u_3, \tag{3.15}$$

$$2 = u_1 + u_2, \tag{3.16}$$

$$4 = 2u_1 + 2u_2, \tag{3.17}$$

$$7 = 2u_2 + u_3. \tag{3.18}$$

We can see that in the system obtained, Eqs. (3.16) and (3.17) are linearly dependent, so it was not in vain that we have found the 4th smooth number. To solve the system, subtract (3.15) from (3.16). We obtain

$$1 = u_2 - u_3. \tag{3.19}$$

Add (3.19) to (3.18). We obtain

$$8 = 3u_2. \tag{3.20}$$

From (3.20) we immediately find u_2 (recall that the logarithms are reduced modulo $47 - 1 = 46$):

$$u_2 = (8/3) \bmod 46 = 8 \cdot 3^{-1} \bmod 46 = 8 \cdot 31 \bmod 46 = 18.$$

We can make a check by computing $10^{18} \bmod 47 = 3$, so u_2 is actually the logarithm of 3. Now from (3.19) find u_3:

$$u_3 = u_2 - 1 = 18 - 1 = 17$$

(actually, $10^{17} \bmod 47 = 5$). Finally, from (3.16) find u_1:

$$u_1 = 2 - u_2 = (2 - 18) \bmod 46 = -16 \bmod 46 = 30$$

($10^{30} \bmod 47 = 2$).

Thus we know the logarithms of the elements of S. The most complex part of the algorithm is left behind. Proceed to the fourth step. Select (randomly) $r = 3$ and compute

$$37 \cdot 10^3 \bmod 47 = 37 \cdot 13 \bmod 47 = 11.$$

The number 11 is not 5-smooth, so try the next r:

$$37 \cdot 10^4 \bmod 47 = 37 \cdot 36 \bmod 47 = 16 = 2 \cdot 2 \cdot 2 \cdot 2.$$

The number 16 is 5-smooth and the fourth step is completed.

Turn to logarithms in the last equality (this is the fifth step) and obtain the final result:

$$\log_{10} 37 = 4 \log_{10} 2 - 4 = (4 \cdot 30 - 4) \bmod 46 = 24.$$

We have found the solution of Eq. (3.14) $x = 24$. We may check it: $10^{24} \bmod 47 = 37$.

The fastest to the date is the variant of the described index calculus algorithm called Number Field Sieve, see [Lenstra and Lenstra (1993)]. This method is based upon subtle algebraic constructions so we do not describe it in this book. Its time complexity is estimated as

$$t_{\text{n.f.s.}} < c_1 \cdot 2^{(c_2 + o(1)) \sqrt[3]{\log p (\log \log p)^2}} \tag{3.21}$$

where c_1, c_2 are some positive constants. It is this method which dictates the conditions for choosing the length of modules in the cryptosystem that rely on intractability of discrete logarithm problem (among the systems considered in Chap. 2 these are Diffie–Hellman, Shamir, and ElGamal schemes). To achieve long-term security it is recommended that the length of modulus be at least 1024 bits (as for 2005).

Remark at the conclusion that in our book, we do not consider the methods of breaking the cryptosystems whose security is based on integer factorisation problem (such as RSA). The fact is that this discussion would require to introduce some extra notions and algorithms from number theory that are of no use elsewhere in this book. However we may say that to date the fastest methods of factorisation are characterised by the same estimate of complexity as given by Eq. (3.21). As a consequence, to ensure long-term security of RSA system the modulus length must also be at least 1024 bits (i.e. prime numbers producing a modulus must be at least 512 bits each).

Problems and Exercises

3.1 Using the baby-step giant-step algorithm, solve the following equations:

(a) $2^x \bmod 29 = 21$,
(b) $3^x \bmod 31 = 25$,
(c) $2^x \bmod 37 = 12$,
(d) $6^x \bmod 41 = 21$,
(e) $3^x \bmod 43 = 11$.

3.2 Using the index calculus algorithm, solve the following equations:

(a) $2^x \bmod 53 = 24$,
(b) $2^x \bmod 59 = 13$,
(c) $2^x \bmod 61 = 45$,
(d) $2^x \bmod 67 = 41$,
(e) $7^x \bmod 71 = 41$.

Themes for Labs

3.3 Create programs implementing the baby-step giant-step and index calculus algorithms and solve on a computer the following equations:

(a) $2^x \bmod 30203 = 24322$,
(b) $2^x \bmod 30323 = 21740$,
(c) $2^x \bmod 30539 = 28620$,
(d) $2^x \bmod 30803 = 16190$,
(e) $5^x \bmod 31607 = 30994$

(due to lack of time, program implementation of only some steps of the algorithms would be enough).

Chapter 4

Digital Signatures

4.1 RSA Digital Signature

Public-key cryptography has made a real revolution in contemporary computer and network technologies. There emerged a possibility to solve problems that earlier had seemed insoluble but now are widely called for in practice. One of the important elements of these new technologies is digital signature. In many countries, including USA and Russia, digital signature standards are adopted and the notion of digital signature is made part of civil legislation.

Before studying cryptographic digital signatures, let us formulate the main requirements which, ideally, should be met by any signature (including handwritten).

(1) It must be only the entity A that could sign documents on behalf of A, i.e. no one should be able to forge signatures.
(2) If the signed document is somehow altered or damaged, the signature must become invalid.
(3) The author of signature should not be able to repudiate it.
(4) The signature must be verifiable by all interested parties, and moreover, a third party (e.g. the court) should be able to decide on the authenticity of signature in case of contention.

Of course, digital signatures should meet all these requirements but the signer and verifier may be thousands of kilometres from each other and communicate via an open computer network (e.g. the Internet).

In this section, we consider a digital signature scheme based on the RSA algorithm [Rivest *et al.* (1978)]. Historically, it was the first method discovered for creating digital signatures. Let's proceed to its description.

Suppose Alice intends to sign documents. Then she has to choose the RSA parameters in the same way as was described in Sec. 2.6. To do that, Alice selects two large primes P and Q, computes $N = PQ$ and $\phi = (P-1)(Q-1)$. Then she selects a number d relatively prime to ϕ and finds

$$c = d^{-1} \bmod \phi. \tag{4.1}$$

At last, she publishes the numbers N and d (her public key), e.g. exposes them at her Internet site in association with her name, and keeps secret the number c (her private key, the other numbers P, Q, and ϕ are no longer required). Now Alice is ready to sign documents and messages.

Assume that Alice wishes to sign a message $\bar{m} = m_1, \dots, m_n$. First, she computes a so-called *hash function*

$$h = h(m_1, \dots, m_n)$$

which maps the message $\bar{m}$ into a number h. It is assumed that the hash function algorithm is publicly known. For the time being, we shall not speak of the properties and ways of computation of hash functions, as this question will be considered in detail in Sec. 8.5. Point out only the property most important for us here: it is practically impossible to alter the main text $m_1, \dots, m_n$ without altering $h(\bar{m})$. So, it is enough for Alice to sign only the number h, and this will act as a signature to the whole message $\bar{m}$.

Alice computes the number

$$s = h^c \bmod N, \tag{4.2}$$

i.e. she raises h to her secret power. The number s is nothing else but the digital signature. Alice simply appends s to the message $\bar{m}$ and obtains the signed message

$$\langle \bar{m}, \ s \rangle. \tag{4.3}$$

Now everybody who knows Alice's public key, i.e. the numbers N and d associated with her name, can verify the authenticity of her signature. To do that, given the signed message (4.3), one needs to compute hash function $h(\bar{m})$ and the number

$$w = s^d \bmod N, \tag{4.4}$$

after which to check the equality $w = h(\bar{m})$.

Proposition 4.1 *If the signature is authentic, $w = h(\bar{m})$.*

Proof. It follows from (4.4), (4.2) and (4.1) that

$$w = s^d \bmod N = h^{cd} \bmod N = h = h(\bar{m}).$$

$\square$

Proposition 4.2 *The described digital signature satisfies all the requirements the signature must meet.*

Proof. The first requirement is met since nobody who knows only the public parameters N and d can derive secret c which is needed to produce a signature (we have already discussed this problem in Sec. 2.6). The second requirement is fulfilled due to hash function: any change in the message contents will (with overwhelming probability) also change the value of h, which makes the previously computed signature invalid. The third requirement is met as a consequence of the former two (the author cannot repudiate the signature since nobody is able to alter the document and forge the signature). Finally, everybody who knows the public parameters N and d can verify the signature. In case of contention, the court can reproduce all computations.

$\square$

Example 4.1 Let $P = 5$, $Q = 11$. Then $N = 5 \cdot 11 = 55$, $\phi = 4 \cdot 10 = 40$. Let $d = 3$. Such a choice of d is valid since $\gcd(40, 3) = 1$. Compute the private key $c = 3^{-1} \bmod 40$ with the extended Euclidean algorithm (see Sec. 2.3), $c = 27$.

Assume that Alice wishes to sign the message $\bar{m} = abbbaa$, the value of hash function being, say, 13:

$$h = h(abbbaa) = 13.$$

Alice computes by (4.2)

$$s = 13^{27} \bmod 55 = 7$$

and obtains the signed message

$$\langle abbbaa,\ 7 \rangle .$$

Now the one who knows Alice's public key $N = 55$, $d = 3$ can verify the signature. Having received the signed message, one computes hash function

$$h(abbbaa) = 13$$

(if the contents of the message are not changed, the value of hash function equals that computed by Alice) and compute by (4.4)

$$w = 7^3 \bmod 55 = 13 \, .$$

The values of w and the hash function are equal, hence, the signature is valid.

Remark   Notice that the same RSA scheme generated by Alice can be used for solving two problems. First, Alice can sign messages as was shown in the present section, by utilising her *secret key c*. Second, anybody can encrypt messages to be read by Alice as was shown in Sec. 2.6, by utilising her *public key d*.

4.2   ElGamal Digital Signature

In the previous section, a digital signature scheme was described whose security is based on intractability of integer factorisation problem. In this section, we present a scheme that relies upon another hard problem, namely, computing discrete logarithms. This scheme was suggested in [ElGamal (1985)] and utilises the ElGamal encryption (see Sec. 2.5).

Assume as before that Alice is going to sign documents. Alice chooses a large prime p and a number g such that different powers of g are different numbers modulo p (see Sec. 2.2). These numbers are transmitted or stored in clear and may be used by the whole community of users. Alice then selects a random number x, $1 < x < p - 1$, which she keeps secret. This is her private key unknown to anybody. Alice computes the number

$$y = g^x \bmod p \tag{4.5}$$

and publishes it as her public key. Due to the hardness of discrete logarithm problem, it is assumed impossible to find x given p and y.

Now Alice is ready to sign messages. Suppose she wants to sign a message $\bar{m} = m_1, \ldots, m_n$. Describe the steps needed to create a signature.

Alice begins with computing a hash function of the message $h = h(\bar{m})$, $1 < h < p$. Then Alice selects a random number k ($1 < k < p-1$) relatively prime to $p - 1$, and computes

$$r = g^k \bmod p \, . \tag{4.6}$$

Then Alice computes

$$u = (h - xr) \bmod (p - 1) \, , \tag{4.7}$$

$$s = k^{-1} u \bmod (p - 1) \, . \tag{4.8}$$

(Remark that k^{-1} in (4.8) denotes a number satisfying the equality

$$k^{-1}k \bmod (p-1) = 1. \tag{4.9}$$

Such a k^{-1} exists since k and $p-1$ are coprime, and can be found with the extended Euclidean algorithm.) Eventually, Alice forms the signed message

$$\langle \bar{m};\ r,\ s \rangle. \tag{4.10}$$

The receiver of the signed message (4.10), first of all, computes again the hash function $h = h(\bar{m})$. Then he verifies the signature using the equality

$$y^r r^s = g^h \bmod p. \tag{4.11}$$

Proposition 4.3 *If the signature is authentic then (4.11) holds.*

Proof. Recall that in all computations the exponents are reduced modulo $p-1$. Substitute y and r in Eq. (4.11) by their defining equations (4.5) and (4.6), and then replace s by (4.8), (4.7):

$$
\begin{aligned}
y^r r^s &= (g^x)^r \left(g^k \right)^s = g^{xr} g^{k\left(k^{-1}(h-xr)\right)} \\
&= g^{xr} g^h g^{-xr} = g^h \bmod p.
\end{aligned}
$$

The proof is complete. $\square$

Proposition 4.4 *The described digital signature satisfies all the requirements the signature must meet.*

Proof. The proof is virtually the same as for RSA signature. First, a secret number x is used in the process of signature generation, moreover, the factor xr in (4.7) changes from message to message since k is selected at random. Therefore nobody can forge the signature. Second, the hash function protects from altering signed messages. Third, the author cannot repudiate the signature as a consequence of the former items. Finally, everybody who knows the public key y and common parameters p and g can verify the signature. In case of contention, the court can reproduce all computations. $\square$

Example 4.2 Let common parameters for a community of users be $p = 23$, $g = 5$. Alice chooses her private key $x = 7$ and computes her public key y by (4.5):

$$y = 5^7 \bmod 23 = 17.$$

Let Alice create the document $\bar{m} = baaaab$ and wish to sign it.

Proceed to signature generation. First of all, Alice computes the hash function of the message. Let $h(\bar{m}) = 3$. Then Alice selects a random number k, e.g. $k = 5$. Computations by (4.6), (4.7) give

$$r = 5^5 \bmod 23 = 20 \,,$$

$$u = (3 - 7 \cdot 20) \bmod 22 = 17 \,.$$

Then Alice finds $k^{-1} \bmod 22$:

$$k^{-1} \bmod 22 = 5^{-1} \bmod 22 = 9 \,.$$

Computations by (4.8) give

$$s = 9 \cdot 17 \bmod 22 = 21 \,.$$

At last, Alice forms the signed message (4.10) that looks like

$$\langle baaaab,\ 20,\ 21 \rangle \,.$$

The signed message is transmitted. Bob (or someone else) receives it and verifies the signature. First, he computes the hash function

$$h(baaaab) = 3 \,,$$

then he computes the left of (4.11)

$$17^{20} \cdot 20^{21} \bmod 23 = 16 \cdot 15 \bmod 23 = 10$$

and the right of (4.11)

$$5^3 \bmod 23 = 10 \,.$$

Since the results of both computations are the same, Bob concludes that the signature is valid, i.e. the message is authentic.

The considered digital signature scheme is somewhat more complex than RSA but its security is based on a different one-way function. It is important for cryptography because should one system be broken or compromised, the other may be used instead. Besides, ElGamal signature is a basis for a more efficient algorithm in which computation time is substantially reduced due to the use of "short" exponents. Such an algorithm is presented in the following section.

4.3   Digital Signature Standards

Today, digital signature standards exist in many countries. In this section, we describe the US standard [FIPS 186-2 (2000)] and Russian GOST R34.10-94. Both standards are based on essentially the same algorithm called DSA (Digital Signature Algorithm) which, in turn, is a variant of ElGamal signature. We consider in detail an American version of the algorithm and then show the distinctive features of the Russian variant.

As a preliminary setup, for a community of users, common open parameters are to be chosen. First, two prime numbers, q (of length 160 bits) and p (of length up to 1024 bits) are chosen related by the equation

$$p = bq + 1 \tag{4.12}$$

for some integer b. The most significant bits in p and q must be 1. Second, a number $a > 1$ is chosen such that

$$a^q \bmod p = 1. \tag{4.13}$$

As a result, we have the three common parameters p, q, and a.

Note that Eq. (4.13) means that, operating modulo p, the exponents of a are reduced modulo q, i.e.

$$a^c \bmod p = a^{c \bmod q} \bmod p \quad \text{for all } c. \tag{4.14}$$

Indeed, if $c = mq + r$, where $0 \le r < q$, then $a^c \bmod p = (a^q)^m \cdot a^r \bmod p = 1 \cdot a^r \bmod p$, see (4.13). This reduction will always be made during signature generation and verification to ensure that the length of exponents will never exceed 160 bit, which simplifies computations.

Every user then chooses a random number x satisfying the condition $0 < x < q$ and computes

$$y = a^x \bmod p. \tag{4.15}$$

The number x will be the private key of the user and the number y the public key. It is assumed that the public keys for all users are collected in a non-secret but "certified" directory which is made available to the whole community. Note that nowadays it is impossible to find x given y under the length of p indicated above. This completes the setup stage of the scheme and now all users are ready to generate and verify signatures.

Let there be given a message $\bar{m}$ to be signed. Signature generation is done as follows.

1 Compute hash function $h = h(\bar{m})$ for message m, the hash function value should lie within the limits $0 < h < q$ (in American standard, SHA-1 hash function [FIPS 180-1 (1995)] must be used).

2 Select a random integer k, $0 < k < q$.

3 Compute $r = \left(a^k \bmod p\right) \bmod q$. If $r = 0$, revert to Step 2.

4 Compute $s = k^{-1}(h + xr) \bmod q$. If $s = 0$, revert to Step 2.

5 Obtain the signed message $\langle \bar{m};\ r,\ s \rangle$.

To verify the signature do the following.

6 Compute hash function of the message $h = h(\bar{m})$.

7 Verify that $0 < r < q$ and $0 < s < q$.

8 Compute $u_1 = h \cdot s^{-1} \bmod q$, $u_2 = r \cdot s^{-1} \bmod q$.

9 Compute $v = (a^{u_1} y^{u_2} \bmod p) \bmod q$.

10 Verify that $v = r$.

If at least one test at Step 7 or 10 fails one should reject the signature. And vice versa, if all the tests pass, the signature is declared valid.

Proposition 4.5 *If the signature on the message was created by a legitimate user, i.e. by the owner of private key x, then $v = r$.*

Proof. Recall that Eq. (4.14) holds for all exponentials with base a. Since y defined by Eq. (4.15) is a power of a, Eq. (4.14) also holds for all exponentials with y as a base. Now, using the definition of v (Step 9) and substituting the defining equations for u_1, u_2 (Step 8) we obtain

$$v = \left(a^{hs^{-1}} y^{rs^{-1}} \bmod p\right) \bmod q. \qquad (4.16)$$

Using the definition of s (Step 4) we can write

$$s^{-1} \bmod q = k(h + xr)^{-1} \bmod q. \qquad (4.17)$$

Substituting the right of Eq. (4.17) for s^{-1} in Eq. (4.16) we obtain

$$v = \left(a^{hk(h+xr)^{-1}} a^{xrk(h+xr)^{-1}} \bmod p\right) \bmod q$$
$$= \left(a^{(h+xr)^{-1}(h+xr)k} \bmod p\right) \bmod q$$
$$= \left(a^k \bmod p\right) \bmod q.$$

Taking into account the definition of r (Step 3) we conclude that $v = r$ which completes the proof. $\qquad \square$

Remark To find an integer a satisfying (4.13) the following method is recommended. Select a random integer $g > 1$ and compute

$$a = g^{(p-1)/q} \bmod p. \tag{4.18}$$

If $a > 1$ then it is what we need. Indeed, by (4.18) and Fermat's theorem

$$a^q \bmod p = g^{((p-1)/q)q} \bmod p = g^{p-1} \bmod p = 1,$$

i.e. (4.13) holds. If after computation by (4.18) we obtain $a = 1$ (extremely improbable case) then we should try another value of g.

Example 4.3 Choose common parameters

$$q = 11, \quad p = 6q + 1 = 67,$$

select $g = 10$ and compute

$$a = 10^6 \bmod 67 = 25.$$

Choose a private key $x = 6$ and compute the corresponding public key

$$y = 25^6 \bmod 67 = 62.$$

Generate a signature for the message $\bar{m} = baaaab$. Let hash function $h(\bar{m}) = 3$. Select randomly an integer $k = 8$. Compute

$$r = \left(25^8 \bmod 67\right) \bmod 11 = 24 \bmod 11 = 2,$$
$$k^{-1} \bmod q = 8^{-1} \bmod 11 = 7,$$
$$s = (7(3 + 6 \cdot 2) \bmod 11 = 105 \bmod 11 = 6.$$

We obtain the signed message

$$\langle baaaab;\ 2,\ 6 \rangle.$$

Now verify the signature. If the message is intact then $h = 3$. Compute

$$s^{-1} \bmod q = 6^{-1} \bmod 11 = 2,$$
$$u_1 = 3 \cdot 2 \bmod 11 = 6,$$
$$u_2 = 2 \cdot 2 \bmod 11 = 4,$$
$$v = \left(25^6 \cdot 62^4 \bmod 67\right) \bmod 11$$
$$= (62 \cdot 22 \bmod 67) \bmod 11 = 24 \bmod 11 = 2.$$

We see that $v = r$, hence, the signature is valid.

Let us now discuss the differences of the Russian standard with respect to the American. These are only the following.

(1) The length of q is 256 bits.
(2) As a hash function, Russian GOST R34.11-94 is used.
(3) In signature generation at Step 4, the parameter s is computed by the formula $s = (kh + xr) \bmod q$.
(4) In signature verification at Step 8, u_1 and u_2 are computed by the formulas $u_1 = s \cdot h^{-1} \bmod q$, $u_2 = -r \cdot h^{-1} \bmod q$.

Taking into account these differences one can easily rewrite the whole scheme in "Russian" style. The proof of correctness is quite similar.

Problems and Exercises

Assume in all tasks that $h(m) = m$ for all m.

4.1 Generate RSA signature on m given the following parameters:

(a) $P = 5$, $Q = 11$, $c = 27$, $m = 7$;
(b) $P = 5$, $Q = 13$, $c = 29$, $m = 10$;
(c) $P = 7$, $Q = 11$, $c = 43$, $m = 5$;
(d) $P = 7$, $Q = 13$, $c = 29$, $m = 15$;
(e) $P = 3$, $Q = 11$, $c = 7$, $m = 24$.

4.2 For the specified public keys of RSA user, verify the authenticity of signed messages

(a) $N = 55$, $d = 3$: $\langle 7, 28 \rangle$, $\langle 22, 15 \rangle$, $\langle 16, 36 \rangle$;
(b) $N = 65$, $d = 5$: $\langle 6, 42 \rangle$, $\langle 10, 30 \rangle$, $\langle 6, 41 \rangle$;
(c) $N = 77$, $d = 7$: $\langle 13, 41 \rangle$, $\langle 11, 28 \rangle$, $\langle 5, 26 \rangle$;
(d) $N = 91$, $d = 5$: $\langle 15, 71 \rangle$, $\langle 11, 46 \rangle$, $\langle 16, 74 \rangle$;
(e) $N = 33$, $d = 3$: $\langle 10, 14 \rangle$, $\langle 24, 18 \rangle$, $\langle 17, 8 \rangle$.

4.3 The users of some network apply the ElGamal signature with common parameters $p = 23$, $g = 5$. For the specified private key, find corresponding public key and generate a signature for message m.

(a) $x = 11$, $k = 3$, $m = h = 15$;
(b) $x = 10$, $k = 15$, $m = h = 5$;
(c) $x = 3$, $k = 13$, $m = h = 8$;
(d) $x = 18$, $k = 7$, $m = h = 5$;
(e) $x = 9$, $k = 19$, $m = h = 15$.

4.4 For the specified public key (y) of the ElGamal system with common parameters $p = 23$, $g = 5$, verify the authenticity of signed messages

    (a) $y = 22$: $\langle 15; 20, 3 \rangle$, $\langle 15; 10, 5 \rangle$, $\langle 15; 19, 3 \rangle$;

    (b) $y = 9$: $\langle 5; 19, 17 \rangle$, $\langle 7; 17, 8 \rangle$, $\langle 6; 17, 8 \rangle$;

    (c) $y = 10$: $\langle 3; 17, 12 \rangle$, $\langle 2; 17, 12 \rangle$, $\langle 8; 21, 11 \rangle$;

    (d) $y = 6$: $\langle 5; 17, 1 \rangle$, $\langle 5; 11, 3 \rangle$, $\langle 5; 17, 10 \rangle$;

    (e) $y = 11$: $\langle 15; 7, 1 \rangle$, $\langle 10; 15, 3 \rangle$, $\langle 15; 7, 16 \rangle$.

4.5 A community of DSA users have the common parameters $q = 11$, $p = 67$, $a = 25$. Compute the public key (y) and generate a signature for message m given the following secret parameters:

    (a) $x = 3$, $h = m = 10$, $k = 1$;

    (b) $x = 8$, $h = m = 1$, $k = 3$;

    (c) $x = 5$, $h = m = 5$, $k = 9$;

    (d) $x = 2$, $h = m = 6$, $k = 7$;

    (e) $x = 9$, $h = m = 7$, $k = 5$.

4.6 For the specified public keys of DSA users with common parameters $q = 11$, $p = 67$, $a = 25$, verify the authenticity of signed messages

    (a) $y = 14$: $\langle 10; 4, 5 \rangle$, $\langle 10; 7, 4 \rangle$, $\langle 10; 3, 8 \rangle$;

    (b) $y = 24$: $\langle 1; 3, 1 \rangle$, $\langle 1; 9, 1 \rangle$, $\langle 1; 4, 5 \rangle$;

    (c) $y = 40$: $\langle 7; 7, 4 \rangle$, $\langle 7; 9, 2 \rangle$, $\langle 5; 9, 8 \rangle$;

    (d) $y = 22$: $\langle 6; 9, 5 \rangle$, $\langle 8; 8, 3 \rangle$, $\langle 7; 4, 7 \rangle$;

    (e) $y = 64$: $\langle 10; 7, 8 \rangle$, $\langle 7; 7, 3 \rangle$, $\langle 8; 7, 5 \rangle$.

Themes for Labs

4.7 Work out programs for generation and verification of RSA signatures. The user parameters should be chosen on one's own. To test the signature verification program, the signed message $\langle 500, 46514 \rangle$ constructed under the public parameters $N = 52891$, $d = 3$ may be used (assume that $h(m) = m$). This message should be declared authentic. Any change in components of the signed message, with high probability, should make the signature invalid.

4.8 Work out programs for generation and verification of ElGamal signatures. The recommended values of common parameters are $p = 31259$, $g = 2$. The other parameters should be chosen on one's own. To test the signature verification program, the signed message $\langle 500; 27665, 26022 \rangle$ constructed under the public key $y = 16196$

may be used (assume that $h(m) = m$). This message should be declared authentic. Any change in components of the signed message, with high probability, should make the signature invalid.

4.9 Work out programs for generation and verification of DSA signatures. The recommended values of common parameters are $q = 787$, $p = 31481$, $a = 1928$. The other parameters should be chosen on one's own. To test the signature verification program, the signed message $\langle 500; 655, 441 \rangle$ constructed under the public key $y = 12785$ may be used (assume that $h(m) = m$). This message should be declared authentic. Any change in components of the signed message, with high probability, should make the signature invalid.

Chapter 5

Cryptographic Protocols

The cryptographic methods considered in the previous chapters are often used as tools for solving many other important problems. Not long ago some of those problems seemed completely insoluble. For example, it seemed impossible to securely commit commercial transactions between remote participants connected through open communications media, to make secure money transfers over public channels, to conduct elections without personal attendance and so on. Now all these problems can be solved by applying cryptographic techniques. The methods involved are usually described in a form of so-called *cryptographic protocols*. Several such protocols will be presented in this chapter.

Notice that cryptographic algorithms not only offer new facilities to the user (e.g. she can use a home computer and does not need to go to the bank to make payments) but are able to provide a considerably higher level of security compared to traditional mechanisms. For example, a traditional paper bank note can be fabricated, and the acts of fabricating money occur quite frequently, but by contrast, a digital bank note created with the use of cryptographic methods is practically impossible to fabricate.

Quite often important problems are formulated in a form of amusing game in order to make a solution "pure", not overladen with technical details. One of such problems, "mental poker", is considered in the next section.

5.1 Mental Poker

Consider a problem of playing a fair card game when the players are far from each other and can communicate only via some public channel, e.g. exchange messages via electronic mail. We consider an extremely simplified version of the problem where there are only two players and three cards. Nevertheless, all basic ideas will be demonstrated with obvious generalisations to other cases.

The problem is stated as follows. There are two players, Alice and Bob, and three cards, α, β, γ. It is required to deal cards so that each player gets one card and one card remains in the deck. Moreover, at the end of the game the following conditions must be fulfilled:

(1) each player gets any of three cards with equal probabilities;
(2) each player knows only his/her card but not the card of the opponent and/or the deck;
(3) in case of contention, a third party is able to judge who has cheated;
(4) anyone who overhears transmitted messages is unable to determine which cards are dealt to.

Let's describe the protocol that allows to arrange such distribution of cards. A preliminary stage is needed for selecting the parameters of protocol. The participants publicly choose a large prime p. Then Alice randomly selects a number c_A coprime to $p-1$ and finds with the extended Gaussian algorithm the number d_A such that

$$c_A d_A \bmod (p-1) = 1. \tag{5.1}$$

Independently and similarly, Bob finds a pair c_B, d_B such that

$$c_B d_B \bmod (p-1) = 1. \tag{5.2}$$

These numbers are kept secret by each player. Then Alice randomly selects three different numbers $\hat{\alpha}$, $\hat{\beta}$, $\hat{\gamma}$ in the interval from 1 to $p-1$, sends them to Bob in clear and tells that $\hat{\alpha}$ corresponds to α, $\hat{\beta}$ to β, $\hat{\gamma}$ to γ (e.g. 3756 denotes the ace).

After that we go to the second stage — the distribution of cards which is described by the following steps.

Step 1 Alice computes the numbers

$$u_1 = \hat{\alpha}^{c_A} \bmod p,$$
$$u_2 = \hat{\beta}^{c_A} \bmod p,$$
$$u_3 = \hat{\gamma}^{c_A} \bmod p,$$

and sends u_1, u_2, u_3 to Bob having shuffled them beforehand.

Step 2 Bob receives the three numbers, selects randomly one of them, say, u_2, and sends it back to Alice. It will be the card dealt to her in the game. Upon the receipt of u_2, Alice can compute

$$\hat{u} = u_2^{d_A} \bmod p = \hat{\beta}^{c_A d_A} \bmod p = \hat{\beta}, \tag{5.3}$$

i.e. she learns that her hand is β (she could learn this without computation since she knows the correspondence between all u_i and the cards).

Step 3 Bob continues. He computes for the two numbers left

$$v_1 = u_1^{c_B} \bmod p, \tag{5.4}$$

$$v_3 = u_3^{c_B} \bmod p. \tag{5.5}$$

With probability $1/2$ he rearranges v_1 and v_3 and sends them to Alice.

Step 4 Alice selects randomly one of the numbers received, say, v_1, computes the number

$$w_1 = v_1^{d_A} \bmod p \tag{5.6}$$

and sends w_1 to Bob. Bob computes

$$z = w_1^{d_B} \bmod p \tag{5.7}$$

and learns his card (his hand is $\hat{\alpha}$). Indeed,

$$z = w_1^{d_B} = v_1^{d_A d_B} = u_1^{c_B d_B d_A} = \hat{\alpha}^{c_A c_B d_A d_B} = \hat{\alpha} \bmod p.$$

The card corresponding to v_2 remains in the deck.

Proposition 5.1 *The described protocol satisfies all requirements to fair distribution of cards.*

Proof. We give only the idea of proof. Alice shuffles the numbers u_1, u_2, u_3 prior to sending them to Bob. Then Bob selects one of these numbers without any knowledge of what corresponds to what. If he selects a number randomly, Alice gets any card with probability $1/3$. Similarly, if Alice selects one of the two remaining cards randomly (with equal probabilities) then Bob gets the card which can be any card with probability $1/3$. It is plain that under these conditions, the card in the deck can also be any card with probability $1/3$.

It is interesting to note that if any of the players will violate the protocol specifications, it may be used against that player. Therefore each player is concerned with exact observance of rules. Let's check it assuming that the game repeats many times.

Suppose that Alice does not shuffle the numbers u_1, u_2, u_3, but always sends them in one order or follows some other simple rule. If the distribution of cards is carried out several times, Bob can benefit from Alice's behaviour (e.g. he will always send back to Alice the first number and will know what card she is dealt). So it is advantageous to Alice to shuffle the cards. Similarly, it can be easily checked that it is better for Bob to shuffle and select cards randomly (with equal probabilities).

Check the second requirement to a fair card game. When Bob selects u_i to be Alice's card (Step 2) he does not know the secret c_A, so he cannot determine to which card u_i corresponds and computation of c_A given u_i is equivalent to solving the discrete logarithm problem which is impossible when p is large. As a matter of fact, when Alice selects a card for Bob, and Bob for Alice, neither of them can determine the value of the card because it is encrypted with either c_A or c_B.

Notice also that neither Alice nor Bob can determine the card remaining in the deck because the corresponding number has the form $a^{c_A c_B}$ (see (5.4) and (5.5)). Alice does not know d_B and Bob does not know d_A to decrypt this.

Check the third requirement. In case of contention between Alice and Bob, they reveal their cards together with the record of all computations to the judge who is able to repeat all computations and bring in a verdict.

Finally, check the fourth requirement. Eve, who overhears all communication between Alice and Bob, has the numbers u_1, u_2, u_3, v_1, v_2, v_3, and w_1. Each of these numbers can be represented as $a^x \bmod p$ where x is unknown to Eve. But to find x one have to solve the discrete logarithm problem which is practically impossible. So Eve cannot learn anything. □

Example 5.1   Assume that Alice and Bob wish to honestly deal the three cards: the three (α), the seven (β), and the ace (γ). (More exactly, it is usually assumed in cryptography that neither of them wants to be cheated and "greater" honesty is not required.) Let the following parameters be chosen at the preliminary stage:

$$p = 23, \quad \hat{\alpha} = 2, \quad \hat{\beta} = 3, \quad \hat{\gamma} = 5.$$

Let Alice choose $c_A = 7$ and Bob choose $c_B = 9$. Then they find using the extended Euclidean algorithm $d_A = 19$ and $d_B = 5$.

(Step 1) Alice computes

$$u_1 = 2^7 \bmod 23 = 13,$$
$$u_2 = 3^7 \bmod 23 = 2,$$
$$u_3 = 5^7 \bmod 23 = 17.$$

Then she shuffles u_1, u_2, u_3 and sends them to Bob.

(Step 2) Bob selects one of the numbers received. Let it be 17. He sends the number 17 to Alice. She knows that 17 corresponds to γ and so her hand is the ace.

(Step 3) Bob computes

$$v_1 = 13^9 \bmod 23 = 3,$$
$$v_2 = 2^9 \bmod 23 = 6$$

and sends these numbers to Alice, perhaps, having swapped them.

(Step 4) Alice receives the numbers 3 and 6, selects one of them, let it be 3, and computes the number

$$w_1 = 3^{19} \bmod 23 = 6.$$

She sends this number to Bob, who computes

$$z = 6^5 \bmod 23 = 2$$

and learns his card α, i.e. his hand is the three. The seven remains in the deck but neither Alice nor Bob know that. As for Eve who has intercepted all messages, she cannot learn the cards without having computed the inverse functions of the messages which is impossible when p is large.

5.2 Zero Knowledge Proofs

Consider the following problem which arises in some cryptographic applications. The participants are again Alice and Bob. Alice knows the solution of some complex problem and wishes to convince Bob thereupon but in such a way that he would not learn the solution. In other words, Bob must become sure that Alice knows the solution but must know nothing about that solution. At first glance the very problem statement seems absurd and the possibility of its being settled fantastic! In order to realise the situation better, consider a scenario from the life of pirates. Let Alice knows the map of an island where there is buried treasure. And let Bob be the captain of the ship which can get her to the island. Alice wishes to prove to Bob that she really possesses the map without showing it (or else Bob could manage without her and obtain all the treasure himself).

Similar problem is in demand for computer networks in the cases when Bob (server or domain controller) should decide on Alice's admission to the information stored in the network but Alice does not wish that anybody who overhears the communications channels, including Bob himself, learn something about her password. That is, Bob gets zero knowledge about her password (map) but is sure that Alice possesses that password (or map).

So our goal is to construct a "zero-knowledge proof" protocol. At that we assume that participants can play an unfair game and try to cheat one another.

As a complex problem whose solution is known to Alice, we first consider the graph colouring problem with three colours. We describe a quite simple in a sense of ideas protocol for that problem. Then we consider the problem of finding Hamiltonian cycle in a graph with more complicated in a sense of ideas but more computationally efficient proof protocol. Note that both problems, the graph colouring and finding Hamiltonian cycle, are NP-complete. We do not give a formal definition of NP-completeness which can be found, e.g. in [Aho *et al.* (1976); Papadimitriou (1994)]. For the reader who is not familiar with this definition, note only that, informally, NP-completeness means the exponential growth of problem solving time as the problem size (the amount of initial data) increases.

5.2.1 *Graph Colouring Problem*

In the problem of graph colouring, a graph is considered with the set of vertices V and set of edges E (denote the number of elements in these sets by $|V|$ and $|E|$). Alice knows the right colouring of the graph with three colours, red (R), blue (B), and yellow (Y). The right colouring is the one where any two adjacent vertices, i.e. connected by an edge, are coloured with different colours. Consider an example (Fig. 5.1).

For finding a correct colouring with three colours, only exponential algorithms are known, i.e. those whose computation time grows exponentially as the number of vertices and edges in a graph increases. Therefore, in case of large $|V|$ and $|E|$ this problem is intractable.

So, Alice knows a right colouring in a graph with large $|V|$ and $|E|$. She wishes to prove that to Bob in such a way that he would not learn the

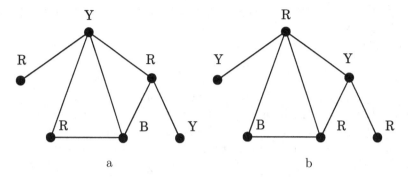

Fig. 5.1   Colouring: a — right colouring, b — wrong colouring

colouring.

The protocol of proof consists of a number of realisations of the following procedure.

Step 1 Alice chooses a random permutation Π of three letters R, B, Y and changes the colouring of graph according to that permutation. Obviously, the colouring remains correct. For example, if Π = (Y, R, B) then the colouring on the left (Fig. 5.1) turn into the colouring shown in Fig. 5.2.

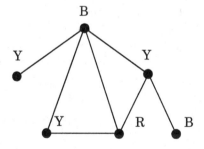

Fig. 5.2   Another variant of colouring

Step 2 For every vertex *v* from set *V*, Alice generates a large random integer *r* and replaces its two least significant bits by the colour code: 00 for red, 01 for blue, 10 for yellow.

Step 3 For every vertex v, Alice generates the data used in RSA, namely, P_v, Q_v, $N_v = P_v Q_v$, c_v, and d_v.

Step 4 Alice computes

$$Z_v = r_v^{d_v} \bmod N_v$$

and sends Bob the values N_v, d_v, and Z_v, for each vertex.

Step 5 Bob selects randomly one edge from set E and tells Alice what edge he has selected. Alice responds with the numbers c_{v_1} and c_{v_2} corresponding to the vertices of this edge. After that Bob computes

$$\hat{Z}_{v_1} = Z_{v_1}^{c_{v_1}} \bmod N_{v_1} = r_{v_1}\,, \quad \hat{Z}_{v_2} = Z_{v_2}^{c_{v_2}} \bmod N_{v_2} = r_{v_2}$$

and checks two least significant bits in these numbers. Under the right colouring, the least significant bits in $\hat{Z}_{v_1}$ and $\hat{Z}_{v_2}$ must be different. If it is not the case, Alice is declared cheating and the protocol stops. Otherwise, the described procedure repeats once again. The total number of repetitions is $a|E|$ where $a > 0$ is a protocol parameter.

Proposition 5.2 *If Alice does not know the right colouring of the graph then the probability of deceiving Bob does not exceed e^{-a} where $e \approx 2.718$ is the Euler number (the base of natural logarithm).*

Remark If one takes a large a then the probability of deception can be made as small as desired. For instance, with $a = 5$ this probability is less than 0.01.

Proof. Assume that Alice does not know the right colouring, i.e. her colouring is not correct. In this case, at least for one edge the vertices are equally coloured. If Alice obeys the protocol then the probability of selecting that edge by Bob is not less than $1/|E|$ (in this case Alice is denounced). Hence, the probability that Alice can deceive at one realisation of the protocol procedure does not exceed $1 - 1/|E|$ and, consequently, the probability that Alice can deceive at $a|E|$ realisations does not exceed $(1 - 1/|E|)^{a|E|}$. Using a well-known inequality $1 - x \le e^{-x}$ we obtain

$$(1 - 1/|E|)^{a|E|} \le \left(e^{-1/|E|} \right)^{a|E|} = e^{-a}\,. \qquad \square$$

Check the properties zero-knowledge proof must have.

(1) We see that the probability of Alice's deception can be made as small as desired by selecting large a.

(2) Let us explain why Bob does not receive any information about colouring. Because the colours are permuted randomly in each realisation (see Step 1) he cannot learn the right colouring examining all edges one

after another. All he learns is that two adjacent vertices are differently coloured but it gives no information about colouring. Besides, he cannot find the codes of colours given the set of N_v and d_v since r_v is random (Step 2). He also cannot decrypt Z_v since he does not know c_v (these are not sent for all vertices) and cannot compute c_v without P_v and Q_v.

(3) Consider one more chance to deceive that Alice seems to have. It seems that Alice can substitute c_{v_1} and c_{v_2} with other values at Step 5. But it is impossible since c_v satisfying the equation

$$c_v d_v \bmod ((P_v - 1)(Q_v - 1)) = 1$$

is unique and Bob knows d_v.

So, all requirements are fulfilled:

(1) Alice proves to Bob that she knows the problem solution and the probability of deception does not exceed e^{-a};
(2) Bob obtains no information about the colouring.

Consider the last chance of deception for all participants. What will ensue should they disobey the described protocol by making their choices not randomly?

Let, for instance, Bob ask edges not randomly but by some simple rule (e.g. in their order). In this case Alice, not actually knowing the colouring, can deceive him by preparing "right" colours only for the edges he will ask. Therefore Bob is interested in making random selections without any regularity.

Tho oocurity of othcr protocol actions is determined by security of RSA and under large P_v and Q_v the system is quite reliable.

5.2.2 *Hamiltonian Cycle Problem*

The problem considered in this subsection not only gives us an opportunity to describe one more scheme of constructing zero-knowledge proofs but also plays an important theoretical role. Manuel Blum showed that, speaking informally, any mathematical statement can be represented as a graph, the proof of the statement being in correspondence with the Hamiltonian cycle of the graph (see [Goldreich *et al.* (1987); Schneier (1996)]). Therefore the existence of zero-knowledge proof for Hamiltonian cycle implies that the proof of any mathematical statement can be presented in the form of zero-knowledge proof.

Definition 5.1   *Hamiltonian cycle* in a graph is a continuous circular path that passes through all vertices, each vertex visited exactly once.

Example 5.2   Consider the graph shown in Fig. 5.3.

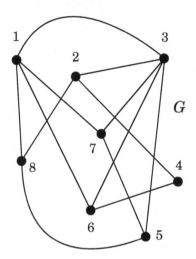

Fig. 5.3   Graph with Hamiltonian cycle (8, 2, 4, 6, 3, 5, 7, 1)

The path that sequentially passes through vertices 8, 2, 4, 6, 3, 5, 7, 1, is a Hamiltonian cycle. Actually, this path contains all vertices of the graph and each vertex is visited only once.

It is plain that if a Hamiltonian cycle exists in a graph G with n vertices then, under a certain numbering of vertices, it will pass exactly through vertices with sequential numbers $1, 2, 3, \ldots, n$. So by examining all possible enumerations of vertices we shall necessarily find a Hamiltonian cycle. But the number of enumerations equals $n!$ and therefore, already under moderately large n, say, $n = 100$, this approach becomes infeasible in practice. It is proved that the problem of finding a Hamiltonian cycle in a graph is NP-complete (we have already mentioned this). Informally, NP-completeness of the considered problem means that, for solving it, no algorithms exist (more exactly, no algorithms are known) which are essentially faster than the exhaustive search method mentioned above.

Our task is to construct a protocol that shall be used by Alice to prove to Bob that she knows a Hamiltonian cycle in a certain graph G in such a way that Bob will not get any knowledge of this cycle. The first construction of the protocol was suggested in [Blum (1986)]. Recall once more that "zero knowledge" means that, independently of the number of realisations of the protocol, Bob will have the same knowledge about Hamiltonian cycle as he might have if he had just studied the graph G.

So, assume that Alice knows a Hamiltonian cycle in graph G. She can prove this to Bob (and anybody else who has the graph) with the help of a protocol described below. She may use this proof, e.g. for her personal identification. But before giving the protocol description, let us agree on some notation.

We shall denote graphs by letters G, H, F, implying simultaneously corresponding adjacency matrices. The matrix element $H_{i,j} = 1$ if there is an edge in graph H which connects the vertices i and j; $H_{i,j} = 0$ otherwise. The symbol $\|$ will denote concatenation of two numbers, more exactly, of two corresponding binary words. For example, $10010\|1 = 100101$. We need a public-key cipher. Generally speaking, it may be any cipher, but for concreteness we shall use RSA (Sec. 2.6). Assume that Alice has generated the RSA system with public parameters N and d. It is essential that the messages encrypted with that system can only be decrypted by Alice and no one else (since only Alice knows the corresponding private key).

Proceed now to the description of the protocol. Each protocol realisation comprises the following four steps (explanations will be given below).

Step 1 Alice constructs a graph H which is the copy of G with a new (random) numbering of vertices. In terms of graph theory, H is said to be isomorphic to G. Alternatively, H is obtained by some permutation of vertices in G (preserving connections between vertices). Alice encodes matrix H by ascribing to initial zeroes and ones random numbers $r_{i,j}$ according to the scheme $\tilde{H}_{i,j} = r_{i,j}\|H_{i,j}$. Then she encrypts the elements of matrix $\tilde{H}$ and obtains the encrypted matrix F, $F_{i,j} = \tilde{H}_{i,j}^d \bmod N$. Alice sends matrix F to Bob.

Step 2 Upon the receipt of encrypted matrix F, Bob asks Alice one of two questions:

  (1) What is the Hamiltonian cycle in graph H?
  (2) Whether graph H is isomorphic to G?

Step 3 Alice answers the corresponding question of Bob:

  (1) In response to the first question, she decrypts in F the edges that constitute the Hamiltonian cycle.
  (2) In response to the second question, she decrypts F completely (in

fact, she sends Bob the graph $\tilde{H}$) and reveals the permutations used to produce graph H from G.

Step 4 Having received the reply, Bob checks the correctness of decrypting by repeated encrypting and comparing to F and makes certain that either the edges decrypted constitute a Hamiltonian cycle, or the permutations revealed convert graph G to graph H.

The described process repeats t times.

We discuss briefly several issues on the protocol construction in the form of questions and answers.

(1) Why does Alice construct an isomorphic graph? If she had not done that, Bob, upon the reply to his Question 1, would have learned the Hamiltonian cycle in graph G.

(2) Why does Alice encode the matrix H? We have already met with this trick when encrypting colours of vertices. The matter is that it is impossible to encrypt individual zeroes and ones (with RSA cipher they are not changed at all). Even if we replace 0 and 1 by some numbers a and b then we will obtain as few as two different ciphertexts and it will be straight to determine their correspondence to a and b, i.e. the graph's structure will not be concealed. Here we face a typical situation where a so-called *randomised cipher* is necessary. And this cipher is constructed by introducing random numbers into the matrix H prior to encrypting. The encoded matrix $\tilde{H}$ completely describes the graph (odd numbers denote the presence of edge, even numbers the absence of it) but after encryption the graph's structure becomes completely concealed.

(3) Why does Bob ask two questions? If he had asked only Question 1 which is, in a sense, the main then Alice, not actually knowing a Hamiltonian cycle in graph G, would have been able to present another graph with the same number of vertices and artificially enclosed Hamiltonian cycle. Therefore Bob sometimes asks Alice to prove the isomorphism of H and G. The point is that Alice does not know in advance what question she will be asked.

(4) Why cannot Bob ask the two questions at once? In this case he would have learned the Hamiltonian cycle in G, since he had obtained a Hamiltonian cycle in H and the way of converting H into G.

(5) Why does Bob check the correctness of decrypting? If he had not done that then Alice at Step 4 would have sent some "favourable" information not connected with that sent at Step 2.

The main details of the protocol are more strictly justified in the proofs of the following two propositions.

Proposition 5.3 *The probability of deception under t protocol realisations does not exceed* 2^{-t}.

Proof. First we show that the probability of deception in one realisation of the protocol equals $1/2$. Notice that if Alice knows the Hamiltonian cycle in graph G, she can answer right to any question of Bob. On the contrary, if she does not know the Hamiltonian cycle then the most she can do is to prepare an answer to either the first or the second question. In expectation of Question 1 she creates a new graph with artificially enclosed Hamiltonian cycle. But in this case she will not be able to prove its isomorphism to graph G. In expectation of Question 2 she creates a graph isomorphic to G. But in this case she will not be able to show a Hamiltonian cycle therein. So the probability of deception equals the probability of guessing the question number. Assuming that Bob puts both questions with equal probabilities we obtain that the probability of deception equals $1/2$.

Since Bob stops the game upon a first incorrect answer, the probability of deception under t realisations of the protocol does not exceed $(1/2)^t$. $\square$

Proposition 5.4 *The described protocol implements a zero-knowledge proof.*

Proof. In order to prove that Bob does not get any knowledge in realisation of the protocol it suffices to show that all he receives from Alice he would obtain himself without entering into any communication with Alice.

Let's begin with the second question of Bob. As a reply to this question he receives a graph isomorphic to G. But he could himself construct as many isomorphic graphs as he wished and what he obtains from Alice is one of such graphs.

The case of the first Bob's question is not that simple. As a reply to his first question he obtains a Hamiltonian cycle in a graph isomorphic to graph G. At first glance it may seem that this provides Bob with some information. But it is not so. Notice that if G possesses a Hamiltonian cycle then under some numbering of vertices, there exist an isomorphic graph defined by the adjacency matrix of the form

$$
\begin{pmatrix}
* & 1 & * & \cdots & * & * & * \\
* & * & 1 & \cdots & * & * & * \\
 & & & \cdots & & & \\
* & * & * & \cdots & * & 1 & * \\
* & * & * & \cdots & * & * & 1 \\
1 & * & * & \cdots & * & * & *
\end{pmatrix},
\tag{5.8}
$$

where $*$ denotes the uncertainty in the presence or absence of edge. Under such a numbering the Hamiltonian cycle passes through the vertices in the order of increasing numbers. By changing the numbering of vertices Bob can construct from (5.8) various isomorphic matrices. When Alice replying to the first question of Bob reveals the Hamiltonian cycle, Bob obtains just one of these matrices.

So, Bob does not obtain any additional information from Alice which he could not obtain himself.   □

Consider an example to illustrate all steps and operations of the described protocol.

Example 5.3   Take as a basis the graph G shown in Fig. 5.3. Its adjacency matrix is

$$
G = \begin{pmatrix}
 & 1 & 2 & 3 & 4 & 5 & 6 & 7 & 8 \\
1 & 0 & 0 & 1 & 0 & 0 & 1 & 1 & \boxed{1} \\
2 & 0 & 0 & 1 & \boxed{1} & 0 & 0 & 0 & 1 \\
3 & 1 & 1 & 0 & 0 & \boxed{1} & 1 & 1 & 0 \\
4 & 0 & 1 & 0 & 0 & 0 & \boxed{1} & 0 & 0 \\
5 & 0 & 0 & 1 & 0 & 0 & 0 & \boxed{1} & 1 \\
6 & 1 & 0 & \boxed{1} & 1 & 0 & 0 & 0 & 0 \\
7 & \boxed{1} & 0 & 1 & 0 & 1 & 0 & 0 & 0 \\
8 & 1 & \boxed{1} & 0 & 0 & 1 & 0 & 0 & 0
\end{pmatrix}.
$$

The box $\boxed{\cdot}$ is used to show the Hamiltonian cycle. Let's use the RSA system with public parameters $N = 55$, $d = 3$ for encryption.

At Step 1 of the protocol, Alice chooses a random numbering of vertices, say, 7, 4, 5, 3, 1, 2, 8, 6, and constructs an isomorphic graph

$$
H = \begin{array}{c} \\ 7 \\ 4 \\ 5 \\ 3 \\ 1 \\ 2 \\ 8 \\ 6 \end{array}
\begin{pmatrix}
7 & 4 & 5 & 3 & 1 & 2 & 8 & 6 \\
0 & 0 & 1 & 1 & \boxed{1} & 0 & 0 & 0 \\
0 & 0 & 0 & 0 & 0 & 1 & 0 & \boxed{1} \\
\boxed{1} & 0 & 0 & 1 & 0 & 0 & 1 & 0 \\
1 & 0 & \boxed{1} & 0 & 1 & 1 & 0 & 1 \\
1 & 0 & 0 & 1 & 0 & 0 & \boxed{1} & 1 \\
0 & \boxed{1} & 0 & 1 & 0 & 0 & 1 & 0 \\
0 & 0 & 1 & 0 & 1 & \boxed{1} & 0 & 0 \\
0 & 1 & 0 & \boxed{1} & 1 & 0 & 0 & 0
\end{pmatrix}.
$$

Next, she must encode H by ascribing to zeroes and ones some random numbers. In this particular example let her simply ascribe to the left of each element a randomly chosen digit from the set $\{1, 2, 3, 4, 5\}$:

$$
\tilde{H} = \begin{pmatrix}
50 & 20 & 11 & 31 & 21 & 40 & 20 & 10 \\
40 & 30 & 50 & 20 & 10 & 41 & 50 & 21 \\
41 & 30 & 50 & 11 & 30 & 20 & 51 & 40 \\
11 & 10 & 41 & 30 & 51 & 41 & 30 & 21 \\
31 & 20 & 40 & 11 & 50 & 10 & 41 & 31 \\
50 & 41 & 20 & 21 & 40 & 10 & 21 & 50 \\
40 & 30 & 31 & 50 & 41 & 21 & 30 & 40 \\
20 & 41 & 10 & 51 & 41 & 20 & 30 & 40
\end{pmatrix}.
$$

Now she encrypts the matrix $\overset{\tiny **}{H}$ by cubing each element modulo 55:

$$
F = \begin{pmatrix}
40 & 25 & 11 & 36 & 21 & 35 & 25 & 10 \\
35 & 50 & 40 & 25 & 10 & 06 & 40 & 21 \\
06 & 50 & 40 & 11 & 50 & 25 & 46 & 35 \\
11 & 10 & 06 & 50 & 46 & 06 & 50 & 21 \\
36 & 25 & 35 & 11 & 40 & 10 & 06 & 36 \\
40 & 06 & 25 & 21 & 35 & 10 & 21 & 40 \\
35 & 50 & 36 & 40 & 06 & 21 & 50 & 35 \\
25 & 06 & 10 & 46 & 06 & 25 & 50 & 35
\end{pmatrix}.
$$

(It may seem at attentive examination of matrix F that the cipher used poorly hides the initial matrix H. It is explained by small value of the modulus $N = 55$ and, as a consequence, a great number of elements in $\tilde{H}$

that are not coprime to the modulus. For any "real" RSA system where N is large this situation is practically impossible.)

At Step 2, Bob receives the matrix F and asks one of the two questions. If he asks to prove the isomorphism of the graphs, Alice simply sends him the encoded matrix $\tilde{H}$ and the numbering used 7, 4, 5, 3, 1, 2, 8, 6 (Step 3). At Step 4, Bob checks the correspondence of $\tilde{H}$ to F, i.e. the equalities $50^3 \bmod 55 = 40$, $20^3 \bmod 55 = 25$ and so on. Next, Bob obtains from $\tilde{H}$ the graph H (by discarding the high-order digits). Then he permutes the vertices of G with respect to the received numbering, as Alice did, and makes sure that H and G are the same graph (up to the numbering of vertices).

If at Step 2 Bob asks to show the Hamiltonian cycle, Alice sends him the corresponding list of (encoded) edges of graph H: (1, 5, 21), (5, 7, 41), (7, 6, 21), ..., (3, 1, 41). Each element contains the vertex numbers and the code of edge (Step 3). At Step 4, Bob checks the correspondence of the edges in the list to matrix F, for instance, $21^3 \bmod 55 = 21 = F_{1,5}$, $41^3 \bmod 55 = 06 = F_{5,7}$ and so on. Then he makes sure that the path specified by the list passes through all vertices, each vertex being visited only once.

5.3   Digital Cash

Nowadays in many countries people pay for purchases by electronic cards, order plane tickets over the Internet, buy various goods in Internet shops *etc.* The information about purchases is accumulated in the shops and banks. As a consequence, a new problem has arisen which is sometimes called a "Big Brother problem".

The essence of this problem is that anonymity of purchase is lost, i.e. the information about purchases of any person may be known to a third party and used against the person. For instance, the information about purchasing train or plane tickets may be of interest to criminals, the information about purchases of alcoholic drinks by a politician can be used against him by his opponents *etc.*

Therefore the idea emerged to work out such schemes of electronic payments that would preserve the anonymity of purchaser to the same extent as payments by cash. The corresponding protocols have got the name of "Digital cash" which emphasises their main property — to ensure the same degree of anonymity as ordinary cash. The scheme described below was suggested by David Chaum[Chaum (1983); Chaum (1985)], see also [Gold-wasser and Bellare (2001)].

For ease of understanding, we first consider two "bad" schemes and then a "good" one.

We begin with a more precise setting of the problem. There are three participants: the Bank, the User (customer), and the Vendor (shop). Both User and Vendor have corresponding accounts in the Bank, and the User wants to buy something from the Vendor. The purchase is done by means of the following three-step process:

(1) the User withdraws a sum, in a form of bank note, from her bank account;
(2) the User pays the Vendor with the note;
(3) the Vendor gives the note to the Bank to credit his account and the User takes her purchase.

We assume that all communications between the participants are carried out over a secured channel which may be created by using the public-key cryptographic methods such as those considered in Chap. 2.

Our goal is to construct an electronic payment scheme that

• makes forgery or fabricating bank notes impossible;
• preserves customer's anonymity.

We shall user RSA as an underlying cryptographic tool. Let the Bank have the following RSA parameters: secret numbers P, Q, c and public

$$N - PQ,$$
$$d = c^{-1} \bmod (P - 1)(Q - 1). \tag{5.9}$$

We shall first consider the case when a bank note of only one denomination, say, £100 may be used.

Now let's describe the first "bad" scheme. Suppose the User decided to spend £100. Then she must create together with the Bank a digital bank note. To do that the User sends to the Bank a number n which will be the serial number of bank note (it is usually required that n be a random number in the interval $[2, \ N - 1]$).

The Bank computes

$$s = n^c \bmod N \tag{5.10}$$

and makes a note $\langle n, \ s \rangle$. The Bank debits the User account with £100 and sends the note back to the User. The parameter s in the note is the Bank's signature. Nobody can forge the signature since the number c is secret.

The User pays (perhaps by sending over the network) the note $\langle n, s \rangle$ to the Vendor in order to buy some goods. The Vendor relays the note to the Bank. First of all, the Bank verifies the signature (it could be done by the Vendor, as well). But, besides, the Bank stores all serial numbers of the notes accepted earlier and now searches for n in that list. If n is found in the list then the payment is rejected (somebody tries to double-spend the note) of which the Bank informs the Vendor. Otherwise, if all tests are successful, the Bank credits £100 to the Vendor account and the Vendor gives the goods to the User.

The drawback of the described scheme is the absence of anonymity. The Bank could have memorised the association between the serial number n and the User and therefore is able to learn who and where has spent the bank note.

Consider the second "bad" scheme which, however, provides anonymity. It is based on the so-called *blind signature*.

Again the User wants to buy some goods. Now she generates a serial number n which will not be sent to the Bank. She generates another random number r, coprime to N, and computes

$$\hat{n} = (n \cdot r^d) \bmod N \qquad (5.11)$$

(recall that the pair N, d is the Bank's public key). The number $\hat{n}$ is sent to the Bank.

The Bank computes

$$\hat{s} = \hat{n}^c \bmod N \qquad (5.12)$$

and sends the number $\hat{s}$ back to the User (with debiting the User account with £100).

The User computes $r^{-1} \bmod N$ and

$$s = (\hat{s} \cdot r^{-1}) \bmod N. \qquad (5.13)$$

Notice that, taking into account the equations (5.12), (5.11), and (5.9), we have

$$s = \hat{n}^c \cdot r^{-1} = (n \cdot r^d)^c \cdot r^{-1} = n^c r^{dc} \cdot r^{-1} = n^c r^1 r^{-1} = n^c \bmod N,$$

i.e. we obtain the Bank's signature to the number n (see (5.10)) but n is unknown to the Bank (and whatever else). Computation (5.12) is called *blind signature* since the signer cannot see the real message (n) and cannot ever "extract" it from $\hat{n}$ since r is an unknown random number.

As a result, the User has the number n, which has never been transmitted over communications channels and is unknown to anybody, and the Bank's signature s which is equal to the one computed by (5.10). The User makes a bank note $\langle n, s \rangle$ and acts the same way as before. But now the note is really anonymous like an ordinary paper note.

The actions of the Vendor and Bank upon the receipt of the note do not differ from those described in the first scheme.

But why we called the present scheme bad? It has the following flaw: one can fabricate a new bank note given at least two genuine notes. Let a counterfeiter have two genuine notes $\langle n_1, s_1 \rangle$ and $\langle n_2, s_2 \rangle$. Then he can easily make a fake note $\langle n_3, s_3 \rangle$ by computing

$$n_3 = n_1 n_2 \bmod N,$$
$$s_3 = s_1 s_2 \bmod N.$$

Actually,

$$n_3^c = (n_1 n_2)^c = n_1^c n_2^c = s_1 s_2 = s_3 \bmod N, \qquad (5.14)$$

i.e. s_3 is a valid signature on n_3 and the Bank has no reason to reject this fake note (it cannot be differentiated from the genuine). Equation (5.14) represents a so-called *multiplicative property* of RSA.

Describe, at last, a "good" scheme free of all drawbacks of the former two. The first variant uses some one-way function

$$f : \{1, \ldots, N\} \to \{1, \ldots, N\},$$

(f can be computed easily but the inverse function f^{-1} is practically uncomputable). Function f is publicly known (i.e. known to the User, Vendor, and Bank).

A bank note is now defined as a pair of numbers $\langle n, s_f \rangle$ where

$$s_f = (f(n))^c \bmod N,$$

i.e. not n is signed but $f(n)$.

The User generates n (keeping it secret), computes $f(n)$, obtains the blind signature of the Bank on $f(n)$ and makes a note $\langle n, s_f \rangle$. This note possesses all the good properties as in the second scheme and, at the same time, cannot be fabricated since it is impossible to compute f^{-1}. For signature verification (i.e. for authentication of the note) one needs to compute

$f(n)$ and check that

$$s_f^d \bmod N = f(n).$$

Note that the one-way function must be judiciously chosen. For instance, the function $f(n) = n^2 \bmod N$ which is indeed one-way does not fit for the protocol in question. The reader may verify that the notes created with this function will still possess the multiplicative property (5.14). In practice, cryptographic hash functions (described in Sec. 8.5) are usually employed.

All other actions of the Vendor and Bank remain the same as in the schemes described earlier.

The second, simpler way to overcome the multiplicative property of RSA, is to introduce some redundancy into the message. Suppose the length of the modulus N is 1024 bits. So can be the length of n. Put a (randomly selected) serial number of a note only into the 512 low-order bits of n, and allocate the 512 high-order bits of n for some fixed number. This fixed number may contain some useful information, such as the denomination of a note, the name of a bank, *etc.* (512 bits are enough to represent a string of 64 ASCII symbols). Now the Bank upon the receipt of the note will require a mandatory fixed heading in parameter n and reject the note in case of absence thereof. The probability of the event that after multiplying two numbers modulo N the product will coincide with the factors in 512 bits is negligibly small. Therefore it is impossible to fabricate a note by using the formula (5.14).

Example 5.4 Let the private parameters of the Bank be $P = 17$, $Q = 7$, $c = 77$. The corresponding public parameters are $N = 119$, $d = 5$.

To preclude fabricating notes the admissible serial numbers will be those consisted of two identical decimal digits, e.g. 11, 77, 99.

When the User wants to obtain a note she first randomly selects its serial number (from the set of admissible numbers). Suppose the User has selected $n = 33$. Then she selects a random number r coprime to 119. Let $r = 67$, $\gcd(67, 119) = 1$. Then the User computes

$$\hat{n} = (33 \cdot 67^5) \bmod 119 = (33 \cdot 16) \bmod 119 = 52.$$

It is the number 52 that she sends to the Bank.

The Bank debits the User account with £100 and sends her back the number

$$\hat{s} = 52^{77} \bmod 119 = 103.$$

The User computes $r^{-1} = 67^{-1} \bmod 119 = 16$, $s = 103 \cdot 16 \bmod 119 = 101$ and makes a note

$$\langle n, s \rangle = \langle 33, 101 \rangle .$$

She pays this note to the Vendor to obtain some goods.

The Vendor forwards the note to the Bank. The Bank verifies:

(1) the serial number ($n = 33$) consists of two identical digits (i.e. contains the required redundancy);
(2) a note with this serial number has not been spent before;
(3) the Bank's signature is valid, i.e. $33^5 \bmod 119 = 101$.

All tests being successful, the Bank credits £100 to the Vendor account. The Vendor serves goods to the User.

At the conclusion we discuss two more issues regarding the digital cash protocol considered.

In the presented scheme, independently acting users or even one user who does not remember the numbers of notes produced earlier, can by chance generate two or more notes with equal numbers. Under the conditions of the protocol, only one of these notes (which is submitted first) will be accepted by the Bank. But let's take into account the lengths of numbers used in the protocol. If the serial number of note is a 512-bit integer and the users generate it randomly then the probability to ever obtain any equal numbers is negligible.

The second issue is that in the scheme presented, the notes of only one denomination are used which is, of course, inconvenient for the users. This can be surmounted as follows. The Bank acquires several pairs (c_i, d_i) subject to (5.9) and declares that, say, d_1 corresponds to £1000, d_2 to £500, and so on. When the User requests the Bank for a blind signature she additionally specifies the desired denomination of note. The Bank debits the User account with the specified amount and uses the corresponding secret number c_i to generate the signature. When afterwards the Bank receives a signed note it uses one after another the numbers d_1, d_2, etc. for signature verification. If the signature occurs valid for some d_i then the note of ith denomination is accepted. In the variant where the parameter n of the note contains a fixed heading with indication of denomination, the Bank directly applies the relevant key d_i.

5.4   Mutual Identification with Key Establishment

In the present section, we consider a cryptographically secure protocol that allows two users A and B to mutually identify each other (i.e. A makes sure that she deals with B, and B makes sure that he deals with A) and to create a common secret key that may be used for further encryption of transmitted messages. In real life A and B may be a user and a computer system, or two computer systems, it does not matter for the protocol described below.

In the course of our study we consider more and more subtle types of attacks and means of protection against them. Thus we have considered earlier (see Secs. 2.1 and 2.2) the approaches to solve the problem of identification and key establishment. But we implicitly assumed then that the adversary can only overhear the information transmitted over open channels. However, in contemporary communications networks, e.g. in the Internet, the user data is transmitted through a number of intermediate nodes (such as routers, gates, mail servers, *etc.*) that are not controlled by the user. As a result, an adversary settled down on one of such nodes is able not only to overhear the information, i.e. play just a passive role, but also to perform some active operations, e.g. alter, install, or delete messages.

Look into a typical attack on Diffie–Hellman system in a network with active adversary. Alice chooses her secret number X_A and sends Bob g^{X_A}. Bob chooses his secret number X_B and sends Alice g^{X_B}. But Eve intercepts these numbers and sends Alice and Bob g^{X_E} instead, where X_E is her number. All these numbers look like completely random, so neither Alice nor Bob suspect anything. Alice ends up with the key $K_A = g^{X_E X_A}$, and Bob with $K_B = g^{X_E X_B}$. Both these keys can also be computed by Eve. Now when Alice sends Bob a message enciphered with K_A, Eve deciphers it, re-enciphers with K_B and sends Bob. She does similarly in case of reverse transmission. Alice and Bob believe that they communicate securely but actually Eve reads all their messages.

Such an attack becomes impossible if Alice and Bob do not transmit their public keys (in the Diffie–Hellman system these are $Y_A = g^{X_A}$ and $Y_B = g^{X_B}$) but take them out of a table or directory obtained earlier from a "reliable" source (as it was assumed in Sec. 2.2).

As a matter of fact, the majority of public key systems require some organisational structure providing for public key certification. Such a structure may look like the following. There is a "trusted" user Trent in the network to which Alice and Bob belong. Trent has no own interests but to ensure a reliable and secure functioning of the network (most likely it is not a human but a heavily-guarded computer operating upon a hardcored program). Trent makes use of some reliable cryptosystem (e.g. RSA with the modulus length of about 10000 bits) with corresponding private keys and performs only two tasks:

(1) he adds to his database the information about the public key of a user sent to him as a message encrypted with the use of Trent's public key;
(2) he provides the information about the public key of a user supplied with Trent's signature.

Trent's public keys are submitted to all users by some way precluding any interference of Eve, e.g. they are published in a form of advertisement in a newspaper. Now Alice having computed her public key creates a message consisted of her name and key, encrypts it with the use of Trent's public key and sends to Trent (nobody but Trent can decrypt this message). When Bob needs Alice's public key he sends Trent a request, and Trent answers him with the signed Alice's public key (nobody can forge Trent's signature). Bob verifies the signature using Trent's public key and accepts Alice's key as valid. By implementing this procedure, each user of the network obtains trustworthy information about users' public keys and Eve cannot interfere in this process.

So, if Alice and Bob use the authentic public keys, the Diffie-Hellman scheme tackles the problem of establishing secret key. However it provides no explicit identification of the users. Indeed, if Eve tries to act as Alice then she and Bob will end up with different secret keys but it will become evident only in the future, e.g. when Bob will have been unable to decipher a received message or have detected that "Alice" does not understand what he sends her. Often it is required to provide an explicit identification, i.e. to let the parties know exactly who is who at the end of the protocol.

The Diffie–Hellman scheme has yet another disadvantage: the secret key established by Alice and Bob will always be the same until they change their public keys. But changing keys is a relatively slow process (e.g. it may be necessary to inform about the change of key all users in the network to let them correct their public key directories). It is desirable to have a protocol which would allow for instantaneous creation of different, randomly selected secret keys.

The solution is to use some public-key cipher for transporting secret keys. Denote the ciphertext for message x produced with the aid of A's public key by $P_A(x)$. (For example, $P_A(x)$ may be RSA or ElGamal encryption. In case of RSA, $P_A(x) = x^{d_A} \mod N_A$ where the pair of numbers

d_A and N_A is the public key of user A.) All who know A's public key can compute $P_A(x)$ for message x. At the same time, only A, who knows the corresponding private key, can recover x out of $y = P_A(x)$. Similarly, we shall denote by $P_B(x)$ the ciphertext produced with the aid of B's public key. Let, as before, the symbol $\|$ denote concatenation of numbers. We shall describe the protocol through a series of improvements so that the reader can understand better the details.

Recall that we are to solve the following problem: Alice and Bob wish to mutually identify each other and establish a common secret key. Consider first the following (flawed) 3-step protocol to discuss several issues.

Step 1 Alice devises a secret key k_1, encrypts it with Bob's public key and sends to Bob:

$$A \longrightarrow B: \quad P_B(k_1). \tag{5.15}$$

Step 2 Bob decrypts k_1, re-encrypts it with Alice's public key and sends to Alice:

$$A \longleftarrow B: \quad P_A(k_1). \tag{5.16}$$

Step 3 Alice decrypts k_1 and compares it to the key she has devised at Step 1.

What do we have as a result of this protocol? First, Alice and Bob have established a common secret key k_1, unknown to Eve (she cannot decrypt either $P_B(k_1)$ or $P_A(k_1)$). Second, Alice has got a cryptographically secure identification of Bob since nobody but him could have decrypted k_1. Obviously, with the present protocol, Bob does not get any identification of Alice (the message (5.15) could be sent by everybody). He could initiate a symmetric protocol:

$$A \longleftarrow B: \quad P_A(k_2), \tag{5.17}$$

$$A \longrightarrow B: \quad P_B(k_2), \tag{5.18}$$

and obtain such identification. However, the issue here is in logical independence of the two protocols which gives no guarantee that both protocols are conducted by the same participants.

But there is yet a more subtle issue. Alice can use this protocol to break the cryptosystem of Bob! This can be done as follows. Suppose Alice has intercepted an encrypted message y intended to Bob, i.e. $y = P_B(x)$. She pretends that she wishes to securely communicate with Bob and initiates the protocol (5.15), (5.16). But instead of $P_B(k_1)$ she sends Bob the message y. Since k_1 is an arbitrary integer, Bob does not suspect anything. He performs his step in the protocol and decrypts x for Alice!

The lesson that should be learned from this is the following: one should not decrypt random numbers. It may impair one's security. The method of circumventing such "dangerous" randomness is to introduce redundancy into messages, e.g. to enclose an element that is known and expected by the recipient. Particularly, in (5.15) Alice could send her name. She could construct a message by allocating 512 bits for random number k_1 and the other 512 bits for her name, address, a fragment of public key, and similar easily verifiable information (denote these all by $\hat{A}$), and send to Bob $P_B(k_1\|\hat{A})$. In this case Bob would not have sent Alice the message x as above because its corresponding 512 bits had certainly not contained $\hat{A}$.

All the above-stated leads us to the following protocol due to Needham and Schroeder[Needham and Schroeder (1978)], see also [Menezes *et al.* (1996)], which completely solves the problem stated in the beginning of the section.

Step 1 Alice devises a number k_1, connects to it her public data $\hat{A}$ and sends to Bob

$$A \longrightarrow B: \quad P_B(k_1\|\hat{A}). \tag{5.19}$$

Step 2 Bob decrypts (5.19) and verifies that the message contains Alice's public data $\hat{A}$. Next he devises a number k_2, connects to it k_1 and sends to Alice

$$A \longleftarrow B: \quad P_A(k_1\|k_2). \tag{5.20}$$

Step 3 Alice decrypts (5.20) and verifies that the message contains k_1. This gives her secure identification of Bob since nobody else could have extracted k_1 from (5.19). Alice sends to Bob

$$A \longrightarrow B: \quad P_B(k_2). \tag{5.21}$$

Step 4 Bob decrypts (5.21) and verifies that it is k_2. This gives him secure identification of Alice since nobody else could have extracted k_2 from (5.20).

Now Alice and Bob can construct from k_1, k_2 a common key, e.g. $k = k_1 \oplus k_2$ where $\oplus$ is bitwise summation modulo 2, or they can use k_1 and k_2 separately for enciphering incoming and outcoming messages.

Example 5.5 Let in some network the ElGamal cipher be used with common public parameters $p = 107$, $g = 2$. Users A and B have public keys $d_A = 58$, $d_B = 28$, to whom the private $c_A = 33$, $c_B = 45$ correspond. Consider a realisation of Needham–Schroeder protocol for mutual identification of users A and B and secret key establishment. Due to small value of modulus p in our example we shall use one decimal digit as the user's identificator. Let $\hat{A} = 1$, $\hat{B} = 2$, and the intended secret key be also one digit.

At the first step of the protocol A devises a secret key, say, $k_1 = 3$, and constructs a message $m = k_1 \| \hat{A} = 31$. This message is encrypted by ElGamal cipher with B's public key:

$$k = 15, \quad r = g^k \bmod p = 2^{15} \bmod 107 = 26,$$
$$e = m \cdot d_B{}^k \bmod p = 31 \cdot 28^{15} \bmod 107 = 47.$$

The pair of numbers $(26, 47)$ is the ciphertext to be sent to B. In the notation of the protocol, $P_B(k_1 \| \hat{A}) = (26, 47)$ and

$$A \longrightarrow B: \quad (26, 47).$$

At the second step B decrypts $(26, 47)$ applying his private key:

$$m' = e \cdot r^{p-1-c_B} \bmod p = 47 \cdot 26^{106-45} \bmod 107 = 31.$$

B verifies that the low-order digit equals the identification number of user A and extracts $k_1 = 3$. Then he selects his secret number, say, $k_2 = 7$, constructs a message $m = k_1 \| k_2 = 37$ and encrypts it using A's public key:

$$k = 77, \quad r = g^k \bmod p = 2^{77} \bmod 107 = 63,$$
$$e = m \cdot d_A{}^k \bmod p = 37 \cdot 58^{77} \bmod 107 = 18.$$

The pair of numbers $(63, 18)$ is what he shall send to A. That is $P_A(k_1 \| k_2) = (63, 18)$ and

$$A \longleftarrow B: \quad (63, 18).$$

At the third step A decrypts $(63, 18)$:

$$m' = e \cdot r^{p-1-c_A} \bmod p = 18 \cdot 63^{106-33} \bmod 107 = 37.$$

A verifies that the high-order digit contains $k_1 = 3$ and extracts $k_2 = 7$.

Now A encrypts k_2 for B:

$$k = 41, \quad r = g^k \bmod p = 2^{41} \bmod 107 = 82,$$
$$e = m \cdot d_B^{\ k} \bmod p = 7 \cdot 28^{41} \bmod 107 = 49,$$

and sends to B

$$A \longrightarrow B: \quad (82, 49).$$

At the fourth step B decrypts $(82, 49)$:

$$m' = e \cdot r^{p-1-c_B} \bmod p = 49 \cdot 82^{106-45} \bmod 107 = 7.$$

B verifies that he obtains his secret number $k_2 = 7$.

Now A and B can make a common key by a method agreed in advance, e.g.

$$k = k_1 \oplus k_2 \bmod 10 = 3 \oplus 7 = (011)_2 \oplus (111)_2 = (100)_2 = 4.$$

Problems and Exercises

5.1 For realization of the "Mental poker" protocol the following common parameters are chosen: $p = 23$, $\hat{\alpha} = 5$, $\hat{\beta} = 7$, $\hat{\gamma} = 14$. Besides, there are the following variants for Alice and Bob:

(a) $c_A = 13$, $c_B = 5$, Alice shuffles cards by the rule $(1, 2, 3) \to (3, 2, 1)$, Bob selects the first number and uses the permutation $(1, 2) \to (2, 1)$. Alice selects the second number.

(b) $c_A = 7$, $c_B = 15$, Alice shuffles cards by the rule $(1, 2, 3) \to (1, 3, 2)$, Bob selects the second number and uses the permutation $(1, 2) \to (1, 2)$. Alice selects the first number.

(c) $c_A = 19$, $c_B = 3$, Alice shuffles cards by the rule $(1, 2, 3) \to (2, 1, 3)$, Bob selects the second number and uses the permutation $(1, 2) \to (2, 1)$. Alice selects the second number.

(d) $c_A = 9$, $c_B = 7$, Alice shuffles cards by the rule $(1, 2, 3) \to (3, 2, 1)$, Bob selects the third number and uses the permutation $(1, 2) \to (1, 2)$. Alice selects the second number.

(e) $c_A = 15$, $c_B = 5$, Alice shuffles cards by the rule $(1, 2, 3) \to (1, 2, 3)$, Bob selects the first number and uses the permutation $(1, 2) \to (2, 1)$. Alice selects the first number.

Determine which cards will be Alice's and Bob's hand. What numbers transmitted will Eve observe?

5.2 In the digital cache system the secret parameters of the Bank are $P = 17$, $Q = 7$, $c = 77$, and the corresponding public parameters $N = 119$, $d = 5$. Make digital bank notes with the following serial number:

    (a) $n = 11$ under $r = 5$,
    (b) $n = 99$ under $r = 6$,
    (c) $n = 55$ under $r = 10$,
    (d) $n = 44$ under $r = 15$,
    (e) $n = 77$ under $r = 30$.

Themes for Labs

In all tasks below, we suggest the reader to select the necessary parameters and cryptographic tools at his/her discretion.

5.3 Make a computer implementation of the "Mental poker" protocol.

5.4 Make a computer implementation of the zero-knowledge protocol based on the graph colouring problem.

5.5 Make a computer implementation of the zero-knowledge protocol based on the Hamiltonian cycle problem.

5.6 Make a computer implementation of the digital cache protocol.

5.7 Make a computer implementation of the Needham–Schroeder mutual identification protocol.

Chapter 6

Elliptic Curve Cryptosystems

6.1 Introduction

In this chapter, we consider one of the new directions of public-key cryptography, elliptic curve systems. Elliptic curves have been studied in mathematics for a long time, but their use in cryptographic applications was first suggested by Neal Koblitz [Koblitz (1987)] and Victor Miller [Miller (1986)]. About 20 years of active investigations have confirmed the beneficial properties of these systems and led to the invention of efficient implementation methods. Since the end of XX century the use of elliptic curves for production of cryptographic primitives, such as digital signatures, has begun to put into standards. We have now, for instance, the US standards ANSI X9.62 and FIPS 186-2 (2000), and Russian standard GOST R34.10-2001 (2001).

The main advantage of elliptic curve cryptosystems is that compared to "conventional" systems studied in the previous chapters, they offer a significantly greater level of security within the same computational complexity, or, *vice versa*, significantly lower complexity within the given level of security. It is explained by the fact that for computing inverse functions on elliptic curves only exponential-time algorithms are known whereas subexponential algorithms exist in case of conventional cryptosystems. As a result, the level of security achieved, say, in RSA with 1024-bit modulus, can be attained in elliptic curve systems with 160-bit modulus which allows for a simpler hardware and software implementation.

The profound study of elliptic curves requires the knowledge of higher algebra and especially algebraic geometry. We shall however try to set out the matter without resorting to any higher-algebraic concepts. Nevertheless it will be sufficient for understanding construction principles and functioning of the corresponding cryptosystems. A more detailed treatment of the elliptic curves and their use in cryptography can be found in [Blake *et al.* (1999); Menezes (1993); Silverman (1986)]. Sections 6.5 and 6.6 are rather technical and may be omitted at first reading.

6.2 Mathematical Foundations

A cubic curve E defined by the equation

$$E: \quad Y^2 = X^3 + aX + b \tag{6.1}$$

is called *elliptic curve* (in fact, Eq. (6.1) is derived by transformation of variables from a more general equation which we are not interested in).

Since $Y = \pm\sqrt{X^3 + aX + b}$ the graph of the curve is symmetric with respect to the horizontal axis. To find the points of intersection between the graph and horizontal axis one needs to solve the cubic equation

$$X^3 + aX + b = 0. \tag{6.2}$$

This can be done using the well-known formulas by Cardano. The discriminant of the equation

$$D = \left(\frac{a}{3}\right)^3 + \left(\frac{b}{2}\right)^2. \tag{6.3}$$

If $D < 0$ then (6.2) has three different real roots α, β, γ; if $D = 0$ then (6.2) has three real roots, say, α, β, β, of which at least two are equal; at last, if $D > 0$ then (6.2) has one real root α and two complex conjugate. The shape of the curve in all three cases is shown in Figs. 6.1–6.3.

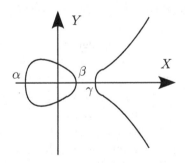

Fig. 6.1   Elliptic curve, $D < 0$

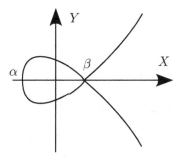

Fig. 6.2   Elliptic curve, $D = 0$

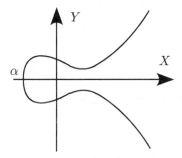

Fig. 6.3   Elliptic curve, $D > 0$

The curve shown in Fig. 6.2 is called *singular*. In its singularity point $(\beta, 0)$, there are two tangents to the curve. We shall exclude singular curves. Therefore, when defining a curve by specifying parameters a and b, we shall require that the condition $D \neq 0$ hold, which is equivalent to

$$4a^3 + 27b^2 \neq 0. \tag{6.4}$$

So, let elliptic curve E be defined by Eq. (6.1) with the constraint (6.4). Define the operation of point composition on the curve. Take any two points $P = (x_1, y_1)$, $Q = (x_2, y_2) \in E$ and plot a straight line through the points (Fig. 6.4). This line will necessarily intersect the curve at a third point which we denote by R'. (The third point necessarily exists. The fact is that the cubic equation obtained after substitution of the line equation into (6.1) has two real roots corresponding to points P and Q, consequently, the third root corresponding to point R' is also real.) The resultant point

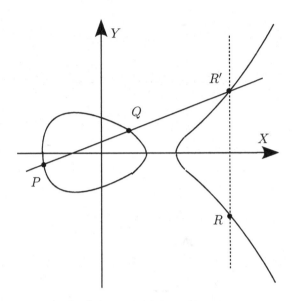

Fig. 6.4   Point composition $R = P + Q$

$R = (x_3, y_3)$ is obtained by changing the sign of y-coordinate of point R'. We shall denote the described composition of points by $R = P + Q$.

Let point $P \in E$ have coordinates (x, y). Then the point with coordinates $(x, -y)$ will be denoted by $-P$. We shall assume that the vertical line passing through P and $-P$ intersects the curve at a point at infinity $\mathcal{O}$, i.e. $P + (-P) = \mathcal{O}$. By convention, $P + \mathcal{O} = \mathcal{O} + P = P$. As we shall see later, point at infinity $\mathcal{O}$ plays the role of zero in elliptic curve arithmetic.

Suppose now that points P and Q (Fig. 6.4) are approaching each other and eventually merge into one point $P = Q = (x_1, y_1)$. Then the composition $R = (x_3, y_3) = P + Q = P + P$ is obtained by plotting the tangent line to the curve at point P and reflecting its second intersection with the curve R' with respect to the horizontal axis (Fig. 6.5). We shall use the following notation: $R = P + P = [2]P$.

Let us derive formulas for determining the coordinates of the resulting point $R = (x_3, y_3)$ on the basis of coordinates of initial points $P = (x_1, y_1)$ and $Q = (x_2, y_2)$. First consider the case when $P \neq \pm Q$, $R = P + Q$ (Fig. 6.4). Denote by k the angular coefficient of the line passing through

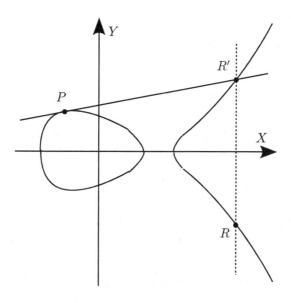

Fig. 6.5   Point doubling $R = P + P = [2]P$

P and Q. It is obvious that

$$k = \frac{y_2 - y_1}{x_2 - x_1} \,. \tag{6.5}$$

Then the line equation will be $Y - y_1 = k(X - x_1)$, so

$$Y = y_1 + k(X - x_1) \,. \tag{6.6}$$

Substitute the expression for variable Y into the curve equation (6.1). We obtain

$$(y_1 + k(X - x_1))^2 = X^3 + aX + b \,.$$

From this by squaring and grouping similar terms we obtain the cubic equation

$$X^3 - k^2 X^2 + \cdots = 0$$

(here $\cdots$ stand for terms not interesting for us). It is known that the sum of roots of cubic equation equals the coefficient under X^2, taken with the minus sign (Viète theorem for cubic equations), i.e.

$$x_1 + x_2 + x_3 = k^2 \,,$$

hence

$$x_3 = k^2 - x_1 - x_2 \,. \tag{6.7}$$

Substitute the expression for x_3 into the line equation (6.6) and find the y-coordinate of point R', $y_3' = y_1 + k(x_3 - x_1)$, and by changing the sign, we obtain

$$y_3 = k(x_1 - x_3) - y_1 \,. \tag{6.8}$$

So we have found the coordinates of the point of interest R.

Consider now the case when $P = Q$ and resulting point $R = [2]P$ (Fig. 6.5). By differentiating both sides of (6.1) with respect to X, we obtain

$$2YY' = 3X^2 + a \,.$$

The angular coefficient of the tangent line equals the value of derivative in point P,

$$k = \frac{3x_1^2 + a}{2y_1} \,. \tag{6.9}$$

Further argumentation is analogous to the former case and the coordinates of point R are determined by the same formulas (6.7) and (6.8). Notice that if the y-coordinate of point P is zero then the tangent line passes in parallel to the vertical axis and $[2]P = \mathcal{O}$.

By using the derived formulas for point composition and accepted conventions as to point at infinity one may verify the following properties of points on elliptic curve:

(1) $P + Q = Q + P$ for all points $P, Q \in E$;
(2) $P + (Q + S) = (P + Q) + S$ for all points $P, Q, S \in E$;
(3) there exists a null element $\mathcal{O}$ (point at infinity) such that $P + \mathcal{O} = \mathcal{O} + P = P$ for all $P \in E$;
(4) for every point $P \in E$ there exists an opposite point $-P \in E$ such that $P + (-P) = \mathcal{O}$.

The listed properties of points match the properties of integer numbers under the summation operation. Therefore point composition is often called *point addition* and operation $[2]P$ *point doubling*.

The analogy with the integers being continued, it is convenient to introduce the following notation. For integer m

$$[m]P = \underbrace{P + P + \cdots + P}_{m},$$

$$[0]P = \mathcal{O},$$

$$[-m]P = -\underbrace{(P + P + \cdots + P)}_{m}.$$

Now we are ready to take the first step toward the cryptographic use of elliptic curves. We can see that computation of point composition (see Eqs. (6.5), (6.9), (6.7), and (6.8)) involves only the operations of addition, subtraction, multiplication, and division of numbers. It means that all the above equalities will hold if we operate with integer numbers modulo a prime p. In this case, addition and multiplication are done modulo p, the difference $u - v$ is calculated as $u + (p - v) \bmod p$, and division u/v is performed by multiplying u by $v^{-1} \bmod p$ (the primality of the modulus guarantees that for any positive integer $v < p$ there exists a number v^{-1} such that $vv^{-1} \bmod p = 1$).

As a result, we obtain a curve

$$E: \quad Y^2 = X^3 + aX + b \pmod{p}. \tag{6.10}$$

In Eq. (6.10), variables X, Y and coefficients a, b take on integer values and all computations are carried out modulo p. In accordance with (6.4), coefficients a, b are subject to the constraint

$$(4a^3 + 27b^2) \bmod p \neq 0. \tag{6.11}$$

The set $E_p(a,b)$ consists of all points (x,y), $0 \leq x,y < p$, satisfying Eq. (6.10) and the point at infinity $\mathcal{O}$. Denote the number of points in $E_p(a,b)$ by $\#E_p(a,b)$. This quantity is of great importance for cryptographic applications of elliptic curves.

Example 6.1 Consider the curve

$$E_7(2,6): \quad Y^2 = X^3 + 2X + 6 \pmod{7}. \tag{6.12}$$

Check condition (6.11):

$$4 \cdot 2^3 + 27 \cdot 6^2 = 4 \cdot 1 + 6 \cdot 1 = 3 \neq 0 \pmod{7}.$$

So this curve is non-singular. Let's find a (random) point in $E_7(2,6)$. Let $x = 5$. Then

$$Y^2 = 5^3 + 2 \cdot 5 + 6 = 6 + 3 + 6 = 1 \pmod 7$$

and $y = 1 \pmod 7$ or $y = -1 = 6 \pmod 7$. We have found two points: $(5,1)$ and $(5,6)$. Let's find more points by computing compositions. First find $[2](5,1)$. Using (6.9), (6.7), and (6.8), we compute

$$k = \frac{3 \cdot 5^2 + 2}{2 \cdot 1} = \frac{0}{2} = 0 \pmod 7,$$

$$x_3 = 0 - 2 \cdot 5 = 4 \pmod 7,$$

$$y_3 = 0 \cdot (5 - 4) - 1 = 6 \pmod 7.$$

We obtain $[2](5,1) = (4,6)$ (one can verify that the point obtained belongs to the curve by substituting its coordinates in Eq. (6.12)). Find a point $[3](5,1) = (5,1) + (4,6)$. Using (6.5), (6.7), and (6.8), we compute

$$k = \frac{6 - 1}{4 - 5} = \frac{5}{6} = 5 \cdot 6 = 2 \pmod 7,$$

$$x_3 = 2^2 - 5 - 4 = 2 \pmod 7,$$

$$y_3 = 2 \cdot (5 - 2) - 1 = 2 \cdot 3 - 1 = 5 \pmod 7.$$

We obtain $[3](5,1) = (2,5)$. So we have found four points. For cryptographic use of the curve we must know the total number of points in the set $E_7(2,6)$. We shall find the answer in Sec. 6.6.

Some words about the properties of the set of points $E_p(a,b)$: It is obvious that this set is finite since it consists of only points with integer coordinates $0 \leq x, y < p$. There exists a direct analogy between $E_p(a,b)$ and the set of integer powers reduced modulo p. Thus $E_p(a,b)$ has a generator, i.e. such a point G that the sequence $G, [2]G, [3]G, \ldots, [n]G$, where $n = \#E_p(a,b)$, contains all points from $E_p(a,b)$, $[n]G = \mathcal{O}$ (compare this to the similar property of generator g in Sec. 2.2). The number of points on elliptic curve upon a proper choice of parameters p, a, and b, can be a prime, $\#E_p(a,b) = q$. In this case any point (except $\mathcal{O}$) is a generator of the whole set of points. Such a curve is beneficial in many respects and can always be found for acceptable time. If by some reasons such a curve cannot be found and $\#E_p(a,b) = hq$ where q is again prime then a subset of $E_p(a,b)$ exists which contains q points with a generator to be any point

$G \neq \mathcal{O}$ such that $[q]G = \mathcal{O}$. In the sequel, without lost of generality, we shall assume that we work with such a subset of cardinality q (and when selecting the curve parameters we shall strive to obtain $q = \#E_p(a,b)$).

The main cryptographic operation on elliptic curve is *point multiplication*, i.e. computation

$$Q = [m]P = \underbrace{P + P + \cdots + P}_{m} \,. \tag{6.13}$$

This operation may be performed quite efficiently with not more than $2\log m$ point compositions. The methods of its implementation are completely the same as of modular exponentiation. For example, to find the point $Q = [21]P$ compute $[2]P$, $[4]P$, $[8]P$, $[16]P$, each time doubling the preceding point, and sum up $P + [4]P + [16]P = Q$ (in total, 4 point doublings and 2 point additions).

The inverse problem which is traditionally called *elliptic curve discrete logarithm* problem if formulated as follows. Given points P and Q find an integer m such that $[m]P = Q$. This problem is difficult. If the curve parameters are carefully chosen (as described in the next section) then the best algorithms known to date are analogues of baby-step giant-step algorithm (Sec. 3.2) and require the number of curve operations proportional to $\sqrt{q}$ where q is the cardinality of the set of points generated by Q. All computations on the curve are carried out modulo p, i.e. with numbers of length $t \approx \log p$ bit. For cryptographic applications, $\log q \approx \log p$ so $\sqrt{q} \approx 2^{t/2}$ which means exponential growth of complexity with the length of numbers increasing.

6.3 Choosing Curve Parameters

In this section, we consider the main recommendations as to the choice of the elliptic curve parameters, namely, coefficients a, b and modulus p, in order to obtain a curve suitable for cryptographic applications. In fact, the criterion of the choice is the impossibility of maintaining some kinds of attacks suggested for elliptic curve cryptosystems. The recommendations below follow the strategy of choosing a *random* curve. This strategy is regarded as the most reliable with respect to security of the resulting cryptosystem. The alternative approach, not considered here, is to systematically construct the curve with desired properties which occurs more efficient from the computational point of view. There are special methods suggested for implementing this approach but the curves obtained are in fact chosen from a relatively small set of curves and are suspected to have some special features which may allow, in the course of time, to invent efficient attacks against them.

Let us describe in steps the process of selecting a good random curve.

(1) Select randomly a prime number p. As will be shown in Sec. 6.6, the number of points on the curve is of the same order as p. So the bitlength of p, $t = \lfloor \log p \rfloor + 1$, must be sufficiently great to prevent the use of general methods for computing discrete logarithms on the curve whose complexity is proportional to $2^{t/2}$ operations. The value of $t = 128$ bits (4 machine words on 32-bit computers) is not sufficient today because there are reports of breaking corresponding curves for several months of intensive distributed computations. But the value of $t = 160$ bits (5 machine words) is nowadays inaccessible by cryptanalysts and may serve as a starting point. Another reasoning is based on the demand that the elliptic curve cipher be no less secure than the block cipher AES (which is now the US standard, see Sec. 8.2.3). It is believed that the security of AES is provided by the full key length which is 128, 196, or 256 bits. Since the security of elliptic curve cipher is determined by the value of $t/2$ the length of the modulus must be 256, 392, or 512 bits, respectively.

(2) Select random integers a and b such that $a, b \neq 0 \pmod{p}$ and $4a^3 + 27b^2 \neq 0 \pmod{p}$. Notice, however, that parameter b does not appear anywhere in the formulas for computing compositions. So it is sometimes recommended, for the sake of computational efficiency, to randomly select only b while taking a equal to a small integer. Thus the US standard FIPS 186-2 assumes the use of curves with $a = -3$ which, as we shall see in Sec. 6.5, slightly simplifies computations.

(3) Determine the number of point on the curve $n = \#E_p(a, b)$ (this is the most complicated step in the described process, its basic algorithm being considered in Sec. 6.6). It is important that n have a large prime divisor q, or better be itself prime, $n = q$. If n has only small factors then many small subsets with their own generators exist in $E_p(a, b)$, and the Pohlig–Hellman algorithm [Pohlig and Hellman (1978); Menezes *et al.* (1996)] can quickly find the general logarithm through the logarithms in these small subsets. If the search for the curve with $n = q$ takes up too much time then one may admit $n = hq$ where h is a small integer. Recall that security of elliptic curve cryptosystem is determined not by modulus p but by the number of points in the working subset q. If h is small then q is of the same order as p. If the number of points on the curve does not

satisfy the requirements, revert to Step 2.

(4) Verify whether the inequalities $p^k - 1 \bmod q \neq 0$ hold for all k, $0 < k < 32$. If not, revert to Step 2. This check prevents the MOV-attack [Menezes (1993)] (called after the names of its inventors Menezes, Okamoto, Vanstone) and, as well, excludes the so-called supersingular curves and the curves with $\#E_p(a, b) = p - 1$. The MOV-attack and the special types of curves mentioned allow to reduce the elliptic curve discrete logarithm problem to simpler problems.

(5) Verify whether the inequality $q \neq p$ holds. If not, revert to Step 2. The matter is that for the curves with $q = p$ which are called anomalous, efficient methods of computing discrete logarithms are suggested.

(6) At this step a suitable curve for cryptographic applications has been obtained. We have parameters p, a, b, the number of points n, and the cardinality of the working subset q. It is usually required to find a point G, the generator of the working subset. If $q = n$ then any point (except $\mathcal{O}$) is the generator. If $q < n$ then select random points G' until $G = [n/q]G' \neq \mathcal{O}$ is obtained. To find a random point on the curve take a random number $x < p$, compute $e = (x^3 + ax + b) \bmod p$ and try to extract the square root $y = \sqrt{e} \bmod p$. If the square root exists, we obtain the point (x, y), otherwise try another number x. The algorithms for computing square roots modulo a prime can be found, e.g. in [Menezes *et al.* (1996), Chap. 3].

6.4 Constructing Cryptosystems

Any cryptosystem based on discrete logarithms can be easily extended to elliptic curves. The basic principle is to replace the operation $y = g^x \bmod p$ by $Y = [x]G \bmod p$ (the indication of the modulus here is not generally accepted but, in fact, all computations are carried out modulo p). One should, however, remember that in case of elliptic curve with cardinality of working subset q, the values of x effectively lie in the interval $0 < x < q$. This is because $[q]G = \mathcal{O}$ and hence the integer factors in point multiplication are reduced modulo q. Another difference is that y is a number but Y is a point and it is usually required to convert a point into an integer. The simplest way to do that is to use the x-coordinate of the point.

It is also possible to construct an analogue of RSA on elliptic curves. In this case the curve is defined modulo a composite N. But we do not gain any advantage here since the length of the modulus remains the same in order to make its factorisation intractable.

We demonstrate the technique of using elliptic curves by the examples of the ElGamal cipher and DSA signature.

6.4.1   Elliptic Curve ElGamal Encryption

For the community of users of a network, an elliptic curve $E_p(a, b)$ is chosen and a point G thereon such that G, $[2]G$, $[3]G$, ..., $[q]G$ are different points and $[q]G = \mathcal{O}$ for some prime q.

Every user U selects a number c_U, $0 < c_U < q$ to be his/her private key and computes the point $D_U = [c_U]G$ which is the corresponding public key. The common parameters and public keys are submitted to all users.

Suppose user A wants to send a message to user B. Assume that the message is represented as a number $m < p$. A does the following:

1 selects a random integer k, $0 < k < q$;
2 computes $R = [k]G$, $P = [k]D_B = (x, y)$;
3 encrypts $e = m\,x \bmod p$;
4 sends B the ciphertext (R, e).

User B, upon receiving (R, e),

5 computes $Q = [c_B]R = (x, y)$;
6 decrypts $m' = ex^{-1} \bmod p$.

Let's give a justification of the protocol. Using the definitions of point Q at Step 5 and point R at Step 2 we can write

$$Q = [c_B]R = [c_B]([k]G) = [k]([c_B]G)\,.$$

The public key of user B, by definition, is $D_B = [c_B]G$. So we can see that $Q = [k]D_B$, i.e. Q is the same point as P at Step 2. Hence the coordinate x at Step 3 equals that at Step 6. Therefore $m' = m$.

The coordinate x of point Q remains secret for the adversary because she does not know the secret number k. The adversary may try to recover k from R but to do that she must solve the elliptic curve discrete logarithm problem which is believed to be impossible.

In the most likely use of the presented protocol, the message m will be the secret key for some block or stream cipher. In this case it makes sense to choose the curve parameters so that $\log q$ be about twice the length of the cipher key.

6.4.2 *Elliptic Curve Digital Signature Algorithm*

The algorithm presented here is quite analogous to digital signature algorithm (DSA) described in Sec. 4.3 but exponentiations are replaced by point multiplications on the curve. As in the preceding subsection, for the community of users, an elliptic curve $E_p(a, b)$ is chosen and a point G thereon such that G, $[2]G$, $[3]G$, ..., $[q]G$ are different points and $[q]G = \mathcal{O}$ for some prime q (the bitlength of p and q is 160 bits).

Every user U selects a number x_U, $0 < x_U < q$ to be his/her private key and computes the point $Y_U = [x_U]G$ which is the corresponding public key. The common parameters and public keys are submitted to all users.

To sign a message $\bar{m}$ user A does the following:

1 computes hash function $h = h(\bar{m})$;
2 selects a random integer k, $0 < k < q$;
3 computes $P = [k]G = (x, y)$;
4 computes $r = x \bmod q$ (if $r = 0$, revert to Step 2);
5 computes $s = k^{-1}(h + rx_A) \bmod q$ (if $s = 0$, revert to Step 2);
6 signs on the message with the pair of numbers (r, s).

For verification of the signed message $(\bar{m}; r, s)$, any user who knows the public key Y_A does the following:

7 computes $h = h(\bar{m})$;
8 verifies that $0 < r, s < q$;
9 computes $u_1 = h \cdot s^{-1} \bmod q$ and $u_2 = r \cdot s^{-1} \bmod q$;
10 computes the composition of points $P = [u_1]G + [u_2]Y_A = (x, y)$;
11 verifies that $P \neq \mathcal{O}$ and $x \bmod q = r$.

The user rejects the signature if at least one test at Step 8 or 11 fails. Otherwise, the user accepts the signature as authentic.

The proof of correctness for this protocol can be done in the same way as in Sec. 4.3.

6.5 Efficient Implementation of Operations

In this section, we consider the main approaches to making efficient computations on elliptic curves. As we have already discussed, the point multiplication by m, i.e. computing $[m]P$ where m is a large integer and P is a point on the curve, can be performed using the same methods as for exponentiation (upon replacement of ordinary modular multiplication by point addition). Here, for the sake of concreteness, we describe explicitly one of the simplest methods — left-to-right point multiplication (cf. Algorithm 2.4). There are other more efficient methods for exponentiation which may be successfully applied to elliptic curve point multiplication. But the gain is usually not so great (about 25%) and these methods go beyond the scope of our book (see their description in, e.g. [Menezes *et al.* (1996); Blake *et al.* (1999)]).

Algorithm 6.1   POINT MULTIPLICATION (FROM LEFT TO RIGHT).

INPUT: Point P, integer $m = (m_t m_{t-1} \ldots m_1)_2$.
OUTPUT: Point $Q = [m]P$.

1. $Q \leftarrow \mathcal{O}$;
2.   FOR $i = t, t - 1, \ldots, 1$ DO
3. $Q \leftarrow [2]Q$,
4.   IF $m_i = 1$ THEN $Q \leftarrow Q + P$;
5.   RETURN Q.

This algorithm requires not more than t point additions and t point doublings (on average, t doublings and $t/2$ additions).

Example 6.2   Let's demonstrate the work of the algorithm by computation of $[21]P$. Here $21 = (10101)_2 = m_1 m_2 m_3 m_4 m_5$, $t = 5$. We show what happens on each iteration.

$$
\begin{aligned}
&[i = 5 \ m_5 = 1] : Q \leftarrow \mathcal{O}, && Q \leftarrow Q + P = P; \\
&[i = 4 \ m_4 = 0] : Q \leftarrow [2]Q = [2]P; \\
&[i = 3 \ m_3 = 1] : Q \leftarrow [2]Q = [4]P, && Q \leftarrow Q + P = [5]P; \\
&[i = 2 \ m_2 = 0] : Q \leftarrow [2]Q = [10]P; \\
&[i = 1 \ m_1 = 1] : Q \leftarrow [2]Q = [20]P, \ Q \leftarrow Q + P = [21]P.
\end{aligned}
$$

For ease of exposition, reproduce here the formulas for point addition and doubling derived in Sec. 6.2. Denote the points participating in these operations by $P_1 = (x_1, y_1)$, $P_2 = (x_2, y_2)$, and $P_3 = (x_3, y_3)$. The point addition $P_3 = P_1 + P_2$ where $P_1, P_2 \neq \mathcal{O}$ and $P_1 \neq \pm P_2$ is computed by the formulas

$$k = \frac{y_2 - y_1}{x_2 - x_1},$$

$$x_3 = k^2 - x_1 - x_2,$$

$$y_3 = k(x_1 - x_3) - y_1 \qquad (\text{mod } p).$$

(6.14)

If $P_1 = \mathcal{O}$ then $P_3 = \mathcal{O} + P_2 = P_2$, and similarly with $P_2 = \mathcal{O}$. If $P_1 = -P_2$ then $P_3 = \mathcal{O}$. Finally, if $P_1 = P_2$ then we must perform doubling.

The point doubling $P_3 = [2]P_1$ where $P_1 \neq \mathcal{O}$ and $y_1 \neq 0$ is computed by the formulas

$$k = \frac{3x_1^2 + a}{2y_1},$$

$$x_3 = k^2 - 2x_1,$$

$$y_3 = k(x_1 - x_3) - y_1 \qquad (\text{mod } p).$$

(6.15)

If $P_1 = \mathcal{O}$ or $y_1 = 0$ then $P_3 = \mathcal{O}$.

Computations by (6.14) and (6.15) have been considered in Example 6.1.

One speaks that in computations by (6.14) and (6.15) the *affine* representation of points is used, i.e. a point P is represented by its two coordinates $P = (x, y)$. Point at infinity $\mathcal{O}$ has no such representation because its coordinates must be ∞. But recall that it plays the role of zero in point operations. So, technically, in Algorithm 6.1 $\mathcal{O}$ is simply a flag indicating that one should omit the operations $Q \leftarrow [2]Q$ until the first addition $Q \leftarrow Q + P$ which is performed as an assignment $Q \leftarrow P$.

The formulas (6.14) and (6.15) are used to perform computations at Lines 3 and 4 of Algorithm 6.1 with obvious substitutions. Notice that if computations on the curve are carried out in a subset of points of cardinality q and q is prime (as we always assume) and factor m lies in the interval $0 < m < q$ then the conditions for point addition formulas (i.e. $P_1, P_2 \neq \mathcal{O}$ and $P_1 \neq \pm P_2$) and point doubling formulas ($P_1 \neq \mathcal{O}$ and $y_1 \neq 0$) are automatically fulfilled at Lines 3 and 4 of Algorithm 6.1 and need not be checked (provided the first doublings omitted and the first addition replaced by assignment, as discussed above).

Now let's consider some issues of computational efficiency of point operations. Denote by M and I, respectively, the cost (time) of multiplication and inversion modulo p. Then it follows from (6.14) and (6.15) that under the affine point representation, the cost of point addition equals $1I + 3M$ and the cost of doubling is $1I + 4M$ (operations of addition with and multiplication by small integers are of no noticeable effect to the cost).

The relation between the costs of multiplication and inversion may differ depending on implementation, but I is always greater than M. If multiplication is implemented by summations and shifts, it will be but a little faster than inversion (by a factor of 2–3). In this case the use of affine representation is appropriate. But if the processor that performs computations is supplied with embedded parallel multiplier (as, e.g. Pentium$^{\circledR}$) then inversion may be significantly slower than multiplication. We can roughly estimate the costs of corresponding computations. If t is the bitlength of numbers then multiplication requires at most on the order of $(t/32)^2 = t^2/1024$ machine operations (the word size is 32 bits). On the other hand, the number of iterations in the extended Euclidean algorithm which computes inversion, is proportional to t by its nature. Even if we manage on each iteration to implement linear in t computations with 32-bit numbers (which is possible) then we obtain the total complexity on the order of $t(t/32) = t^2/32$ machine operations, i.e. one inversion will correspond to 32 multiplications. In reality, each iteration of Euclidean algorithm involves several operations and multiplication can be done with faster methods, so $I > 32M$.

Consider another approach to implementing point operations. We can get rid of inversions at each step of Algorithm 6.1 if operating with coordinates as rational numbers, making computations separately with numerator and denominator. The following transformation of variables is the most beneficial:

$$x \to \frac{X}{Z^2}, \quad y \to \frac{Y}{Z^3}. \tag{6.16}$$

A point on the curve is represented by a triplet (X, Y, Z) and one speaks of transition to *weighted projective* representation (for simplicity, we shall omit the word "weighted"). Conversion from affine to projective coordinates is quite simple:

$$(x, y) \to (x, y, 1). \tag{6.17}$$

After that all computations are carried out in projective coordinates (without computing inversions). The reverse conversion from projective to affine coordinates is done as follows:

$$(X, Y, Z) \to (X/Z^2, Y/Z^3), \tag{6.18}$$

and costs $1I + 4M$ (one computation of Z^{-1}, two multiplications for obtaining Z^{-2} and Z^{-3} and, finally, two multiplications XZ^{-2} and YZ^{-3}).

Derive the formulas for point addition in projective representation. First in Eq. (6.14) for x_3, transform variables according to (6.16). After reducing to a common denominator and cancelling we obtain

$$x_3 = \frac{X_3}{Z_3^2} = \frac{(Y_2 Z_1^3 - Y_1 Z_2^3)^2 - (X_1 Z_2^2 + X_2 Z_1^2)(X_2 Z_1^2 - X_1 Z_2^2)^2}{Z_1^2 Z_2^2 (X_2 Z_1^2 - X_1 Z_2^2)^2}. \qquad (6.19)$$

From this we find the expressions for X_3 and Z_3 taking, respectively, the numerator and the square root from denominator of the right side of (6.19). To obtain an expression for Y_3, resort to a trick that allows to save one multiplication. Notice that $P_1 + P_2 = P_2 + P_1$ and hence

$$y_3 = \left((x_1 - x_3)\frac{y_2 - y_1}{x_2 - x_1} - y_1 + (x_2 - x_3)\frac{y_2 - y_1}{x_2 - x_1} - y_2 \right) / 2.$$

Transform variables according to (6.16) and, instead of Z_3, use its representation from (6.19). After reducing to a common denominator, cancelling, and reducing the similar terms we obtain

$$y_3 = \frac{Y_3}{Z_3^3} = \frac{\left((X_1 Z_2^2 + X_2 Z_1^2)(X_2 Z_1^2 - X_1 Z_2^2)^2 - 2X_3 \right)(Y_2 Z_1^3 - Y_1 Z_2^3)}{2 Z_1^3 Z_2^3 (X_2 Z_1^2 - X_1 Z_2^2)^3}$$

$$\frac{(Y_1 Z_2^3 + Y_2 Z_1^3)(X_2 Z_1^2 - X_1 Z_2^2)^3}{2 Z_1^3 Z_2^3 (X_2 Z_1^2 - X_1 Z_2^2)^3}. \qquad (6.20)$$

Based on Eqs. (6.19) and (6.20), write Algorithm 6.2.

As it follows from the algorithm's description, the cost of addition in projective coordinates equals $16M$. We do not count simple operations of addition, subtraction, as well as multiplication and division by 2 (to explain how to compute $v/2 \bmod p$ notice that if v is even then $v/2 \bmod p = v/2$ (right shift per 1 bit); if v is odd then $v/2 \bmod p = (v + p)/2 \bmod p$, $v + p$ even, so $v/2 \bmod p = (v + p)/2$).

If one of the points, say, P_2 is given in affine coordinates, i.e. $Z_2 = 1$ then the cost of addition decreases to $11M$. It is called *mixed* addition. Algorithm 6.1 is constructed so that mixed additions can always be used, i.e. the cost of computations at Line 4 equals $11M$.

Algorithm 6.2 ADDITION IN PROJECTIVE REPRESENTATION.

INPUT: $P_1 = (X_1, Y_1, Z_1)$, $P_2 = (X_2, Y_2, Z_2)$,
$P_1, P_2 \neq \mathcal{O}$, $P_1 \neq \pm P_2$

OUTPUT: $P_3 = (X_3, Y_3, Z_3) = P_1 + P_2$
(all computations are modulo p)

$$
\begin{array}{lll}
\lambda_1 &= X_1 Z_2^2 & 2M \\
\lambda_2 &= X_2 Z_1^2 & 2M \\
\lambda_3 &= \lambda_2 - \lambda_1 & \\
\lambda_4 &= Y_1 Z_2^3 & 2M \\
\lambda_5 &= Y_2 Z_1^3 & 2M \\
\lambda_6 &= \lambda_5 - \lambda_4 & \\
\lambda_7 &= \lambda_1 + \lambda_2 & \\
\lambda_8 &= \lambda_4 + \lambda_5 & \\
Z_3 &= Z_1 Z_2 \lambda_3 & 2M \\
X_3 &= \lambda_6^2 - \lambda_7 \lambda_3^2 & 3M \\
\lambda_9 &= \lambda_7 \lambda_3^2 - 2X_3 & \\
Y_3 &= (\lambda_9 \lambda_6 - \lambda_8 \lambda_3^3)/2 & \underline{3M} \\
& & 16M
\end{array}
$$

Example 6.3 Compute the sum $(5,1) + (4,6)$ in projective coordinates for the curve of Example 6.1 (all operations are modulo 7).

$$
\begin{aligned}
P_1 &= (5,1,1), \quad P_2 = (4,6,1). \\
\lambda_1 &= 5 \cdot 1 = 5, \\
\lambda_2 &= 4 \cdot 1 = 4, \\
\lambda_3 &= 4 - 5 = 6, \lambda_4 = 1 \cdot 1 = 1, \\
\lambda_5 &= 6 \cdot 1 = 6, \\
\lambda_6 &= 6 - 1 = 5, \\
\lambda_7 &= 5 + 4 = 2, \\
\lambda_8 &= 1 + 6 = 0, \\
Z_3 &= 1 \cdot 1 \cdot 6 = 6, \\
X_3 &= 5^2 - 2 \cdot 6^2 = 2, \\
\lambda_9 &= 2 \cdot 6^2 - 2 \cdot 2 = 2 - 4 = 5, \\
Y_3 &= (5 \cdot 5 - 0 \cdot 6^3)/2 = 25/2 = (25 + 7)/2 = 16 = 2; \\
P_3 &= (2,2,6).
\end{aligned}
$$

To check the result convert point P_3 to affine representation. For that purpose compute

$$6^{-1} = 6, \quad 6^{-2} = 6 \cdot 6 = 1, \quad 6^{-3} = 1 \cdot 6 = 6.$$

We finally obtain

$$P_3 = (2 \cdot 1, 2 \cdot 6) = (2, 5)$$

which coincides with the result of Example 6.1.

Note that condition $P_1, P_2 \neq \mathcal{O}$ is equivalent to $Z_1, Z_2 \neq 0$ and condition $P_1 \neq \pm P_2$ equivalent to $X_1 \neq X_2$.

To derive the formulas for doubling a point in projective representation substitute (6.16) in (6.15):

$$x_3 = \frac{X_3}{Z_3^2} = \frac{(3X_1^2 + aZ_1^4)^2 - 8X_1Y_1^2}{(2Z_1Y_1)^2}, \tag{6.21}$$

$$y_3 = \frac{Y_3}{Z_3^3} = \frac{(4X_1Y_1^2 - X_3)(3X_1^2 + aZ_1^4)Z_1^2 - 8Y_1^4}{(2Z_1Y_1)^3}, \tag{6.22}$$

which leads to the following Algorithm 6.3.

Algorithm 6.3 DOUBLING IN PROJECTIVE REPRESENTATION.

INPUT: $P_1 = (X_1, Y_1, Z_1)$, $P_1 \neq \mathcal{O}$
OUTPUT: $P_3 = (X_3, Y_3, Z_3) = [2]P_1$

$\lambda_1 = 3X_1^2 + aZ_1^4$	$4M$
$\lambda_2 = 4X_1Y_1^2$	$2M$
$Z_3 = 2Y_1Z_1$	$1M$
$X_3 = \lambda_1^2 - 2\lambda_2$	$1M$
$\lambda_3 = 8Y_1^4$	$1M$
$Y_3 = \lambda_1(\lambda_2 - X_3) - \lambda_3$	$1M$
	$10M$

We can see that the cost of doubling in projective coordinates equals $10M$. But if the curve parameter $a = -3$ then $\lambda_1 = 3(X_1 - Z_1^2)(X_1 + Z_1^2)$ and the cost of doubling decreases to $8M$.

Notice once again that in all the above algorithms computations are performed modulo p. Therefore much depends on the efficiency of modular arithmetic. For randomly selected moduli, the best to the date approach is the use of Montgomery representation for integers [Montgomery (1985)], see also [Menezes *et al.* (1996)]. In Montgomery representation, multiplication modulo p is equivalent to two ordinary multiplications.

6.6 Counting Points on Elliptic Curve

In this section, we consider the algorithm by René Schoof suggested in [Schoof (1995)] for finding $\#E_p(a, b)$, i.e. the number of points whose coordinates satisfy the curve equation (6.10) and are positive integers less than p (plus point at infinity $\mathcal{O}$). Schoof's algorithm was the first polynomial-time algorithm for counting points, its complexity is estimated as $O(\log^6 p)$ modular operations. This algorithm forms a basis for all modern methods used for random curves.

We begin with the theorem proved by Helmut Hasse in 1933 (proofs for all theorems may be found in [Silverman (1986)]).

Theorem 6.1 (Hasse) $\#E_p(a, b)$ *satisfies the inequalities*

$$p + 1 - 2\sqrt{p} \leq \#E_p(a, b) \leq p + 1 + 2\sqrt{p}.$$

It is useful to represent $\#E_p(a, b)$ in the form

$$\#E_p(a, b) = p + 1 - t. \tag{6.23}$$

Parameter t in (6.23) can be zero, positive or negative integer and is called the *trace of Frobenius* for $E_p(a, b)$. If we could find t we would be able to obtain the number of points on curve by Eq. (6.23). The trace of Frobenius is remarkably related to the modulus p.

Theorem 6.2 *For all complex numbers x and y satisfying the curve equation (6.10) the equality holds*

$$(x^{p^2}, y^{p^2}) + [p](x, y) = [t](x^p, y^p) \tag{6.24}$$

(addition in the formula means composition of points).

Now our task is to solve Eq. (6.24) with respect to the unknown t. Notice that the point composition of the form $Q = [m]P$ can be expressed through the coordinates of point P. For instance,

$$[2](x, y) = \left(x' = \left(\frac{3x^2 + a}{2y} \right)^2 - 2x, \ y' = \frac{3x^2 + a}{2y}(x - x') - y \right)$$

$$= \left(\frac{x^4 - 2ax^2 - 8bx + a^2}{4y^2} , \right.$$

$$\left. \frac{x^6 + 5ax^4 + 20bx^3 - 5a^2x^2 - 4abx - 8b^2 - a^3}{8y^3} \right) .$$

The point $[3](x, y)$ can be obtained as $[2](x, y) + (x, y)$ by substituting the obtained coordinates for the point $[2](x, y)$ in Eqs. (6.5), (6.7), (6.8) (the interested reader may do that). The process of obtaining expressions for subsequent points seems much too complicated, nevertheless, it can be described by the following simple recurrence scheme:

$$\psi_0 = 0 \,,$$
$$\psi_1 = 1 \,,$$
$$\psi_2 = 2y \,,$$
$$\psi_3 = 3x^4 + 6ax^2 + 12bx - a^2 \,,$$
$$\psi_4 = 4y(x^6 + 5ax^4 + 20bx^3 - 5a^2x^2 - 4abx - 8b^2 - a^3) \,,$$
$$\psi_{2m+1} = \psi_{m+2}\psi_m^3 - \psi_{m-1}\psi_{m+1}^3 \,, \quad m \geq 2 \,,$$
$$\psi_{2m} = (\psi_{m+2}\psi_{m-1}^2 - \psi_{m-2}\psi_{m+1}^2)\psi_m / 2y \,, \quad m > 2 \,.$$

For $m \geq 2$ and $P = (x, y)$

$$[m]P = \left(\frac{\psi_m^2 x - \psi_{m-1}\psi_{m+1}}{\psi_m^2} , \frac{\psi_{m+2}\psi_{m-1}^2 - \psi_{m-2}\psi_{m+1}^2}{4y\psi_m^3} \right) . \tag{6.25}$$

Polynomial $\psi_m(x, y)$ is called the *division polynomial* of order m. As we consider the curve reduced modulo p, the coefficients of all polynomials ψ are also reduced modulo p. With the aid of the above scheme the division polynomial of order m can be computed for $O(\log m)$ steps (the reader not familiar with polynomial arithmetic may consult [Knuth (1981)]). Notice that under an odd m, polynomials ψ_m depend on only one variable x since the other variable y enters only in even powers and y^2 is replaced by the right side of the curve equation (6.10). Notice also that the polynomials of the "second layer" (ψ_{2m}, ψ_{2m+1}) include the products of 4 polynomials of the "first layer" (from ψ_{m-2} to ψ_{m+2}), therefore, the degree of polynomial ψ_m grows as $O(m^2)$.

A complex point P on curve E is called the *torsion point* of order m if $[m]P = \mathcal{O}$. Due to (6.25) it is quite obvious that a point $P = (x, y)$ is a torsion point of order m if and only if $\psi_m(x, y) = 0$.

The idea of Schoof's algorithm is to search for solutions of Eq. (6.24) (with respect to t) over the sets of torsion points of small orders with subsequent determination of the general solution. For torsion point of order

m the factors are reduced modulo m and polynomials reduced modulo ψ_m, so Eq. (6.24) takes the form

$$(x^{p^2}, y^{p^2})_m + [p_m](x, y) = [t_m](x^p, y^p)_m \qquad (6.26)$$

where $p_m = p \bmod m$, $t_m = t \bmod m$, $(x^k, y^k)_m = (x^k \bmod \psi_m, y^k \bmod \psi_m)$, besides, x and y are linked by the curve equation $y^2 = x^3 + ax + b$. According to the Hasse theorem

$$|t| \le 2\sqrt{p}. \qquad (6.27)$$

Let us take for the values of m prime numbers up to $m_{\max}$ such that

$$\prod_{\substack{m \text{ prime} \\ 2 \le m \le m_{\max}}} m > 4\sqrt{p}. \qquad (6.28)$$

Then having obtained t_m we shall uniquely determine the trace of Frobenius t satisfying (6.27) by Chinese Remainder Theorem (see [Knuth (1981); Menezes *et al.* (1996)]).

Consider briefly the method of solving Eq. (6.26) for the case $m > 2$. First compute the polynomial ψ_m. Since m is odd, $\psi_m = \psi_m(x)$. (Further on, all operations with polynomials are carried out modulo ψ_m, the power of y is reduced to 1 by the curve equation, coefficients are computed modulo p.) Compute the polynomials x^p, y^p, x^{p^2}, y^{p^2} using the same exponentiation algorithm as for integers. By (6.25) compute $Q = [p_m](x, y)$ and using the point addition formulas find in symbolic form the composition $R = (x^{p^2}, y^{p^2})_m + Q$. If $R = \mathcal{O}$ then $t_m = 0$. Otherwise, in order to find t_m compute the x-coordinates of points $P = [\tau](x^p, y^p)_m$ for all τ, $0 < \tau < m$. For each τ we must verify the equality between x_R and x_P. To do that we represent the difference of x-coordinates in the form $x_R - x_P = u(x) - yv(x) = 0$. Take from this $y = u(x)/v(x)$, substitute it in the curve equation and obtain some polynomial $h_x(x) = 0$. If $h_x \bmod \psi_m \ne 0$ then x_R and x_P are different and we must try another value of τ. Otherwise, if $x_R = x_P$ then compute the y-coordinate of point P and, by similar techniques, transform the difference $y_R - y_P$ in a polynomial $h_y(x) = 0$. If $h_y \bmod \psi_m = 0$ then $t_m = \tau$, otherwise $t_m = -\tau \bmod m$.

When $m = 2$, $\psi_2 = y$ and the difficulty arises with computation of $x^p \bmod y$. But here one simple observation helps. Since we exclude singular curves, our curve may have either one or three intersections with the horizontal axis. All other points appear in pairs (x, y), $(x, -y)$ and there is one point at infinity $\mathcal{O}$. So the number of points on the curve is even or odd depending on whether $X^3 + aX + b$ can be factored modulo p or not. A simple criterion is known for making such a decision (see, e.g. [Menezes *et al.* (1996); Gallager (1968)]).

Theorem 6.3 *A third-degree polynomial $F(X)$ cannot be factored modulo p if and only if*

$$\gcd(F(X), X^p - X) = 1.$$

As a result we have $t_2 = 1$ if $\gcd(X^3 + aX + b, X^p - X) = 1$, and $t_2 = 0$ otherwise.

Let us estimate the complexity of Schoof's algorithm. First, give the following well-known property of prime numbers (see [Rosen (1992); Menezes *et al.* (1996)]).

Proposition 6.1 *The number of primes less than n is approximately $n/\ln n$.*

It follows from Proposition 6.1 that $m_{\max} = O(\log p)$ and the number of moduli for which the computations are performed is $O(\log p)$. The most time-consuming step in the algorithm is the computation of x^{p^2} and the similar polynomials. If a fast exponentiation method is used, this step requires $O(\log p)$ multiplications with polynomials of degree $O(m^2) = O(\log^2 p)$. Each multiplication requires $O(\log^4 p)$ numerical multiplications modulo p, i.e. there is a total of $O(\log^5 p)$ multiplications modulo p. One multiplication modulo p requires $O(\log^2 p)$ bit operations. So computation of x^{p^2} requires $O(\log^7 p)$ bit operations. Taking into account the number of moduli we obtain the overall complexity $O(\log^8 p)$ bit operations.

Example 6.4 Determine the number of points on the curve used in Example 6.1 on p. 89:

$$Y^2 = X^3 + 2X + 6 \pmod 7 \quad (a = 2, b = 6).$$

First apply the exponential-time algorithm: for all values of X from 0 to 6 find corresponding values of Y (if any). We shall need a list of squares modulo 7:

$$0^2 = 0,$$
$$1^2 = 1,$$
$$2^2 = 4,$$
$$3^2 = 9 = 2,$$
$$4^2 = 2,$$
$$5^2 = 4,$$
$$6^2 = 1 \quad (\text{mod } 7).$$

With the use of this list find the set of points $E_7(2,6)$:

$$x = 0, y^2 = 6, \qquad\qquad y \text{ does not exist,}$$
$$x = 1, y^2 = 1 + 2 + 6 = 9 = 2, \ y = 3 \text{ and } y = -3 = 4,$$
$$x = 2, y^2 = 8 + 4 + 6 = 4, \qquad y = 2 \text{ and } y = -2 = 5,$$
$$x = 3, y^2 = 27 + 6 + 6 = 4, \qquad y = 2 \text{ and } y = -2 = 5,$$
$$x = 4, y^2 = 64 + 8 + 6 = 1, \qquad y = 1 \text{ and } y = -1 = 6,$$
$$x = 5, y^2 = 125 + 10 + 6 = 1, \ y = 1 \text{ and } y = -1 = 6,$$
$$x = 6, y^2 = 216 + 12 + 6 = 3, \ y \text{ does not exist.}$$

Counting the number of points found and adding the point at infinity we obtain

$$\#E_7(2,6) = 11.$$

It is clear that this method cannot be applied if p is large, but we shall use the result for checking.

Begin the execution of Schoof's algorithm. Three moduli $m = 2, 3, 5$ will suffice since $2 \cdot 3 \cdot 5 = 30 > 4\sqrt{7} = 10.58$ (in fact, two moduli $m = 3, 5$ would be enough but we shall use also $m = 2$ for the sake of exposition).

For ease of designation, we shall write polynomials as decimal numbers (the size of the modulus allows us to do that). Thus, for instance,

$$x^4 + 5x^2 + 2 = 1x^4 + 0x^3 + 5x^2 + 0x + 2 = 10502,$$
$$x^4 + x = 1x^4 + 0x^3 + 0x^2 + 1x + 0 = 10010.$$

All operations with coefficients will be performed modulo 7. Compute the necessary division polynomials:

$$\psi_0 = 0\,,$$
$$\psi_1 = 1\,,$$
$$\psi_2 = 2y\,,$$
$$\psi_3 = 30523\,,$$
$$\psi_4 = 4y \cdot 1031115 = 4054446y\,,$$
$$\psi_5 = \psi_4\psi_2^3 - \psi_1\psi_3^3 = 4054446 \cdot 1026^2 - 6025554626356$$
$$= 5055036550230\,.$$

Now we are to solve Eq. (6.26) for $m = 3$. Compute modulo ψ_3:

$$x^7 = 1363\,,$$
$$y^7 = (y^2)^3y = 1026^3y = 1360y\,,$$
$$x^{49} = 10 = x\,,$$
$$y^{49} = 1026^{24}y = 6y\,,$$
$$p_3 = 7 \bmod 3 = 1\,.$$

The left side of (6.26) converts to

$$R = (x, 6y) + (x, y) = \mathcal{O}\,.$$

Hence, $t_3 = 0$.

Now solve Eq. (6.26) for $m = 5$. Compute modulo ψ_5:

$$x^7 = 10000000\,,$$
$$y^7 = 1064524266y\,,$$
$$x^{49} = 531353334500\,,$$
$$y^{49} = 650465522521y\,,$$
$$p_5 = 2\,.$$

Let's find a point $Q = [2](x, y)$. In general case, it is done by Eq. (6.25):

$$Q = \left(\frac{4y^2x - \psi_3}{4y^2}, \frac{\psi_4}{4y^4}\right) = \left(\frac{10314}{4013}, \frac{1031115y}{1045431}\right)\,.$$

We can see that $x_Q \neq x^{49}$, so we shall look for $\tau > 0$. Find a point

$R = (x^{49}, y^{49}) + Q$ by Eqs. (6.5), (6.7), (6.8):

$$k = \frac{\dfrac{1031115y}{1045431} - 650465522521y}{\dfrac{10314}{4013} - 531353334500}$$

$$= \frac{(1031115 - 650465522521 \cdot 1045431)4013y}{1045431(10314 - 531353334500 \cdot 4013}$$

$$= \frac{541024434205y}{115461562234},$$

$$x_R = \frac{541024434205^2 y^2}{115461562234^2} - 531353334500 - \frac{10314}{4013}$$

$$= \frac{552631612401}{533030166456},$$

$$y_R = \left(531353334500 - \frac{552631612401}{533030166456}\right) \cdot \frac{541024434205y}{115461562234} -$$

$$- 650465522521y = \frac{515441613166y}{115165441243}.$$

Let's try $\tau = 1$, $P = (x^7, y^7)$. Verify the hypothesis $x_R - x_P = 0$:

$$h_x = 552631612401 - 533030166456 \cdot 10000000$$
$$= 61115566241 \neq 0 \bmod \psi_5.$$

Try $\tau = 2$. Compute $P = [2](x^7, y^7)$. Here it is convenient to use point addition since we add the point (x^7, y^7) to the previous point P. We obtain

$$k = \frac{3 \cdot 10000000^2 + 2}{2 \cdot 1064524266y} = \frac{434232361462}{2051341455y},$$

$$x_P = \frac{434232361462^2}{2051341455^2 y^2} - 2 \cdot 10000000 = \frac{213203662514}{220445441503}.$$

Verify the hypothesis $x_R - x_P = 0$:

$$h_x = 552631612401 \cdot 220445441503 - 213203662514 \cdot 533030166456$$
$$= 0 \bmod \psi_5.$$

Hence, $x_R = x_P$. Now we need to compare y_R and y_P. We have

$$y_P = \left(10000000 - \frac{213203662514}{220445441503}\right) \cdot \frac{434232361462}{2051341455y} - 1064524266y$$

$$= \frac{510334350655}{221015611231y}.$$

Verify whether $y_R - y_P = 0$:

$$h_y = 515441613166y \cdot 221015611231y - 510334350655 \cdot 115165441243$$
$$= 0 \bmod \psi_5.$$

Hence, $t_5 = 2$.

Finally, determine t_2. We must find the greatest common divisor for $x^3 + ax + b$ and $x^p - x$. Apply the Euclidean algorithm for polynomials. Notice that under the large p used in cryptography, we cannot store in memory and operate with the polynomial $x^p - x$. But at the first step of Euclidean algorithm the remainder is computed $(x^p - x) \bmod (x^3 + ax + b)$, therefore it suffices to set as input not the polynomial $x^p - x$ but the remainder. So we compute $x^p \bmod (x^3 + ax + b)$ using a fast exponentiation algorithm and subtract x. After that preparation we run the Euclidean algorithm. In out example,

$$x^7 = 304 \bmod 1026,$$
$$x^7 - x = 364,$$
$$\gcd(1026, 364) = 1.$$

Hence, $t_2 = 1$.

Now apply the Chinese Remainder Theorem [Knuth (1981); Menezes *et al.* (1996)]. We have

$$t = 1 \bmod 2,$$
$$t = 0 \bmod 3,$$
$$t = 2 \bmod 5,$$
$$N = 2 \cdot 3 \cdot 5 = 30.$$

The solution $t' = t \bmod N$ is found by the formula

$$t' = \sum_{i=1}^{3} a_i N_i M_i \bmod N$$

where

$$a_1 = 1,\, N_1 = 30/2 = 15,\, M_1 = 15^{-1} \bmod 2 = 1,$$
$$a_2 = 0,\, N_2 = 30/3 = 10,\, M_2 = 10^{-1} \bmod 3 = 1,$$
$$a_3 = 2,\, N_3 = 30/5 = 6,\quad M_3 = 6^{-1} \bmod 5 = 1.$$

Substituting the numbers we obtain

$$t' = 1 \cdot 15 \cdot 1 + 0 \cdot 10 \cdot 1 + 2 \cdot 6 \cdot 1 = 27.$$

To make the solution satisfy the inequality (6.27) subtract the modulus:

$$t = t' - N = -3.$$

By Eq. (6.23) find

$$\#E_7(2,6) = 7 + 1 - (-3) = 11.$$

We see that determination of the number of points on the curve is not a simple problem. Solving it requires high-performance computers. In practice, improved versions of Schoof's algorithm are used that involve subtle higher-algebraic constructions. The main feature of these methods is the reduction of the degree of division polynomials from $O(m^2)$ down to $O(m)$. As a result, the complexity is reduced to $O(\log^6 p)$ and may be further decreased down to $O(\log^{4+\epsilon} p)$ owing to the use of asymptotically faster methods of multiplication and division.

6.7   Using Standard Curves

In view of the fact that generating random curves according to the guidelines of Sec. 6.3, especially performing the step of point counting, appears quite difficult, it is enough in practice to use the curves suggested by various standards and other sources. For instance, the US standard FIPS 186-2 [FIPS 186-2 (2000)] suggests specific elliptic curves for several lengths of moduli. Generally speaking, there are no restrictions that one well-chosen elliptic curve be used by all the users over the world. However such a curve, being widely used, will attract considerable forces of cryptanalysts and adversaries. One cannot rule out the possibility that, in the course of time, some attacks on that specific curve will be invented by utilising its hidden properties not taken into account earlier. But this is only a possibility which is considered by many specialists as highly improbable.

Let us give an example of a real curve suggested by FIPS 186-2 (Curve P-256). By a backslash \ we denote the continuation of a number at a next line. It is assumed that the curve is defined by the equation $Y^2 = X^3 + aX + b \bmod p$, the number of points on the curve $\#E_p(a, b) = n$, the point $G = (x_G, y_G)$ is a generator of the working subset of points of cardinality q where q is prime.

$$p = 2^{256} - 2^{224} + 2^{192} + 2^{96} - 1$$

$= 115792\ 089210356\ 248762697\ 446949407\ 573530086\backslash$
143415290 314195533 631308867 097853951

$a = -3$

$b = $ 0x 5ac635d8 aa3a93e7 b3ebbd55 769886bc 651d06b0$\backslash$
cc53b0f6 3bce3c3e 27d2604b

$n = 115792\ 089210356\ 248762697\ 446949407\ 573529996\backslash$
955224135 760342422 259061068 512044369
(prime number)

$q = n$

$x_G = $ 0x 6b17d1f2 e12c4247 f8bce6e5 63a440f2 77037d81$\backslash$
2deb33a0 f4a13945 d898c296

$y_G = $ 0x 4fe342e2 fe1a7f9b 8ee7eb4a 7c0f9e16 2bce3357$\backslash$
6b315ece cbb64068 37bf51f5

We can see that parameters p and a are scarcely be conceived as random, and all "randomness" of the curve is determined by the random choice of parameter b.

The first question that arises when we are given a curve such as the one above: are there no errors in the record of parameters? Three basic tests can be performed to ascertain this.

(1) Verify that p is prime.

(2) Verify that the point $G = (x_G, y_G)$ lies on the curve (satisfies the curve equation).

(3) Verify that n is indeed the number of points on the curve. Note that this check makes sense also if we ourselves compute n, e.g. by the use of Schoof's algorithm. In general case, $n = hq$ where h is a small integer and q prime. First of all, by trial division and testing primality, one should make certain that n complies with the specified form. Then randomly select a point P on the curve (one may take $P = [k]G$ where k is a random integer). The number n is guaranteed to be the number of points if simultaneously $[n]P = \mathcal{O}$ and $[h]P \neq \mathcal{O}$. This condition being unsatisfied, two variants are possible: If $[n]P \neq \mathcal{O}$ then n is not a number of points; but if $[h]P = \mathcal{O}$

(which is extremely unlikely) then one needs to take another point P.

In addition to the proposed tests one may verify all other requirements described in Sec. 6.3.

The second question that arises when we are given a "cooked" curve, is whether it actually was generated randomly? This question is also important for many other cryptographic schemes. May be, the curve suggested possesses some rare property allowing to break the resulting cryptosystem, and the one who has manufactured the curve will be able later on to access the secret information encrypted with the aid of this curve. To prove that the curve was indeed randomly generated, we must prove that its parameters were chosen randomly but not at will. For instance, for the curve recommended above, we must prove that parameter b was selected at random. But how can one prove that some number is random? Actually, what we need is to prove that it was not systematically constructed. This problem is solved as follows. Let $h(x)$ be a cryptographically secure hash function. To generate a number b we select a number s, compute $b = h(s)$ and suggest both b and s. If the hash function satisfies all security requirements (see Sec. 8.5) then b cannot have any prescribed properties and we can rely on it, as it were truly random. The number s is the "certificate" which proves the "purity" of number b (everyone can verify that $b = h(s)$). The elliptic curve described above has such a certificate, based on hash function SHA-1 [FIPS 180-1 (1995)], and the standard specifies the procedure of its usage. Therefore me may be sure that the curve is actually random.

Problems and Exercises

6.1 The elliptic curve is defined by the parameters $p = 11$, $a = 4$, $b = 7$. Determine whether the following points are on the curve: $(1,1)$, $(1,2)$, $(2,1)$, $(2,2)$, $(5,8)$.

6.2 For the elliptic curve with parameters $p = 7$, $a = 2$, $b = 6$ compute the following point compositions: $[2](2,2)$, $[2](4,6)$, $(1,3) + (1,4)$, $(2,2) + (3,2)$, $(3,5) + (5,1)$.

Themes for Labs

In labs, it is recommended to use the elliptic curve with the following parameters:

$$p = 31991, \quad a = -3 = 31988, \quad b = 1000.$$

The number of points on this curve

$$n = 32089 \quad (\text{prime number}).$$

As a generator, one may take the point

$$G = (0, 5585).$$

It is convenient to represent the point at infinity $\mathcal{O}$ as a point with coordinates (0,0).

6.3 Write the set of programs (program functions) for computation of elliptic curve point addition, doubling, and multiplication. We propose several equalities for program testing:

$$(51, 7858) + (91, 5500) = (7252, 18353),$$
$$(7777, 10935) + (16000, 20400) = (12395, 26268),$$
$$(12405, 28624) + (2963, 16300) = (14005, 2313),$$
$$(8020, 1740) + (8020, 30251) = \mathcal{O},$$

$$[2](0, 5585) = (8, 19435),$$
$$[2](23161, 17992) = (26775, 10831),$$
$$[2](110, 13171) = (26948, 16087),$$

$$[10000](31122, 9) = (31180, 29596),$$
$$[12345](13140, 5033) = (9362, 27046),$$
$$[11111](11007, 23704) = (850, 6718).$$

6.4 Make a program implementation of ElGamal cipher on elliptic curve. When debugging and testing the program one may use the following example of cipher:

$$c = 5103\,, \quad D = (12507, 2027)\,;$$
$$m = 10000\,, \quad k = 523\,;$$
$$R = (9767, 11500)\,, \quad P = (25482, 16638)\,;$$
$$e = 11685\,.$$

The obtained ciphertext $((9767, 11500), 11685)$ must decrypt to the message 10000 under the secret key 5103.

6.5 Make a program implementation of the algorithms of elliptic curve signature generation and verification. As usually, assume that $h(m) = m$. As the parameter q take $n = 32089$ (the number of points on curve). The signed message

$$(1000; 4615, 5944)$$

must be declared valid for the signer whose public key is $Y = (12224, 7207)$.

Chapter 7

Theoretical Security of Cryptosystems

7.1 Introduction

One of the first open works on cryptography was [Shannon (1949)]. Shannon considered the classical secret-key cryptosystem as shown schematically in Fig. 1.1 (p. 3). In this system, we have a secure channel for transmitting secret keys. However notice that in our days we may replace the secure channel by a *secured* channel which is virtually created when the secret key is computed by means of public-key cryptographic methods, e.g. Diffie–Hellman key agreement or Needham–Schroeder protocol. In this chapter, we shall consider only the classical scheme with the secret key, but many of the results may be extended to the case of generating secret keys by public-key methods.

We may roughly divide all ciphers into two big classes:

(1) the schemes unbreakable in principle, which can be strictly proved;
(2) the schemes whose security is based on impossibility of searching through a large number of keys (although, in principle, they can be broken).

In this chapter, we shall study the systems from the first class. The second class will be the topic of the next chapter. To expose the matter of this chapter we need some elementary notions and facts from probability theory. We shall use these without giving strict definitions and proofs which may be found in almost any textbook on probability theory, see, e.g. [Feller (1968)]. Many of the results discussed in the following sections are due to [Shannon (1948)] and [Shannon (1949)].

7.2   Theory of Perfect Secrecy

Let $M = \{M_1, M_2, M_3, \ldots, M_m\}$ be the set of all admissible messages (e.g. the set of all texts in English of the length no more than 1000 letters), $K = \{K_1, K_2, K_3, \ldots, K_n\}$ be the set of all possible keys, $E = \{E_1, E_2, \ldots, E_k\}$ be the set of all cryptograms (i.e. enciphered messages). The cryptograms are the functions of the source message and the key, i.e. $E_j = f(M_i, K_l)$.

Assume that the set of messages M obeys a probability distribution P, i.e. a probability $P(M_i)$ is defined for all $i = 1, 2, \ldots, m$. This is an *a priori* distribution which is also known to an adversary. Notation $P(A|B)$ will be used, as usual, for conditional probability of event A given event B (i.e. $P(A|B)$ is the probability of occurrence of event A provided that event B has occurred).

Definition 7.1   A cryptosystem is said to be *perfectly secure* (or to provide *perfect secrecy*) if the equality holds

$$P(M_i|E_j) = P(M_i) \tag{7.1}$$

for all M_i, K_l, and $E_j = f(M_i, K_l)$.

Let's give some explanations. Suppose that Eve overhears the cryptogram E_j. If Eq. (7.1) holds for all admissible messages then Eve does not obtain any information about the message transmitted, i.e. the knowledge of E_j is of no use for her. Consider a schematic

Example 7.1   Let M be the set of all 6-letter words in English. Let it be known *a priori* that

$$\begin{aligned}P(\text{message} = \text{``dollar''}) &= 0.000150\,, \\ P(\text{message} = \text{``bottle''}) &= 0.000012\,, \;\; etc.\end{aligned} \tag{7.2}$$

Suppose we have a non-perfect system and Eve upon interception and computation obtains the following data:

$$\begin{aligned}P(\text{message} = \text{``dollar''}) &= 10^{-20}\,, \\ P(\text{message} = \text{``bottle''}) &= 0.9999\,.\end{aligned}$$

It means that Eve has, in fact, deciphered the message: she is almost sure that the word "bottle" was transmitted because the probability of anything else does not exceed 0.0001.

Suppose now that we have a perfect system. In this case, for any intercepted cryptogram E_j, Eve obtains

$$P(\text{message} = \text{``dollar''}|E_j) = 0.000150\,,$$
$$P(\text{message} = \text{``bottle''}|E_j) = 0.000012\,, \ etc.$$

i.e. her *a posteriori* distribution completely coincides with the *a priori* distribution (7.2). It means that she may pay no attention to the intercepted cryptogram but guess the message based on the source probabilities. We can see that Eq. (7.1) is actually a reasonable definition of perfect secrecy.

Explore the properties of perfect secrecy systems.

Theorem 7.1 *If a system is perfectly secure (Eq. (7.1) holds) then the equality is valid*

$$P\left(E_j|M_i\right) = P\left(E_j\right) \tag{7.3}$$

for all i and j. The converse is also true: if (7.3) holds then the system is perfectly secure.

Proof. By definition of conditional probability

$$P\left(A|B\right) = \frac{P(AB)}{P(B)}$$

under $P(B) \neq 0$. Therefore given $P(E_j) \neq 0$ we can write

$$P(M_i|E_j) = \frac{P(M_iE_j)}{P(E_j)} = \frac{P(M_i)P(E_j|M_i)}{P(E_j)}\,.$$

Taking into account Eq. (7.1) we obtain

$$P\left(M_i|E_j\right) = \frac{P(M_i|E_j)P(E_j|M_i)}{P(E_j)}\,,$$

i.e.

$$\frac{P(E_j|M_i)}{P(E_j)} = 1\,.$$

So Eq. (7.3) is proved. The converse proposition can be proved by the reverse chain of the presented equalities, see [Shannon (1949)]. $\square$

7.3 Vernam Cipher

This cipher was suggested by American engineer Gilbert Vernam [Vernam (1926)] and was used in practice but the proof of its security was given much later in [Shannon (1949)]. The Vernam cipher is sometimes called a *one-time pad*. We shall describe the cipher for the case of binary alphabet.

Let the set of messages M consist of binary words of length n, i.e. there are no more than 2^n messages. In the Vernam cipher, the set of keys consists of the words of the same length n and each key is used with probability $1/2^n$. In other words, all keys are used with equal probabilities.

Let the message be $\bar{m} = m_1 m_2 \ldots m_n$ and the key $\bar{k} = k_1 k_2 \ldots k_n$. Then the ciphertext $\bar{e} = e_1 e_2 \ldots e_n$ is produced by the rule:

$$e_i = m_i \oplus k_i, \quad i = 1, 2, \ldots, n, \tag{7.4}$$

where $\oplus$ denotes addition modulo 2. In other words, the message is enciphered by the scheme

$$
\oplus \frac{\begin{array}{cccc} m_1 & m_2 & \ldots & m_n \\ k_1 & k_2 & \ldots & k_n \end{array}}{\begin{array}{cccc} e_1 & e_2 & \ldots & e_n \end{array}} \ .
$$

Since addition and subtraction modulo 2 are the same, deciphering is done by the rule

$$m_i = e_i \oplus k_i . \tag{7.5}$$

Example 7.2 Let $\bar{m} = 01001$, $\bar{k} = 11010$. Then we obtain $\bar{e} = 10011$. Summing up $\bar{e}$ with $\bar{k}$ we recover $\bar{m} = 01001$.

Theorem 7.2 *The Vernam cipher is perfectly secure.*

Proof. By Theorem 7.1 it suffices to prove that (7.3) holds. We have

$$
\begin{aligned}
P(E_j|M_i) &= P(\bar{e}|\bar{m}) \\
&= P(k_1 = e_1 \oplus m_1, \, k_2 = e_2 \oplus m_2, \, \ldots, \, k_n = e_n \oplus m_n) \\
&= P(\bar{k} = k_1 \ldots k_n) = 2^{-n}
\end{aligned}
$$

(in the last equality we used the assumption that all keys are equiprobable). Find $P(E_j)$. Provided that events M_i are pairwise mutually exclusive, by total probability formula

$$P(E_j) = \sum_{i=1}^{2^n} P(M_i)P(E_j|M_i).$$

Taking into account that $P(E_j|M_i) = 2^{-n}$ we obtain

$$P(E_j) = 2^{-n} \sum_{i=1}^{2^n} P(M_i).$$

Since the sum of probabilities of all messages equals 1 we obtain

$$P(E_j) = 2^{-n}.$$

So, $P(E_j|M_i) = P(E_j) = 2^{-n}$, i.e. Eq. (7.3) holds.   □

It is known that the Vernam cipher was used for securing governmental communications, e.g. on the so-called hot line "Moscow–Washington" [Menezes *et al.* (1996)]. The key was delivered by a trusted courier. There is a point of view that the Vernam cipher is very expensive because the length of the key must be equal to the message length. On the other hand, the cipher can be used in many practical situations. For example, students Alice and Bob can agree to use this cipher for securing their e-mail messages when they part for holidays (we advise the reader to work out the scheme and write the program assuming that the length of letters they will exchange does not exceed 1.44 Mbytes, i.e. the size of a standard floppy disk).

7.4   Elements of Information Theory

We have proved that the Vernam cipher is perfectly secure but it requires the key to be as long as the message. Shannon showed that in any perfect secrecy system the key length must be no less than the message entropy (the notion we shall define below), i.e. proportional to the message length. However in many practical systems, we have to use short keys (say, hundreds or thousands bits) for encrypting long messages (hundreds kilobytes and more). In this case, we may construct the so-called *ideal* cryptosystems described firstly by Shannon. For constructing ideal systems and studying their properties Shannon suggested to use the notions and results of information theory. In this section, we shall define and briefly illustrate these. A sufficiently complete and strict study can be found in many textbooks, e.g. [Gallager (1968); McEliece (1984); Blahut (1987); Welsh (1988)]. It is also useful to consult the pioneering work [Shannon (1948)]. The reader may refer to any of these books for strict definitions and proofs.

We begin with definition of the main notion, the Shannon entropy. Let a discrete random variable ξ be given taking on values $a_1, a_2, \ldots, a_r$ with probabilities $P_1, P_2, \ldots, P_r$, respectively.

Definition 7.2   The *entropy* of random variable ξ is defined by the equation

$$H(\xi) = -\sum_{i=1}^{r} P_i \log P_i \qquad (7.6)$$

assuming $0 \log 0 = 0$.

If one uses binary logarithms (i.e. to the base 2) then the entropy is measured in bits, which is generally accepted in cryptography, information theory, and computer science. In case of natural logarithms, the unity of measure is nat, in case of decimal logarithms — dit.

If $r = 2$, Eq. (7.6) can be written differently with the following notation: $P_1 = p$, $P_2 = 1 - p$. Then

$$H = -\left(p \log p + (1 - p) \log(1 - p)\right). \qquad (7.7)$$

The graph of the entropy for this case is shown in Fig. 7.1.

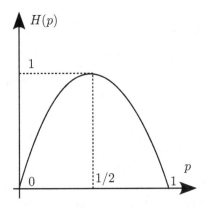

Fig. 7.1   The graph of binary entropy.

Consider the simplest properties of entropy.

Proposition 7.1

(1) $H\left(\xi\right) \geq 0$;
(2) $H\left(\xi\right) \leq \log r$;
(3) $H\left(\xi\right) = \log r$ if $P_i = 1/r$, $i = 1, 2, \ldots, r$.

Proof. The first property is quite obvious (see (7.6)). We prove the second property only for $r = 2$ since the general case is similar. Explore the graph of entropy. We need to find the maximum of function (7.7). For that, we find the first and second derivatives of $H(p)$ assuming for simplicity that the logarithms are natural.

$$H'(p) = -\left(\ln p + p \cdot \frac{1}{p} - \ln(1-p) - \frac{1-p}{1-p}\right) = -\ln p + \ln(1-p).$$

Hence $H'(p) = 0$ if $p = 1/2$. Find the second derivative

$$H''(p) = -\frac{1}{p} - \frac{1}{1-p}.$$

We can see that $H''(p) < 0$ when $p \in (0;\ 1)$. It means that the function $H(p)$ attains the maximum when $p = 1/2$ and is convex in the interval $(0;\ 1)$. So the graph depicted in Fig. 7.1 is justified. It is plain that under any other base of the logarithm the graph will be analogous.

The third property follows directly from the definition of entropy (7.6):

$$H(\xi) = -\sum_{i=1}^{r} \frac{1}{r} \log \frac{1}{r} = -r \cdot \frac{1}{r} \log \frac{1}{r} = \log r.$$

$\square$

The physical sense of the entropy is the quantitative measure of uncertainty. Consider, for instance, three different random variables ξ_1, ξ_2, ξ_3 taking on values a_1 and a_2 ($r = 2$):

$$\xi_1 : P(a_1) = 1, \quad P(a_2) = 0;$$
$$\xi_2 : P(a_1) = 0.5, \quad P(a_2) = 0.5;$$
$$\xi_3 : P(a_1) = 0.01, \quad P(a_2) = 0.99.$$

Intuition suggests that uncertainty of ξ_1 is zero. Actually,

$$H(\xi_1) = -(1 \cdot \log 1 + 0 \cdot \log 0) = 0.$$

Look at ξ_2 and ξ_3. Intuition says that uncertainty of ξ_2 is higher than that of ξ_3. Compute the entropies:

$$H(\xi_2) = 1 \text{ bit}$$

(has been computed above),

$$H(\xi_3) = -(0.01 \cdot \log 0.01 + 0.99 \cdot \log 0.99) \approx 0.08 \text{ bit}.$$

We can see that the entropy is indeed a reasonable measure of uncertainty. But the matter is not the examples of that sort. The entropy plays a key role in many problems of telecommunications and information sciences. In particular, the entropy characterises the maximum attainable degree of data compression. More exactly, if a source with the (defined below) limit entropy h generates a (sufficiently long) message of n symbols, this message can be compressed up to nh bits on average. For example, if $h = 1/2$, the message can be compressed to half of its size. Point out that we speak of so-called lossless compression when the source message can be recovered without distortion.

Consider now a two-dimensional random variable defined by the following distribution

$$P_{ij} = P(\xi_1 = a_i, \ \xi_2 = b_j), \quad 1 \le i \le r, \ 1 \le j \le s. \tag{7.8}$$

Introduce the following notation:

$$P_{i\cdot} = P(\xi_1 = a_i) = \sum_{j=1}^{s} P_{ij},$$
$$P_{\cdot j} = P(\xi_2 = b_j) = \sum_{i=1}^{r} P_{ij}.$$

By analogy with (7.6) define the entropy of two-dimensional random variable

$$H(\xi_1, \xi_2) = -\sum_{i=1}^{r}\sum_{j=1}^{s} P_{ij} \log P_{ij}. \tag{7.9}$$

Similarly, for a three-dimensional random variable (ξ_1, ξ_2, ξ_3) and probability distribution P_{ijk}, define

$$H(\xi_1, \xi_2, \xi_3) = -\sum_{i}\sum_{j}\sum_{k} P_{ijk} \log P_{ijk}. \tag{7.10}$$

The entropy of n-dimensional random variable is defined in the same way.

Suppose now that the value of ξ_1 is known but the value of ξ_2 is not. Then it is natural to define the conditional entropy

$$H(\xi_2|\xi_1) = -\sum_{i=1}^{r} P_{i\cdot} \sum_{j=1}^{s} \frac{P_{ij}}{P_{i\cdot}} \log \frac{P_{ij}}{P_{i\cdot}}. \qquad (7.11)$$

This is the mean conditional entropy of random variable ξ_2 under the condition that the value of ξ_1 is known.

Proposition 7.2 (properties of two-dimensional entropy)

$$H(\xi_1, \xi_2) = H(\xi_1) + H(\xi_2|\xi_1) , \qquad (7.12)$$

in particular, for independent random variables ξ_1 and ξ_2,

$$H(\xi_2|\xi_1) = H(\xi_2) ,$$
$$H(\xi_1, \xi_2) = H(\xi_1) + H(\xi_2) . \qquad (7.13)$$

Recall from probability theory that ξ_1, ξ_2 are independent if $P_{ij} = P_i P_j$ for all i and j. The proof of the proposition is quite simple and can be found in the literature. We confine ourselves only with its interpretation. In the first experiment, let ξ_1 be observed, in the second experiment ξ_2. Then the total uncertainty must be equal to the uncertainty of the first experiment summed up with the conditional uncertainty of the second. In case of independent ξ_1 and ξ_2, the knowledge of one variable does not offer any information about the value of the other, which corresponds to (7.13).

Let an n-dimensional random variable $(\xi_1, \xi_2, \ldots, \xi_n)$ be given. Then the following equation holds:

$$H(\xi_1, \ldots, \xi_n) = H(\xi_1) + H(\xi_2|\xi_1) + H(\xi_3|\xi_1, \xi_2) + \ldots + H(\xi_n|\xi_1, \ldots, \xi_{n-1}) . \qquad (7.14)$$

For independent random variables,

$$H(\xi_1, \ldots, \xi_n) = \sum_{i=1}^{n} H(\xi_i) \qquad (7.15)$$

(observe that (7.12), (7.13) are special cases of (7.14), (7.15)).

In general case,

$$H(\xi_k|\xi_1, \ldots, \xi_{k-1}) \le H(\xi_k) . \qquad (7.16)$$

Consider a sequence of random variables $\xi_1, \xi_2, \xi_3, \ldots$ (ξ_i take on values in A), which may be interpreted as a random process with discrete time. We shall assume that this process is stationary, i.e. informally, probabilities for $(\xi_1, \ldots, \xi_n)$ are the same as for $(\xi_{\Delta+1}, \ldots, \xi_{\Delta+n})$ for all positive integers n and Δ.

Let $H(\xi_1, \ldots, \xi_n)$ be the entropy of n-dimensional random variable $(\xi_1, \ldots, \xi_n)$. Denote by

$$h_n^+ = \frac{1}{n} H(\xi_1, \ldots, \xi_n)$$

the entropy rate of the nth order and define

$$h_n^- = H(\xi_n | \xi_1, \ldots, \xi_{n-1}) \,.$$

Note the following properties:

$$h_n^+ \leq h_{n-1}^+, \quad n > 1 \,, \tag{7.17}$$

$$h_n^- \leq h_n^+ \,, \tag{7.18}$$

$$h_n^- \leq h_{n-1}^-, \quad n > 1 \,. \tag{7.19}$$

For independent $\xi_1, \xi_2, \ldots, \xi_n$ the equalities

$$h_n^+ = h_n^- = h$$

hold. (The process generating independent random variables is said to be the memoryless process.)

Theorem 7.3 *For a stationary process, the limits* $\lim_{n\to\infty} h_n^+$ *and* $\lim_{n\to\infty} h_n^-$ *exist and are equal.*

Denote the common value of these limits by h_∞,

$$h_\infty = \lim_{n\to\infty} h_n^+ = \lim_{n\to\infty} h_n^- \,. \tag{7.20}$$

Let the alphabet $A = (a_1, a_2, \ldots a_r)$ be given. We know that

$$\max H(\xi_1) = \log r$$

for memoryless processes, therefore, taking into account (7.19) and (7.20), we obtain $\max h_\infty = \log r$, the maximum being reached for the memoryless processes with equal probabilities of letters $1/r$. It is natural to introduce the quantity

$$R = \log r - h_\infty \tag{7.21}$$

called *redundancy* (per source letter). Informally, this is, so to speak, "unused" portion of the alphabet. Redundancy is a quantitative measure of mutual dependence and non-uniformity of the letters. Note that in the second example with the Caesar cipher (p. 5), the redundancy of encrypted message equals zero since all letters (decimal digits) are equiprobable and independent, i.e. $h_\infty = \log 10$ and $R = 0$. And this caused the simple Caesar cipher to become unbreakable.

7.5 Unicity Distance for Secret Key Cipher

Consider the secret-key cryptosystem shown in Fig. 1.1 (p. 3). Let the source generate the message $\bar{m} = m_1 m_2 \ldots m_n$. Alice and Bob have the secret key k, known only to them, and let $\bar{e} = e_1 e_2 \ldots e_n$ be the ciphertext produced under that key.

Example 7.3 Let the memoryless source generate letters over the alphabet $A = \{a, b, c\}$ with probabilities $P(a) = 0.8$, $P(b) = 0.15$, $P(c) = 0.05$. Let the encrypter substitutes the letters in the message by the other letters according to some fixed permutation depending on the key k:

$$
\begin{aligned}
(a, b, c) \ & k = 1, \\
(a, c, b) \ & k = 2, \\
(b, a, c) \ & k = 3, \\
(b, c, a) \ & k = 4, \\
(c, a, b) \ & k = 5, \\
(c, b, a) \ & k = 6.
\end{aligned}
$$

That is, there are 6 possible keys (from 1 to 6) and if e.g. $k = 5$, the following substitution is made in the message: $a \to c$, $b \to a$, $c \to b$.

Let Eve has eavesdropped the ciphertext

$$\bar{e} = cccbc$$

and wishes to determine the value of key. Try to do it with her. Compute *a posteriori* probabilities of the keys used. We can do that by the Bayes formula

$$P\left(K_i | E\right) = \frac{P(K_i) P(E|K_i)}{\sum_{j=1}^{t} P(K_j) P(E|K_j)}$$

where E, K_1, ..., K_t are some events, K_i mutually exclusive and $E \subset \sum_{i=1}^{t} K_i$. In our case, event E is the receipt of the ciphertext $\bar{e} = cccbc$, $t = 6$ and K_i means that the key $k = i$ was chosen.

We assume that all keys are equally likely, i.e.

$$P(K_1) = P(K_2) = P(K_3) = P(K_4) = P(K_5) = P(K_6) = 1/6\,.$$

Then

$$P(E|K_1) = P(\bar{m} = cccbc) = 0.05^4 \cdot 0.15 \approx 0.000001\,,$$
$$P(E|K_2) = P(\bar{m} = bbbcb) = 0.15^4 \cdot 0.05 \approx 0.000025\,,$$
$$P(E|K_3) = P(\bar{m} = cccac) = 0.8 \cdot 0.05^4 \approx 0.000005\,,$$
$$P(E|K_4) = P(\bar{m} = bbbab) = 0.8 \cdot 0.15^4 \approx 0.000405\,,$$
$$P(E|K_5) = P(\bar{m} = aaaca) = 0.8^4 \cdot 0.05 \approx 0.020480\,,$$
$$P(E|K_6) = P(\bar{m} = aaaba) = 0.8^4 \cdot 0.15 \approx 0.061440\,.$$

From this we easily find

$$\sum_{j=1}^{6} P(K_j)\, P(E|K_j) \approx 0.013726$$

and obtain by the Bayes formula the *a posteriori* probability that the key $k = 1$ was used given the ciphertext $\bar{e} = cccbc$ is received:

$$P(K_1|E) = P(\bar{m} = cccbc | \bar{e} = cccbc) \approx \frac{(1/6) \cdot 0.000001}{0.013726} \approx 0.000011\,.$$

Continuing similarly, find the *a posteriori* probabilities of the other keys:

$$P(K_2|E) = P(\bar{m} = bbbcb | \bar{e} = cccbc) \approx 0.000304\,,$$
$$P(K_3|E) = P(\bar{m} = cccac | \bar{e} = cccbc) \approx 0.000061\,,$$
$$P(K_4|E) = P(\bar{m} = bbbab | \bar{e} = cccbc) \approx 0.004918\,,$$
$$P(K_5|E) = P(\bar{m} = aaaca | \bar{e} = cccbc) \approx 0.25\,,$$
$$P(K_6|E) = P(\bar{m} = aaaba | \bar{e} = cccbc) \approx 0.75\,.$$

We can see that the most probable keys are $k = 5$ and $k = 6$, the probabilities of all other keys being less than 0.01.

We can see that having eavesdropped only 5 letters Eve is able to determine the key almost surely. So, from this example and from the example with the Caesar cipher (Chapter 1), we can conclude that, evidently, there exists some critical length of ciphertext, n, after which the key can be determined with probability close to 1. More formally it can be written

$$H(K|e_1, \ldots, e_n) \approx 0\,. \tag{7.22}$$

This means that, on average, it suffices to intercept n symbols of ciphertext to determine the key used almost surely. The number n satisfying Eq. (7.22) is called the *unicity distance* of a cipher. The following result from [Shannon (1949)] relates unicity distance with message redundancy and secret key entropy.

Proposition 7.3 (on unicity distance) *Let the secret-key cryptosystem be considered and let $H(K)$ be the entropy of the key and R the message redundancy. Then for unicity distance n, the inequality holds*

$$n \geq \frac{H(K)}{R} . \tag{7.23}$$

Let's give some notes on this proposition before discussing the proof.

(1) We can see that if the message redundancy $R = 0$ then the key will never be determined since $n = \infty$. That is, the cipher cannot be broken (we have demonstrated this in the example with combination lock (p. 5).

(2) The redundancy can be decreased by means of data compression. The point is that lossless compression preserves the entropy while decreasing the length of data. Consequently, in the compressed data, the entropy per symbol (entropy rate) is higher and the redundancy per symbol (redundancy rate) is lower, see (7.21). Therefore after the compression, the unicity distance of a cipher increases.

(3) In practice, it is better to use the systems in which the key changes long before the unicity distance is reached.

Proof. We present only the main idea of the proof. Let the adversary intercepting the ciphertext $\bar{e} = e_1 e_2 \ldots e_n$ have uniquely determined the key and, therefore, the message. It means that her uncertainty is decreased by $H(K) + H(m_1, \ldots, m_n)$ since she has learned both the key and the message. With that she obtains n letters over an r-letter alphabet $\{a_1, \ldots, a_r\}$. We know that the maximum value of the entropy $h_\infty = \log r$, which means that the adversary's uncertainty can be decreased at most by $n \log r$. Hence

$$n \log r \geq H(K) + H(m_1, \ldots, m_n) ,$$

consequently,

$$n \left(\log r - H(m_1, \ldots, m_n) / n \right) \geq H(K) ,$$

from which we obtain that

$$n \geq \frac{H(K)}{\log r - H(m_1, \ldots, m_n) / n} = \frac{H(K)}{R}$$

(here we used the convergence $H(m_1, \ldots, m_n)/n \to h_\infty$ and definition of redundancy (7.21)). $\square$

Example 7.4   Let's estimate the unicity distance for the cipher from Example 7.3. We have $H(K) = \log 6 \approx 2.58$, $\log r = \log 3 \approx 1.58$ and the entropy per source letter

$$H = -(0.8 \log 0.8 + 0.15 \log 0.15 + 0.05 \log 0.05) \approx 0.88.$$

So

$$n \geq \frac{2.58}{1.58 - 0.88} \approx 3.7.$$

We could see that 5 letters were enough to determine the key almost surely and inequality (7.23) corresponds well with our example.

Let's show by one more example how mutual dependence of letters increases redundancy and thereby decreases the unicity distance.

Example 7.5   Let a Markov source be given, i.e. the source with memory in which each next letter probability may depend on the preceding letter. The source is defined by the following transition matrix:

	a	b	c
a	0	0.9	0.1
b	0	0.1	0.9
c	0.4	0.3	0.3

and initial probabilities $P(a) = 0.19$, $P(b) = 0.34$, $P(c) = 0.47$. It means that the first letter is generated with its initial probability, and each next letter is generated with probability given by the row of transition matrix corresponding to the preceding letter, e.g. after the letter a the letters b and c may occur with probabilities 0.9 and 0.1, respectively.

Let, as in Example 7.3, the cipher with 6 possible keys be used and the intercepted ciphertext be

$$\bar{e} = bbacbac.$$

We can see from the transition matrix that the combination aa is impossible (the probability of occurrence of a after the preceding a is zero) and the combination bb unlikely (the probability of b after b equals 0.1). Consequently, the first pair of letters in the message is most likely cc, i.e. the substitution $c \to b$ were used in encryption. Then ac in the ciphertext corresponds to either ab or ba in the message. From the transition matrix, the combination ba is impossible and only ab remains. Therefore we may conclude that, with high probability, the key is 2, i.e. the second permutation was used:

$$k = 2 \quad (a \to a,\ b \to c,\ c \to b).$$

Now compute the exact *a posteriori* probabilities of the keys as in Example 7.3. Note that the probability of a particular source message equals to the product of the first letter initial probability and the probabilities of transitions from one letter to another.

$$P(E|K_1) = P(\bar{m} = bbacbac) = 0.34 \cdot 0.1 \cdot 0 = 0,$$
$$P(E|K_2) = P(\bar{m} = ccabcab) = 0.47 \cdot 0.3 \cdot 0.4 \cdot 0.9 \cdot 0.9 \cdot 0.4 \cdot 0.9$$
$$= 0.016446,\cdot$$
$$P(E|K_3) = P(\bar{m} = aabcabc) = 0.19 \cdot 0 = 0,$$
$$P(E|K_4) = P(\bar{m} = aacbacb) = 0.19 \cdot 0 = 0,$$
$$P(E|K_5) = P(\bar{m} = ccbacba) = 0.47 \cdot 0.3 \cdot 0.3 \cdot 0 = 0,$$
$$P(E|K_6) = P(\bar{m} = bbcabca) = 0.34 \cdot 0.1 \cdot 0.9 \cdot 0.4 \cdot 0.9 \cdot 0.9 \cdot 0.4$$
$$= 0.003966.$$

From this we find

$$\sum_{j-1}^{6} P(K_j)\, P(E|K_j) \approx 0.003402$$

and obtain what we need by the Bayes formula, i.e. *a posteriori* probabilities of keys under the condition that the ciphertext is $\bar{e} = bbacbac$:

$$P(K_1|E) = 0,$$
$$P(K_2|E) = P(\bar{m} = ccabcab|\bar{e} = bbacbac) \approx 0.8,$$
$$P(K_3|E) = 0,$$
$$P(K_4|E) = 0,$$
$$P(K_5|E) = 0,$$
$$P(K_6|E) = P(\bar{m} = bbcabca|\bar{e} = bbacbac) \approx 0.2.$$

These computations confirm the correctness of the above informal observation.

The unicity distance estimation can be used in constructing cryptosystems. For instance, it seems reasonable to change the key as the total length of encrypted messages approaches the unicity distance.

New approaches to constructing theoretically secure cryptosystems connected with the use of special coding methods were suggested in the works [Ryabko and Fionov (1997); Ryabko and Fionov (1999a); Ryabko and Fionov (1999b); Ryabko (2000)]. The suggested methods are complicated for description but efficient from the computational point of view and allow for construction of unbreakable secret-key ciphers. The main idea of these methods is to ensure, by means of special coding, the zero redundancy of the message to be encrypted. One of such methods will be considered in the next section.

7.6 Ideal Cryptosystems

In Sec. 7.2, the notion of perfect secrecy was introduced and it was shown then that the Vernam cipher is perfectly secure. We could see that in this cipher the key length equals the message length and the key is used only once. If we want to use a short long-term key (which is the demand of the majority of practical applications) then what security level can we attain at best? In the notes to Proposition 7.3, it was pointed out that under the null redundancy of the message the unicity distance is infinite. It means that even a short (or, equivalently, applied many times) key used for encrypting a very long message cannot be disclosed. In its turn it means that an adversary who tries to recover the message will face the uncertainty equal to that of the key. Evidently, it is the best that can be reached under the said conditions (it is helpful to recall here again the example with combination lock from Chapter 1). These observations lead us to the notion of a strongly ideal cipher introduced in [Shannon (1949)].

Let the message $m_1 m_2 \ldots m_t$ is encrypted under the secret key $\bar{k} = k_1 k_2 \ldots k_s$ and the ciphertext $\bar{e} = e_1 e_2 \ldots e_t$ is produced. Denote by $H(m_1 m_2 \ldots m_t)$ the entropy of the message, by $H(\bar{e})$ and $H(\bar{k})$ the entropies of the ciphertext and the key, respectively. Then $H(m_1 m_2 \ldots m_t | \bar{e})$ is the uncertainty of the message and $H(\bar{k} | \bar{e})$ the uncertainty of the key given the ciphertext $\bar{e}$.

Definition 7.3 The cipher is called *strongly ideal* if

$$H(m_1 m_2 \ldots m_t | \bar{e}) = H(\bar{k} | \bar{e}) = \min\{H(m_1 m_2 \ldots m_t), H(\bar{k})\}. \quad (7.24)$$

Let's first consider the case when $\min\{H(m_1m_2\ldots m_t), H(\bar{k})\} = H(m_1m_2\ldots m_t)$. In this case the system provides perfect secrecy. Indeed, Eq. (7.24) converts to $H(m_1m_2\ldots m_t|\bar{e}) = H(m_1m_2\ldots m_t)$ which means perfect secrecy by definition, see Eq. (7.1).

In the other case, when the entropy of key is less than the entropy of message, Eq. (7.24) is reduced to

$$H(m_1m_2\ldots m_t|\bar{e}) = H(\bar{k}|\bar{e}) = H(\bar{k}) \qquad (7.25)$$

for all sufficiently large t. Since we shall deal mainly with the case when the message length t is large (or even infinite) we shall use Eq. (7.25) as the definition of a strongly ideal cipher.

Informally, strong ideality of the cipher means that the number of solutions of a cryptogram equals the number of possible keys, all the solutions being equiprobable (as in the example with combination lock).

In this section, we shall consider the construction of ideal system suggested recently in [Ryabko (2000)] but confine ourselves to the description of the main idea only as applied to the case of a binary source with unknown statistics, i.e. to the case when the message consists of letters over the alphabet $A = \{a_1, a_2\}$, the letters being independent but their probabilities unknown.

Let the source generate potentially unbounded messages $m_1m_2\ldots m_t$, $t \to \infty$, and there be a fixed-length key $\bar{k} = k_1k_2\ldots k_s$, $s \geq 1$. (As we mentioned above the per-letter source entropy is assumed to be non-zero since, otherwise, there is no necessity to transmit anything.) We shall split the message into blocks of n letters where $n > 1$ is a parameter of the method. Denote one of such blocks by m. Describe the transformations carried out on each n-letter block.

First determine the number of individual letters a_1 and a_2 in $\bar{m}$. Let there be, say, n_1 letters a_1 and $n_2 = n - n_1$ letters a_2. Define $u(\bar{m})$ as a word of length $\lceil \log(n + 1) \rceil$ bits which encodes n_1.

Now consider the set S of all sequences consisted of n_1 letters a_1 and n_2 letters a_2. There are

$$|S| = \binom{n}{n_1} = \frac{n!}{n_1!(n - n_1)!}$$

elements in this set. Despite the fact that the probabilities of the sequences from S are unknown, one thing may be stated — they are equal to each other (by independence of individual letters). Set a lexicographic order on S (assuming that $a_1 < a_2$) and compute the ordinal number of $\bar{m}$ within

S (the efficient algorithm [Ryabko (1998)] can be used for this computation, but its description goes beyond the scope of the book). Denote the computed ordinal by $\omega(\bar{m})$.

Split the set S into non-overlapping subsets S_0, S_1, ..., S_ν with the numbers of elements equal to the powers of 2 (e.g. if $|S| = 21$ then three subsets may result with cardinalities 16, 4, and 1). Using $\omega(\bar{m})$, determine to what subset $\bar{m}$ belongs (denote the ordinal number of such subset by $v(\bar{m})$) and find the ordinal of $\bar{m}$ within this subset (denote this ordinal by $w(\bar{m})$).

Look attentively at the ordinal of the message within the subset $w(\bar{m})$. What is remarkable, the $w(\bar{m})$ is a completely random sequence of zeroes and ones (i.e. all bits are equiprobable and independent). Indeed, $w(\bar{m})$ is the ordinal of one of equiprobable sequences of letters in a set of 2^b elements (for some b). The ordinals of all such sequences are all possible combinations of b binary digits. But if all combinations of b binary digits are equiprobable, then the individual bits are equiprobable and independent.

So, by processing consecutive blocks of the message in the described way we represent the message in the form

$$u(\bar{m}_1)v(\bar{m}_1)w(\bar{m}_1)u(\bar{m}_2)v(\bar{m}_2)w(\bar{m}_2)\ldots.$$

Now describe the procedure of encrypting the transformed message. It may seem strange at first sight, but the words $u(\cdot)$ and $v(\cdot)$ are not encrypted at all! Only the words $w(\cdot)$ are encrypted under the secret key $\bar{k}$. As one of the possibilities, we may use as the cipher the bitwise sum modulo 2 with periodically continued key. To describe such a cipher enumerate sequentially the symbols of all words $w(\cdot)$ and denote these by $w_1 w_2 w_3 \ldots$. Then the encryption is performed according to the formula

$$z_i = w_i \oplus k_{i \bmod s}.$$

As a result, we have encrypted the source message by the following way:

$$m_1 m_2 \ldots m_t \longrightarrow \bar{e} = u(\bar{m}_1)v(\bar{m}_1)z(\bar{m}_1)u(\bar{m}_2)v(\bar{m}_2)z(\bar{m}_2)\ldots. \qquad (7.26)$$

By the algorithm's construction, it is clear that the message can be recovered from the right side of (7.26) if we know the secret key $\bar{k}$. First we need to decrypt the symbols of the words $w(\cdot)$ by the formula

$$w_i = z_i \oplus k_{i \bmod s}, \qquad (7.27)$$

and then from the words $u(\cdot)v(\cdot)w(\cdot)$ the consecutive blocks of the message can be recovered.

Example 7.6   Let it be required to encrypt the message

$$a_2 a_2 a_1 a_2 a_2 a_2 a_1 a_2 a_2 a_1$$

under the 3-bit key $\bar{k} = 011$. Split the message into two blocks of 5 symbols, $n = 5$.

Perform the transformation for the first block $\bar{m}_1 = a_2 a_2 a_1 a_2 a_2$. For this block, $n_1 = 1$ and $u(\bar{m}_1) = (001)_2$. Consider now the ordered set of all messages consisted of 1 letter a_1 and 4 letters a_2 (see Table 7.1). There are $\frac{5!}{1!4!} = 5$ such messages, so we have two subsets S_0 and S_1 with the number of elements 4 and 1, respectively.

Table 7.1   The set of equiprobable messages; $n_1 = 1$, $n_2 = 4$.

Message	Ordinal in S	S_v	w
$a_1 a_2 a_2 a_2 a_2$	000		00
$a_2 a_1 a_2 a_2 a_2$	001		01
$a_2 a_2 a_1 a_2 a_2$	010	S_0	10
$a_2 a_2 a_2 a_1 a_2$	011		11
$a_2 a_2 a_2 a_2 a_1$	100	S_1	-

We can see that $\bar{m}_1$ enters in S_0 under the ordinal $2 = (10)_2$. So we obtain the following two words: $v(\bar{m}_1) = 0$, $w(\bar{m}_1) = (10)_2$.

Now perform the transformation for the second block of the message. $\bar{m}_2 = a_2 a_1 a_2 a_2 a_1$. For this block, $n_1 = 2$ and $u(\bar{m}_2) = (010)_2$. Consider the ordered set of all messages consisted of 2 letters a_1 and 3 letters a_2 (see Table 7.2). There are $\frac{5!}{2!3!} = 10$ such messages, so we have two subsets S_0 and S_1 with the number of elements 8 and 2, respectively.

We can see that $\bar{m}_2$ enters in S_0 under the ordinal $6 = (110)_2$. So we obtain $v(\bar{m}_2) = 0$, $w(\bar{m}_2) = (110)_2$.

To that point, we have obtained the following binary code of the transformed message:

$$001\ 0\ 10\ 010\ 0\ 110$$

(blank spaces here are only for ease of perception; they are not needed for unique decoding).

Table 7.2   The set of equiprobable messages;
$n_1 = 2$, $n_2 = 3$.

Message	Ordinal in S	S_v	w
$a_1 a_1 a_2 a_2 a_2$	0000		000
$a_1 a_2 a_1 a_2 a_2$	0001		001
$a_1 a_2 a_2 a_1 a_2$	0010		010
$a_1 a_2 a_2 a_2 a_1$	0011	S_0	011
$a_2 a_1 a_1 a_2 a_2$	0100		100
$a_2 a_1 a_2 a_1 a_2$	0101		101
$a_2 a_1 a_2 a_2 a_1$	0110		110
$a_2 a_2 a_1 a_1 a_2$	0111		111
$a_2 a_2 a_1 a_2 a_1$	1000	S_1	0
$a_2 a_2 a_2 a_1 a_1$	1001		1

Now encrypt the transformed message. The periodically continued key looks like $\bar{k} = 011011\ldots$. Bitwise summation modulo 2 of the words $w(\cdot)$ with that key gives

$$\begin{array}{r} 1\,0\,1\,1\,0 \\ \oplus\ 0\,1\,1\,0\,1 \\ \hline 1\,1\,0\,1\,1 \end{array}.$$

The ciphertext looks like this:

$$\bar{e} = 001\ 0\ 11\ 010\ 0\ 011\,.$$

Discuss now the main properties of the described method.

Proposition 7.4   *The cipher constructed is strongly ideal.*

Proof.   Without much rigour, the idea of the proof is the following. As we have already noted in the method description, the word $w(\bar{m})$ for each block $\bar{m}$ consists of equiprobable and independent symbols 0 and 1 (is completely random, for short). Since the blocks of the message are independent, the sequence $w(\bar{m}_1)w(\bar{m}_2)\ldots = w_1 w_2 w_3 \ldots$ in the transformed message is also completely random. But any sequence $w_1 w_2 w_3 \ldots$ corresponds to some message and all such messages are equiprobable. Therefore, under substitution of any key in deciphering equation (7.27), we obtain some solution, all the solutions being equiprobable. As a result, having only the ciphertext, we cannot say anything about the key used, i.e.

$$H(\bar{k}|\bar{e}) = H(\bar{k})\,.$$

Further, each individual message $m_1 m_2 \ldots m_t$ converts to one and only one sequence $w_1 w_2 w_3 \ldots$ and, under a sufficiently large t, namely, such that the length of the sequence $w_1 w_2 w_3 \ldots$ is no less than the key length, each different key, being used in (7.27), will produce different equiprobable messages. Therefore

$$H(m_1 m_2 \ldots m_t | \bar{e}) = H(\bar{k}).$$

Non-zero source entropy guarantees that the required sufficiently large t always exists.

So, we can see that (7.25) holds. □

The peculiarity of the described method is that not all transformed message is encrypted but only a part of it. In the example provided, it may even seem that too much information remains "open". What portion of information is concealed by the cipher? The following proposition answers this question.

Proposition 7.5 *Let the message be generated by a memoryless source with the entropy h per letter. Then for every block $\bar{m}$ of n symbols, the expected length of the encrypted word $w(\bar{m})$ satisfies the inequality*

$$E(|w(\bar{m})|) > nh - 2\log(n+1) \tag{7.28}$$

(here $E(\cdot)$ denotes expectation and $|\cdot|$ the length).

Proof. The code component $u(\bar{m})$ can take on any value from 0 to n, therefore its maximal entropy is $\log(n+1)$.

The word $v(\bar{m})$ can take on any value from 0 to ν which is related with splitting the set S into the subsets S_0, S_1, ..., S_ν. It is obvious that $\nu \leq \lfloor \log |S| \rfloor$. From the well-known inequality $|S| = \binom{n}{n_1} < 2^n$ we obtain $\log |S| < n$ and, hence, $\nu \leq \log |S| < n$. Therefore the maximal entropy of the word $v(\bar{m})$ is less than $\log(n+1)$.

The entropy of the block $H(\bar{m}) = nh$ (since the letters are generated by a memoryless source). The transformation of the block does not change the entropy. Therefore for the entropy of the word $w(\bar{m})$ we have

$$H(w(\bar{m})) > nh - 2\log(n+1)$$

(we subtract from the block entropy the upper bounds for the entropies of $u(\bar{m})$ and $v(\bar{m})$). But as the word $w(\bar{m})$ consists of equiprobable and independent symbols 0 and 1, its average length equals the entropy which completes the proof. □

Informally, Proposition 7.5 says that "almost all" information of the message is contained in the encrypted codeword w if the blocklength n is sufficiently large. In other words, the presented cipher conceals "almost all" information and even the exhaustive search through the whole set of keys does not allow to break the cipher.

Problems and Exercises

7.1 Encrypt the message $\bar{m}$ by the Vernam cipher under the key $\bar{k}$:

(a) $\bar{m} = 1001101011$, $\bar{k} = 0110100101$,
(b) $\bar{m} = 0011101001$, $\bar{k} = 1100011100$,
(c) $\bar{m} = 1000011100$, $\bar{k} = 1001011010$,
(d) $\bar{m} = 0011100010$, $\bar{k} = 0110111001$,
(e) $\bar{m} = 1001101011$, $\bar{k} = 1000111010$.

7.2 Let a memoryless source generate letters over the alphabet $A = \{a, b, c\}$ with probabilities $P(a)$, $P(b)$, $P(c)$. The encrypter substitutes the letters using one of the six possible permutations, as in Example 7.3. Determine the *a posteriori* probabilities of keys given the ciphertext $\bar{e}$:

(a) $P(a) = 0.1$, $P(b) = 0.7$, $P(c) = 0.2$, $\bar{e} = abaacac$,
(b) $P(a) = 0.9$, $P(b) = 0.09$, $P(c) = 0.01$, $\bar{e} = cbaccca$,
(c) $P(a) = 0.14$, $P(b) = 0.06$, $P(c) = 0.8$, $\bar{e} = bbabbcab$,
(d) $P(a) = 0.7$, $P(b) = 0.05$, $P(c) = 0.25$, $\bar{e} = cccacbbc$,
(e) $P(a) = 0.1$, $P(b) = 0.7$, $P(c) = 0.2$, $\bar{e} = abbbbab$.

7.3 For the cipher and sources of Problem 7.2, compute the entropy and unicity distance.

7.4 Given the ciphertext $\bar{e}$ find the *a posteriori* probabilities of keys and corresponding messages if it is known that the cipher of Example 7.3 was used and the messages are generated by the Markov source described in Example 7.5:

(a) $\bar{e} = bcacbcacc$,
(b) $\bar{e} = caaabaaba$,
(c) $\bar{e} = aacabcaac$,
(d) $\bar{e} = bcaaaacaa$,
(e) $\bar{e} = aaacaaaca$.

Chapter 8

Modern Secret Key Ciphers

8.1 Introduction

In this chapter, we shall consider computationally secure secret-key ciphers which can theoretically be broken but this will require a huge amount of computations, e.g. 10^{20} years for a supercomputer. The main advantage of these ciphers is their fast operation. Actually, they encrypt and decrypt data essentially faster than public-key and theoretically secure ciphers. In the subsequent sections we shall describe the most popular ciphers and the modes of operation, but before that, to explain the principles of construction of such ciphers we continue the example with the Caesar cipher from Chap. 1.

In Chap. 1 we have considered the ciphertext-only attack on the Caesar cipher. It was shown that in case of redundant messages, this cipher can be easily broken by the exhaustive key search. Let's look for the means of increasing the security of the Caesar cipher. May be, the first thing that comes to mind is to increase the number of possible keys. In this case, Eve will spend more time while searching for a correct key.

The natural way to increase the number of possible keys for the Caesar cipher is to use different keys for different symbols of the message. For instance, we may encrypt every odd letter with the key k_1 and every even letter with the key k_2. Then the secret key $k = (k_1, k_2)$ will consist of two integers and the number of possible keys will be $26^2 = 676$. Let's encrypt the same message as in Chapter 1 with the key $k = (3,5)$:

$$\text{SEQUENCE} \xrightarrow{3,5} \text{VJTZHSFJ}. \tag{8.1}$$

This scheme can easily be extended to an arbitrary secret key length

$k = (k_1, k_2, \cdots, k_t)_{26}$. With t about 10 or more the exhaustive key search becomes infeasible.

Nevertheless, this cipher is easily disclosed by the so-called *frequency analysis*. This analysis is based on statistics of the language in which the message is written. The key search begins with the keys corresponding to the most frequent letters of combinations. For instance, it is known that in a typical text in English, the letter E occurs more frequently than the other letters. Look at VJTZHSFJ in (8.1) and determine what letters are more frequent at odd and even positions. At even positions, this is the letter J. Make an assumption that it substitutes for the letter E and hence $k_2 = J - E = 5$. At odd positions, all letters are different (just because the message taken for the example is too small). Try to find k_1, as before, by the exhaustive search. After several trials we find $k_1 = 3$. So, in this particular example, to recover the message from the ciphertext we had to check only 4 keys out of 676 (specifically, we have checked $(0,5), (1,5), (2,5), (3,5)$).

Let's try to slightly improve the cipher in order to complicate the frequency analysis. We need somehow to intermingle the letters, to make them affect each other to hide the individual frequencies of occurrence. As before, we shall use the key $k = (k_1, k_2)$ and encrypt the message in two-letter blocks m_i, m_{i+1}. One of the simplest variants of the cipher may look like this:

$$\begin{aligned}
\tilde{m}_i &= m_i + m_{i+1}, \\
\tilde{m}_{i+1} &= m_{i+1} + \tilde{m}_i, \\
c_i &= \tilde{m}_i + k_1, \\
c_{i+1} &= \tilde{m}_{i+1} + k_2 \qquad (\text{mod } 26)
\end{aligned} \tag{8.2}$$

(all operations are modulo 26). Here m_i is an odd letter of the message, m_{i+1} is the even letter, k_1, k_2 are the key digits, and c_i, c_{i+1} the resulting symbols of ciphertext. For instance, the pair of symbols SE is encrypted under the key $k = (3,5)$ by the following way:

$$\begin{aligned}
\tilde{m}_i &= S + E = W, \\
\tilde{m}_{i+1} &= E + W = A, \\
c_i &= W + 3 = Z, \\
c_{i+1} &= A + 5 = F,
\end{aligned}$$

i.e. SE converts to ZF.

Note that this cipher is decipherable. The decryption algorithm usually called the *inverse cipher* is written as follows:

$$\begin{aligned}
\tilde{m}_{i+1} &= c_{i+1} - k_2, \\
\tilde{m}_i &= c_i - k_1, \\
m_{i+1} &= \tilde{m}_{i+1} - \tilde{m}_i, \\
m_i &= \tilde{m}_i - m_{i+1} \quad (\text{mod } 26).
\end{aligned} \tag{8.3}$$

Applying the cipher (8.2) to our message under the key $(3, 5)$ we obtain

$$\text{SEQUENCE} \longrightarrow \text{WAKEREGK} \xrightarrow{3,5} \text{ZFNJUJJP}.$$

Here, for clearness, after the first arrow, the intermediate result is shown obtained after the first two operations in (8.2) (this is an "intermingled" but not yet encrypted text). We can see that this cipher hides the frequencies of letters which complicates the frequency analysis. Of course, the frequencies of the pairs (digrams) are preserved but we can conceal they too if encrypt in blocks of 3 letters *etc.*

So, we have considered two ways of improving the cipher: increasing the length of the key and combining symbols into blocks with mixing transformations. Both methods are widely used in real modern ciphers. Now we shall consider one more trick which is also used in practice. For the sake of simplicity, we proceed with the same example.

The cipher (8.2) is more complicated to Eve compared to the cipher (8.1) and gives us the opportunity to consider another scenario of attack. Up to this point we considered the ciphertext-only attacks. But what will happen if Eve has somehow procured the plaintext corresponding to a ciphertext transmitted earlier? Here we have a situation of the known-plaintext attack (see Chap. 1, p. 5). For instance, Eve has the pair (SEQUENCE, VJTZHSFJ) for the cipher (8.1). Then she immediately computes the secret key $k_1 = \text{V} - \text{S} = 3$, $k_2 = \text{J} - \text{E} = 5$ and is able to decrypt all further messages from Alice to Bob. When the cipher (8.2) is used, the pair (SEQUENCE, ZFNJUJJP) does not allow for such obvious solution, although all is simple too. Eve performs the first two operations from (8.2), which do not require the secret key, to the word SEQUENCE, obtains the intermediate word WAKEREGK and using the pair (WAKEREGK, ZFNJUJJP), as in the previous case, finds the key $k = 3, 5$.

How one can hamper the Eve's actions? The idea is simple. In encryption, we shall use the cipher (8.2) twice. So we obtain:

$$\text{SEQUENCE} \xrightarrow{3,5} \text{ZFNJUJJP} \xrightarrow{3,5} \text{HOZKGRBS}. \tag{8.4}$$

Now having the pair (SEQUENCE, HOZKGRBS) Eve cannot derive the key, at least, her algorithm is not obvious (she cannot obtain the intermediate word ZFNJUJJP since it was constructed with the use of secret key unknown to her).

In the scheme (8.4), the single realisation of the algorithm (8.2) is called the *round* of cipher.

We have illustrated the relation between the security of cipher and such parameters as the length of key, the blocklength, the number of rounds. We have also showed the necessity of "intermingling" transformations. The real ciphers employ the same techniques though enhanced to withstand the advanced methods of cryptanalysis, such as differential and linear cryptanalysis (the reader may consult [Schneier (2000)] as a guide to modern cryptanalytic methods).

8.2 Block Ciphers

The *block cipher* can be defined as a transformation of a word (or a block) X of length n bits dependent on the key K. We shall denote the transformed word by Y. For all ciphers considered in this section, the length of word Y is equal to the length of word X.

In other words, the block cipher is an invertible function E (i.e. a function for which an inverse function exists). The specific look E_K of this function is determined by the key K,

$$Y = E_K(X),$$
$$X = E_K^{-1}(Y) \quad \text{for all } X.$$

Here E_K^{-1} denotes the deciphering transformation and is often called the *inverse cipher*.

For cryptographic applications, a block cipher must meet a number of requirements depending on the situation in which it is used. In most cases it is enough to claim that the cipher be secure with respect to the chosen-plaintext attack. It automatically assumes its security with respect to the known-plaintext and ciphertext-only attacks. One should notice that in the chosen-plaintext attack, the cipher can always be broken by the exhaustive key search. Therefore the requirement for the cipher to be secure may be re-formulated as follows.

The cipher is secure (under the chosen-plaintext attack) if there exist no algorithms for breaking it essentially more efficient than the exhaustive key search.

We shall content ourselves with this loose definition of security. In fact, the compliance to this definition is not proved for any cipher which is in use today. To be more realistic we should mention the following.

The cipher is believed to be secure (under the chosen-plaintext attack) if there are no algorithms known for breaking it essentially faster than the exhaustive key search.

In the rest of the section we consider some popular modern block ciphers. Our task is not just to give the description of the algorithms as it may be found in the literature but also to explain the basic principles of construction of the block ciphers. Besides, our discussion will be helpful for better understanding of the matters set forth in official documents (standards). Then we shall study the techniques of using block ciphers for solving various cryptographic problems.

Until recently, no book on cryptography could do without description of the cipher DES (Data Encryption Standard). This cipher was adopted as a standard of USA in 1977. Its main parameters are: block size 64 bits, key length 56 bits, 16 rounds. This cipher was intensively used for more than 20 years and even today can be met in many working systems. Despite numerous attacks on DES it has not be broken. However, the high level of computer performance today enables one to break DES by exhaustive key search. For instance, in 1993 a technical description was published of the system which costed 1 million dollars and allowed to disclose the DES key for 7 hours. As a result, DES is not recommended to use in newly created cryptosystems. So we do not describe DES. In 2001, after a special competition, a new block cipher standard was adopted in USA, called AES (Advanced Encryption Standard), which is based on the Rijndael block cipher developed by Belgian specialists Vincent Rijmen and Joan Daemen.

The majority of modern block ciphers are constructed by the schemes significantly different from DES. Nevertheless, there is (at least) one active cipher built on the same principles as DES. This is the Russian standard block cipher, GOST 28147-89. Due to its extremely simple design and by historical reasons it will be convenient to begin with.

8.2.1 *The GOST 28147-89 Block Cipher*

The cipher GOST 28147-89, as follows from its designation, was adopted as a standard in 1989 in the USSR and is now used as a standard in Russia (the word GOST is an acronym to GOvernmental STandard). The main parameters of GOST 28147-89 are: key length 256 bits, block size 64 bits, number of rounds 32. GOST 28147-89 is more convenient for program implementation than DES, there are notices about the gain in 1.5 times. Unlike DES, GOST 28147-89 was seemingly not a subject of as thorough analysis by the world "open" cryptographic community. Nevertheless, as the specialists conclude, the conservative design and the size of main parameters (the key length, the blocklength, and the number of rounds) allow to believe that the cipher cannot be weak (see [Schneier (1996)]). No effective attacks against GOST 28147-89 have been published.

GOST 28147-89, as well as DES, is based on the so-called *Feistel structure* [Feistel (1973)]. The block is split into two equal parts, the right R and the left L. The right half is combined with the key element and by a certain algorithm encrypts the left half. Before the next round the parts are replaced with each other. Such a structure allows one to use the same algorithm for decryption as for encryption. It is of special importance in case of hardware implementation because the direct and the inverse ciphers are produced by one and the same device (only the order of feeding key elements differs).

Proceed to the description of GOST 28147-89. Introduce necessary notation and definitions. The sequence of 32 bits is called a word. The plaintext block X (64 bits), as well as the ciphertext block Y, consists of two words, the left L and the right R, L being the high-order word and R low-order. The secret key K (256 bits) is considered to consist of 8 words $K = K_0 K_1 \cdots K_7$. It provides the basis for construction of the so-called *round key* $W = W_0 W_1 \cdots W_{31}$ that contains 32 words (the method of constructing the round key will be given further on).

There are 8 tables needed for the cipher operation S_0, S_1, ..., S_7 (also called S-boxes). Each table contains 16 4-bit elements, numbered from 0 to 15. Denote by $S_i[j]$ the jth element of the ith table. The standard recommends to fill each table with different numbers from the set $\{0, 1, \ldots, 15\}$ permuted randomly. The content of the tables forms an extra secret parameter that may be common for a large group of users. Note that in DES the similar S-boxes are fixed and publicly known.

The following operations are used in the cipher:

+ addition modulo 2^{32};

↤ cyclic shift left the specified number of bits;

⊕ bitwise "exclusive or" of two words, i.e. bitwise addition modulo 2.

Algorithm 8.1 BASIC CYCLE OF GOST 28147-89.

INPUT: Block L, R, round key W.

OUTPUT: Transformed block L, R.

1.   FOR $i = 0, 1, \ldots, 31$ DO

2. $k \leftarrow R + W_i, \quad k = (k_7 \cdots k_0)_{16};$

3.   FOR $j = 0, 1, \ldots, 7$ DO

4. $k_j \leftarrow S_j[k_j];$

5. $L \leftarrow L \oplus (k \hookleftarrow 11);$

6. $L \longleftrightarrow R;$

7.   RETURN L, R.

(At Step 4 of the algorithm distinct 4-bit elements of variable k are used.)

The described "basic cycle" is used for encryption and decryption. To encrypt a block X, construct the round key

$$W = K_0 K_1 K_2 K_3 K_4 K_5 K_6 K_7 K_0 K_1 K_2 K_3 K_4 K_5 K_6 K_7$$
$$K_0 K_1 K_2 K_3 K_4 K_5 K_6 K_7 K_7 K_6 K_5 K_4 K_3 K_2 K_1 K_0, \quad (8.5)$$

put X and W to the input and obtain the encrypted block Y as the output. To decrypt a block, construct the round key

$$W = K_0 K_1 K_2 K_3 K_4 K_5 K_6 K_7 K_7 K_6 K_5 K_4 K_3 K_2 K_1 K_0$$
$$K_7 K_6 K_5 K_4 K_3 K_2 K_1 K_0 K_7 K_6 K_5 K_4 K_3 K_2 K_1 K_0,$$

i.e. (8.5) in the reverse order, input W, Y and obtain X as output.

A program implementation usually requires to rework the loop beginning at Step 3 of Algorithm 8.1 since operating with half-bytes is inefficient. It is clear that the same transformation can be performed with the use of 4 tables, 256 bytes each, or two tables, 65536 half-words each. For instance, when working with bytes, we have $k = (k_3 \cdots k_0)_{256}$ and Steps 3–4 of Algorithm 8.1 are rewritten as follows:

3.   FOR $j = 0, 1, 2, 3$ DO

4. $k_j \leftarrow T_j[k_j].$

The tables T_j, $j = 0, 1, 2, 3$, are computed beforehand from S-boxes:

FOR $i = 0, 1, \ldots, 255$ DO

$\quad T_j[i] \leftarrow S_{2j}[i \bmod 16] + 16 S_{2j+1}[i \operatorname{div} 16].$

The standard says nothing about the rules of generating the keying information except the claim that each S-box should contain a permutation of different numbers. Yet, it can be seen that, for example, zero key or trivially defined S-boxes (mapping k to itself) do not provide the security of the cipher.

8.2.2   *The RC5 and RC6 Ciphers*

The RC5 and RC6 are modern block ciphers designed by Ron Rivest in 1995 and 1998, respectively. The cipher RC5 (see [Menezes *et al.* (1996)]) has been a touchstone for many new cryptanalytic methods. We shall describe one of the attacks involving RC5 in Sec. 9.5. It must be said that RC5 was not completely broken by either of the attacks but some of its "weak spots" were demonstrated followed by increasing demands for parameter values. As a response to these attacks, the cipher RC6 [Rivest *et al.* (1998)] was suggested which may be viewed as an enhanced version of RC5. RC6 took part in the competition for the new US block cipher standard carried out in years 1999–2001, had passed to the finals but lost the first place to another cipher (Rijndael). Nevertheless, intensive investigations of RC6 in the course of competition do not reveal in it any weakness and this cipher is highly esteemed by the specialists. For the sake of completeness and for further references, we shall describe both ciphers but discuss the design rationale only for RC6.

In RC5, the user specifies the word size w (16, 32, or 64 bits), the number of rounds r, and the key length l in bytes. A particular variant of the cipher is denoted by the template RC5-$w/r/l$, e.g. RC5-32/20/16. The block always contains two words. The same round key W of $2r + 2$ words is used in encryption and decryption.

The cipher uses the following operations (all on w-bit words):

$+, -$ addition and subtraction modulo 2^w;

$\oplus$ bitwise "exclusive or" of two words (the sum modulo 2);

$\hookleftarrow, \hookrightarrow$ cyclic left and right shifts by a specified number of bits (note that given the word size of w bits the number of shift positions is reduced modulo w, such a reduction being usually done automatically at machine level — the processor uses only low-order $\log w$ bits of the number defining the shift amount).

The encryption algorithm is as follows.

Algorithm 8.2 RC5: ENCRYPTION.

INPUT: Two-word block (a, b), round key W.
OUTPUT: Encrypted block (a, b).
1. $a \leftarrow a + W_0$, $b \leftarrow b + W_1$;
2.   FOR $i = 1, 2, \ldots, r$ DO
3. $a \leftarrow ((a \oplus b) \hookleftarrow b) + W_{2i}$,
4. $b \leftarrow ((b \oplus a) \hookleftarrow a) + W_{2i+1}$;
5.   RETURN (a, b).

To decrypt, undone the process in reverse order.

Algorithm 8.3 RC5: DECRYPTION.

INPUT: Two-word block (a, b), round key W.
OUTPUT: Decrypted block (a, b).
1.   FOR $i = r, r - 1, \ldots, 1$ DO
2. $b \leftarrow ((b - W_{2i+1}) \hookrightarrow a) \oplus a$,
3. $a \leftarrow ((a - W_{2i}) \hookrightarrow b) \oplus b$;
4. $b \leftarrow b - W_1$, $a \leftarrow a - W_0$;
5.   RETURN (a, b).

The process of round key formation (round key schedule) is more complicated in RC5 and RC6 than in GOST 28147-89, which is typical for most of modern ciphers. In fact, the secret key K is expanded to a longer pseudorandom sequence W in order to harden the cryptanalysis of a cipher.

Denote by c the number of words in the key, $c = 8l/w$. With the round key schedule algorithm the secret key K is expanded to the round key W:

$$K_0 K_1 \cdots K_{c-1} \longrightarrow W_0 W_1 \cdots W_{2r+1}.$$

The following "magic" numbers are used in the algorithm: P_w, the first w bits of the binary expansion for $e - 2$ where $e = 2.718281828\ldots$ is the base of natural logarithm, and Q_w, the first w bits of the binary expansion for $\phi - 1$ where $\phi = (\sqrt{5} - 1)/2$ is the golden section. In Table 8.1 the values of P_w and Q_w are given in hexadecimal system for various word lengths. With all this in mind, the algorithm of round key formation for RC5 is written down as follows.

Algorithm 8.4 RC5: ROUND KEY SCHEDULE.

INPUT: Secret key K.

OUTPUT: Round key W.

1. $W_0 \leftarrow P_w$;

2.   FOR $i = 1, 2, \ldots, 2r + 1$ DO $W_i \leftarrow W_{i-1} + Q_w$;

3. $a \leftarrow 0, \ b \leftarrow 0, \ i \leftarrow 0, \ j \leftarrow 0$;

4. $k \leftarrow 3 \max(c, 2r + 2)$;

5.   DO k times

6. $W_i \leftarrow (W_i + a + b) \hookleftarrow 3, \quad a \leftarrow W_i$,

7. $K_j \leftarrow (K_j + a + b) \hookleftarrow (a + b), \quad b \leftarrow K_j$,

8. $i \leftarrow i + 1 \bmod 2r + 2, \quad j \leftarrow j + 1 \bmod c$;

9.   RETURN W.

Now we describe the cipher RC6. It is quite close to RC5. In RC6, the user also specifies the word size w (16, 32, or 64 bits), the number of rounds r, and the key length l in bytes (from 0 to 255). But, in contrast to RC5, the block consists of 4 words and the round key W of $2r+4$ words. A particular variant of the cipher is denoted similarly by the template RC6-$w/r/l$. For example, RC6-32/20/16 is the variant with the blocksize and key length 128 bits, 20 rounds (this variant had been proposed as a candidate for the US standard).

The cipher uses the same operations as RC5 but one new operation is added:

∗ multiplication modulo 2^w.

Algorithm 8.5 RC6: ENCRYPTION.

INPUT: Four-word block (a, b, c, d), round key W.

OUTPUT: Encrypted block (a, b, c, d).

1. $b \leftarrow b + W_0, \ d \leftarrow d + W_1$;

2.   FOR $i = 1, 2, \ldots, r$ DO

3. $t \leftarrow (b \ast (2b + 1)) \hookleftarrow \log w$,

4. $u \leftarrow (d \ast (2d + 1)) \hookleftarrow \log w$,

5. $a \leftarrow ((a \oplus t) \hookleftarrow u) + W_{2i}$,

6. $c \leftarrow ((c \oplus u) \hookleftarrow t) + W_{2i+1}$,

7. $(a, b, c, d) \leftarrow (b, c, d, a)$;

8. $a \leftarrow a + W_{2r+2}, \ c \leftarrow c + W_{2r+3}$;

9.   RETURN (a, b, c, d).

To decrypt, as in RC5, undo the process in reverse order.

Algorithm 8.6 RC6: DECRYPTION.

INPUT: Four-word block (a, b, c, d), round key W.
OUTPUT: Decrypted block (a, b, c, d).

1. $c \leftarrow c - W_{2r+3}$, $a \leftarrow a - W_{2r+2}$;
2.   FOR $i = r, r - 1, \ldots, 1$ DO
3. $(a, b, c, d) \leftarrow (d, a, b, c)$,
4. $t \leftarrow (b * (2b + 1)) \hookleftarrow \log w$,
5. $u \leftarrow (d * (2d + 1)) \hookleftarrow \log w$,
6. $a \leftarrow ((a - W_{2i}) \hookrightarrow u) \oplus t$,
7. $c \leftarrow ((c - W_{2i+1}) \hookrightarrow t) \oplus u$;
8. $d \leftarrow d - W_1$, $b \leftarrow b - W_0$;
9.   RETURN (a, b, c, d).

To describe the round key formation we use the same notation as for RC5.

Algorithm 8.7 RC6: ROUND KEY SCHEDULE.

INPUT: Secret key K.
OUTPUT: Round key W.

1. $W_0 \leftarrow P_w$;
2.   FOR $i = 1, 2, \ldots, 2r + 3$ DO $W_i \leftarrow W_{i-1} + Q_w$;
3. $a \leftarrow 0$, $b \leftarrow 0$, $i \leftarrow 0$, $j \leftarrow 0$;
4. $k \leftarrow 3 \max(c, 2r + 4)$;
5.   DO k times
6. $W_i \leftarrow (W_i + a + b) \hookleftarrow 3$, $a \leftarrow W_i$,
7. $K_j \leftarrow (K_j + a + b) \hookleftarrow (a + b)$, $b \leftarrow K_j$,
8. $i \leftarrow i + 1 \bmod 2r + 4$, $j \leftarrow j + 1 \bmod c$;
9.   RETURN W.

Discuss briefly the main ideas of RC6 construction. First of all, note that similarly to DES and GOST 28147-89, in each round of RC6, one half of block is used for encrypting the other. Indeed, the values of variables t and u (Lines 3–4 of Algorithm 8.5) are determined only by the words b and d, respectively. Then these variables are used to modify the words a and c prior to summation with the elements of the key (Lines 5–6). Therefore, a

Table 8.1 "Magic" numbers for RC5 and RC6.

w	16	32	64
P_w	b7e1	b7e15163	b7e15162 8aed2a6b
Q_w	9e37	9e3779b9	9e3779b9 7f4a7c15

dependence upon b and d is introduced in a and c. In the next round, the pairs a, c and b, d exchange the roles, b and d transposed (Line 7). Owing to such structure the number of rounds has to be even.

The function $f(x) = (2x^2 + x) \bmod 2^w$ chosen for computation of t and u is known to manifest a strong dependence of high-order bits of its value upon all the bits of the argument. There are the high-order bits of f that must determine the shift amount in Lines 5–6 of the algorithm. So these bits are put in the low-order bits of t and u by means of rotation $\hookleftarrow \log w$. The use of "exclusive or" for modification of a and c is quite traditional but the use of data-dependent rotations is a characteristic feature of RC6 (and RC5).

Lines 1 and 8 are intended to hide the words unmodified in the first and last rounds.

The recommended number of rounds $r = 20$ is connected with the results of investigating the cipher's security with respect to differential and linear cryptanalysis.

In the course of studying the security of RC6 no weak keys were found, i.e. any key, even all zero, ensures the declared security of the cipher. It is believed that for RC6-32/20/16 there exist no attacks more efficient than the brute force attack.

8.2.3   *The Rijndael (AES) Cipher*

This cipher is designed by Belgian specialists Vincent Rijmen and Joan Daemen and has won in the competition AES as was mentioned before. In 2001, Rijndael was adopted as the new US standard (AES). Perhaps, it will play as important role in practical cryptography as was played by DES for decades. Rijndael is noticeably more complicated than RC6 and GOST 28147-89 although its computer implementation occurs to be very fast. We shall describe only the main ideas behind the construction of the cipher. Details and implementation examples may be found in [Daemen and Rijmen (2002); FIPS 197 (2001)].

The Rijndael/AES cipher is characterised by the block size 128 bits, the key length 128, 192, or 256 bits, and the number of rounds 10, 12, or 14 depending on the key length.

Let's agree on notation. The word (32 bits) is the sequence of 4 bytes. The bytes in a word are numbered from 0 (least significant byte) to 3 (most significant byte). The data block consists of 4 words that are also numbered from 0 to 3. For ease of designation, we shall assume that the ordinal numbers of bytes in a word and words in a block are always reduced modulo 4, without explicit indication. A data block is considered as a matrix 4×4 bytes, the words corresponding not to the rows (as usually) but to the columns. For instance, $X_{2,3}$ denotes the 2nd byte of the 3rd word of block X. Nevertheless, the item with only one subscript denotes the word, e.g. X_3 is the 3rd word of the block. We shall follow this agreement in order not to change the connected terminology of Rijndael.

For making transformations in a block, the round key W is used, derived from the secret key K. The length of the secret key l implicates the number of rounds r:

$$l = 128 \Rightarrow r = 10\,,$$
$$l = 192 \Rightarrow r = 12\,,$$
$$l = 256 \Rightarrow r = 14\,.$$

The round key consists of blocks (per 128 bits), the number of blocks being equal to the number of rounds plus 1,

$$W = W_0, W_1, \ldots, W_r\,.$$

Three criteria formed the basis for the design of Rijndael: security with respect to all known attacks, speed and compactness of code, simplicity and clearness of design. As distinct from the previous ciphers considered, Rijndael does not use any analogue of the Feistel structure. Each round consists of three different invertible transformations called layers:

(1) the linear mixing layer guarantees high diffusion between bytes over multiple rounds for masking statistical relations;
(2) the non-linear layer implemented with S-boxes having optimum non-linearity properties precludes the application of the linear, differential, and other methods of cryptanalysis;
(3) the key addition layer performs the encryption.

Encryption begins and ends with the operation of adding the key. This allows to conceal the input of the first round in the known-plaintext attack and to make cryptographically meaningful the result of the last round.

Algorithm 8.8 RIJNDAEL: ENCRYPTION.

INPUT: Block X, round key W.
OUTPUT: Block Y.
1. $Y \leftarrow X \oplus W_0$;
2.   FOR $i = 1, 2, \ldots, r - 1$ DO
3. $Y \leftarrow \text{SubBytes}(Y)$,
4. $Y \leftarrow \text{ShiftRows}(Y)$,
5. $Y \leftarrow \text{MixColumns}(Y)$,
6. $Y \leftarrow Y \oplus W_i$;
7. $Y \leftarrow \text{SubBytes}(Y)$,
8. $Y \leftarrow \text{ShiftRows}(Y)$,
9. $Y \leftarrow Y \oplus W_r$;
10.   RETURN Y.

The SubBytes procedure (byte substitution) implements the non-linear layer. The other procedures, ShiftRows and MixColumns, present the linear mixing layer. The key addition layer is realised by means of bitwise "exclusive or" $\oplus$.

Notice that there is no MixColumns transformation in the last round. It seems at first sight worsening the structure of cipher. But it is not so. Denote the Steps 3–6 of the algorithm by B, R, C, and K, respectively, and write the sequence of operations in the form of linear chain:

$$\text{KBRCKBRCK} \cdots \text{BRCKBRK}. \qquad (8.6)$$

To decrypt a block one has to perform all operations in the reverse order using the inverse functions. As will be shown below, the transformations B and R can be swapped without affecting the result. The transformations C and K can also be swapped provided some changes are made in the round key. Under such alteration the sequence (8.6) is rewritten as

$$\text{KRBKCRBKC} \cdots \text{RBKCRBK}. \qquad (8.7)$$

The sequence (8.7), read from right to left, matches exactly to (8.6). This means that we can decrypt the block using the same sequence of operations as in encryption. It is important that the sequence of operations BRCK (as will be shown below) can be efficiently implemented by table lookups, the tables being constantly defined, i.e. independent of either the key or the data.

Now we proceed immediately to the description of transformations BRC. In order to understand the Rijndael transformations one have to learn polynomial arithmetic (see, e.g. [Knuth (1981)]). However, if the reader is interested mainly in computer implementation of the cipher, he/she may jump immediately to p. 156 where efficient tabular algorithms are presented.

Each data byte in Rijndael is considered as a polynomial with binary coefficients 0 and 1 and all operations with coefficients are performed modulo 2. For example,

$$10010011 = x^7 + x^4 + x + 1,$$

$$10010011 + 01010001 = (x^7 + x^4 + x + 1) + (x^6 + x^4 + 1)$$
$$= x^7 + x^6 + x = 11000010,$$

$$10010011 \cdot 00000010 = (x^7 + x^4 + x + 1) \cdot x$$
$$= x^8 + x^5 + x^2 + x = 100100110.$$

In many of Rijndael's operations, byte-polynomials are multiplied modulo the polynomial $m(x) = x^8 + x^4 + x^3 + x + 1$. For example,

$$10010011 \cdot 00000010 \bmod m(x)$$
$$= (x^7 + x^4 + x + 1) \cdot x \bmod (x^8 + x^4 + x^3 + x + 1)$$
$$= (x^8 + x^5 + x^2 + x) \bmod (x^8 + x^4 + x^3 + x + 1)$$
$$= (x^8 + x^5 + x^2 + x) - (x^8 + x^4 + x^3 + x + 1) = x^5 + x^4 + x^3 + x^2 + 1 = 00111101$$

(subtraction and addition modulo 2 are the same operation).

The selected polynomial $m(x)$ has the following important property: it cannot be represented as the product of other polynomials with binary coefficients (this is an analogue of a prime number in binary polynomial arithmetic). As a result, any polynomial $a(x) \neq 0$ has the inverse, i.e. the polynomial $a^{-1}(x)$ such that $a(x) \cdot a^{-1}(x) \bmod m(x) = 1$ (the inverse is computed by the extended Euclidean algorithm in which all numbers are replaced by polynomials). In terms of the theory of groups, one says that byte-polynomials constitute a field $\mathbb{F}_{2^8}$.

Each word of data, i.e. a sequence of 4 bytes, in Rijndael is represented as a polynomial with coefficients in $\mathbb{F}_{2^8}$, i.e. each byte-coefficient is considered as binary polynomial reduced modulo $m(x)$. For example, the word

7500a302, written in hexadecimal system, consists of 4 bytes (from most to least significant): 75, 00, a3, and 02, and can be represented as polynomial

$$7500a302 = (75)y^3 + (a3)y + 2$$

(here we use the indeterminate y just to avoid confusion between word-polynomials and defined above byte-polynomials). The arithmetic of these word-polynomials is more complicated but we need not go into details. Now we are ready to describe the Rijndael transformations.

The transformation SubBytes(Y) is applied independently to each byte b in block Y:

$$b(x) \leftarrow b^{-1}(x) \bmod m(x) \quad (0 \leftarrow 0)\,,$$

$$b(x) \leftarrow \left((x^7 + x^6 + x^5 + x^4 + 1)b(x) + (x^7 + x^6 + x^2 + x)\right) \bmod (x^8 + 1).$$

The results of this transformation computed for each byte from 0 to 255 beforehand, are stored in the table S (this is an S-box). Then the transformation SubBytes(Y) is reduced to performing for each byte b in Y the operation

$$b \leftarrow S[b]\,.$$

The content of table S is explicitly given in [Daemen and Rijmen (2002)].

The transformation ShiftRows(Y) acts upon each row r_i in block Y, i.e. upon the sequence of ith bytes of block words ($i = 0, 1, 2, 3$). The operation involved is the cyclic shift left a specified number of bytes, denoted by $\hookleftarrow$. The rule of the transformation is

$$r_i \leftarrow (r_i \hookleftarrow i), \quad i = 0, 1, 2, 3\,.$$

For example, show the contents of the block before and after ShiftRows transformation:

Y	ShiftRows(Y)
03 02 01 00	03 02 01 00
13 12 11 10	12 11 10 13
23 22 21 20	21 20 23 22
33 32 31 30	30 33 32 31

The transformation MixColumns(Y) acts upon each column c_i in block Y, i.e. upon each machine word, $i = 0, 1, 2, 3$, by the rule

$$c_i(y) \leftarrow a(y) \cdot c_i(y) \bmod (y^4 + 1)$$

where $a(y) = 3y^3 + y^2 + y + 2$. This operation can be written in a matrix form

$$c_i = \begin{bmatrix} c_{0,i} \\ c_{1,i} \\ c_{2,i} \\ c_{3,i} \end{bmatrix} \leftarrow \begin{bmatrix} 2\ 3\ 1\ 1 \\ 1\ 2\ 3\ 1 \\ 1\ 1\ 2\ 3 \\ 3\ 1\ 1\ 2 \end{bmatrix} \cdot \begin{bmatrix} c_{0,i} \\ c_{1,i} \\ c_{2,i} \\ c_{3,i} \end{bmatrix}. \tag{8.8}$$

Here all "elementary" operations are performed on binary polynomials modulo $m(x)$.

It is obvious that operation SubBytes can be swapped with ShiftRows without affecting the result since these transformations act upon individual bytes. Using the distributivity of polynomial multiplication we can write

$$\mathrm{MixColumns}(Y \oplus W_i) = \mathrm{MixColumns}(Y) \oplus \mathrm{MixColumns}(W_i).$$

So, MixColumns transformation and the key addition can also be swapped under the condition that the corresponding blocks of the round key (except the first and last) were subjected to the inverse transformation $\mathrm{MixColumns}^{-1}(W_i)$. All these proves the identity of operation sequences (8.6) and (8.7) with the modified key. As a result, we obtain the following algorithm for the inverse cipher.

Algorithm 8.9 RIJNDAEL: DECRYPTION.

INPUT: Block Y, round key W.
OUTPUT: Block X.
1. $X \leftarrow Y \oplus W_r$;
2.   FOR $i = r-1, r-2, \ldots, 1$ DO
3. $X \leftarrow \mathrm{SubBytes}^{-1}(X)$,
4. $X \leftarrow \mathrm{ShiftRows}^{-1}(X)$,
5. $X \leftarrow \mathrm{MixColumns}^{-1}(X)$,
6. $X \leftarrow X \oplus W_i$;
7. $X \leftarrow \mathrm{SubBytes}^{-1}(X)$,
8. $X \leftarrow \mathrm{ShiftRows}^{-1}(X)$,
9. $X \leftarrow X \oplus W_0$;
10.   RETURN X.

The inverse transformations used in the algorithm are defined by the natural way.

The transformation SubBytes$^{-1}(X)$ is applied to each byte b in X:

$$b(x) \leftarrow (b(x) - (x^7 + x^6 + x^2 + x))(x^7 + x^5 + x^2) \bmod (x^8 + 1),$$

$$b(x) \leftarrow b^{-1}(x) \bmod m(x) \quad (0 \leftarrow 0),$$

where $x^7 + x^5 + x^2 = (x^7 + x^6 + x^5 + x^4 + 1)^{-1} \bmod (x^8 + 1)$. The results are stored on the table S^{-1}. The content of table S^{-1} is explicitly given in [Daemen and Rijmen (2002)].

The transformation ShiftRows$^{-1}(X)$ acts upon each row r_i in block X according to the rule

$$r_i \leftarrow (r_i \hookrightarrow i)$$

(here $\hookrightarrow$ denotes the cyclic shift right i bytes).

The transformation MixColumns$^{-1}(X)$ acts upon each column c_i in block X by the rule

$$c_i(y) \leftarrow a^{-1}(y) \cdot c_i(y) \bmod (y^4 + 1)$$

where $a^{-1}(y) = 11y^3 + 13y^2 + 9y + 14$. The same in the matrix form looks like this:

$$c_i = \begin{bmatrix} c_{0,i} \\ c_{1,i} \\ c_{2,i} \\ c_{3,i} \end{bmatrix} \leftarrow \begin{bmatrix} 14 & 11 & 13 & 09 \\ 09 & 14 & 11 & 13 \\ 13 & 09 & 14 & 11 \\ 11 & 13 & 09 & 14 \end{bmatrix} \cdot \begin{bmatrix} c_{0,i} \\ c_{1,i} \\ c_{2,i} \\ c_{3,i} \end{bmatrix}. \tag{8.9}$$

Now proceed to the efficient tabular implementation which we consider only for the case of a 32-bit computer. Denote the state of the block by U. The sequence of Steps 3–6 of encryption algorithm converts the data block from the state U to a new state Y. Taking into account the transformations performed at Steps 3–6, we can write the computation of each jth word (i.e. each column) in Y:

$$\begin{bmatrix} Y_{0,j} \\ Y_{1,j} \\ Y_{2,j} \\ Y_{3,j} \end{bmatrix} = \begin{bmatrix} 2 & 3 & 1 & 1 \\ 1 & 2 & 3 & 1 \\ 1 & 1 & 2 & 3 \\ 3 & 1 & 1 & 2 \end{bmatrix} \cdot \begin{bmatrix} S[U_{0,j}] \\ S[U_{1,j-1}] \\ S[U_{2,j-2}] \\ S[U_{3,j-3}] \end{bmatrix} \oplus \begin{bmatrix} W_{i,0,j} \\ W_{i,1,j} \\ W_{i,2,j} \\ W_{i,3,j} \end{bmatrix}$$

(the rightmost column in the expression is the jth word of W_i). Uncovering the matrix multiplication we obtain

$$Y_j = S[U_{0,j}] \cdot \begin{bmatrix} 2 \\ 1 \\ 1 \\ 3 \end{bmatrix} \oplus S[U_{1,j-1}] \cdot \begin{bmatrix} 3 \\ 2 \\ 1 \\ 1 \end{bmatrix}$$

$$\oplus S[U_{2,j-2}] \cdot \begin{bmatrix} 1 \\ 3 \\ 2 \\ 1 \end{bmatrix} \oplus S[U_{0,j-3}] \cdot \begin{bmatrix} 1 \\ 1 \\ 3 \\ 2 \end{bmatrix} \oplus W_{i,j} \, .$$

Define the four tables

$$T_0[b] = \begin{bmatrix} S[b] \cdot 2 \\ S[b] \\ S[b] \\ S[b] \cdot 3 \end{bmatrix}, \; T_1[b] = \begin{bmatrix} S[b] \cdot 3 \\ S[b] \cdot 2 \\ S[b] \\ S[b] \end{bmatrix},$$

$$T_2[b] = \begin{bmatrix} S[b] \\ S[b] \cdot 3 \\ S[b] \cdot 2 \\ S[b] \end{bmatrix}, \; T_3[b] = \begin{bmatrix} S[b] \\ S[b] \\ S[b] \cdot 3 \\ S[b] \cdot 2 \end{bmatrix} \, .$$

Each table is built for b running from 0 to 255 and consists of 256 4-byte words. The multiplication operation in the computations is binary polynomial multiplication modulo $m(x)$. Tables T_i do not depend on either the key or the data and can be computed in advance. Using these tables we can build the jth word of the block as follows:

$$Y_j = T_0[U_{0,j}] \oplus T_1[U_{1,j-1}] \oplus T_2[U_{2,j-2}] \oplus T_3[U_{3,j-3}] \oplus W_{i,j} \, .$$

Now we are ready to write the algorithm in the tabular form (Algorithm 8.10). Note that many S-boxes are contained in tables T_i. For instance, for the S-box at Step 8, one can use low-order bytes of table T_2.

To construct a tabular version for the inverse cipher we must review the observations given above with respect to the inverse transformations. This

Algorithm 8.10 RIJNDAEL: ENCRYPTION (FAST VERSION).

INPUT: Block X, round key W.
OUTPUT: Block Y.

1. $U \leftarrow X \oplus W_0$;
2.   FOR $i = 1, 2, \ldots, r - 1$ DO
3.   FOR $j = 0, 1, 2, 3$ DO
4. $Y_j \leftarrow T_0[U_{0,j}] \oplus T_1[U_{1,j-1}] \oplus T_2[U_{2,j-2}]$
$$\oplus \, T_3[U_{3,j-3}] \oplus W_{i,j};$$
5. $U \leftarrow Y$;
6.   FOR $i = 0, 1, 2, 3$ DO
7.   FOR $j = 0, 1, 2, 3$ DO
8. $Y_{i,j} \leftarrow S[U_{i,j-i}]$;
9. $Y \leftarrow Y \oplus W_r$;
10.   RETURN Y.

results in obtaining the inverse tables T_i^{-1}:

$$T_0^{-1}[b] = \begin{bmatrix} S^{-1}[b] \cdot 14 \\ S^{-1}[b] \cdot 9 \\ S^{-1}[b] \cdot 13 \\ S^{-1}[b] \cdot 11 \end{bmatrix}, \; T_1^{-1}[b] = \begin{bmatrix} S^{-1}[b] \cdot 11 \\ S^{-1}[b] \cdot 14 \\ S^{-1}[b] \cdot 9 \\ S^{-1}[b] \cdot 13 \end{bmatrix},$$

$$T_2^{-1}[b] = \begin{bmatrix} S^{-1}[b] \cdot 13 \\ S^{-1}[b] \cdot 11 \\ S^{-1}[b] \cdot 14 \\ S^{-1}[b] \cdot 9 \end{bmatrix}, \; T_3^{-1}[b] = \begin{bmatrix} S^{-1}[b] \cdot 9 \\ S^{-1}[b] \cdot 13 \\ S^{-1}[b] \cdot 11 \\ S^{-1}[b] \cdot 14 \end{bmatrix}.$$

Given these inverse tables we can write down the decrypting algorithm (Algorithm 8.11).

Note once again that all the tables in a ready-to-use form may be found in [Daemen and Rijmen (2002)].

The last thing to consider is the formation of the round key. In the direct and inverse ciphers, it is convenient to divide the round key W into 4-word blocks. However, the formation of the key must be done in a word mode, so let's denote by the letter w with a subscript a distinct word in W starting numbering from zero. As it follows from the encryption and decryption algorithms, the round key W must consist of $r + 1$ blocks where r is the number of rounds. So the number of words in W equals $4(r + 1)$. In its turn, the number of words in the secret key K, which we shall denote

Algorithm 8.11 RIJNDAEL: DECRYPTION (FAST VERSION).

INPUT: Block Y, round key W.
OUTPUT: Decrypted block X.

1. $U \leftarrow Y \oplus W_0$;
2. FOR $i = r - 1, r - 2, \ldots, 1$ DO
3.   FOR $j = 0, 1, 2, 3$ DO
4. $X_j \leftarrow T_0^{-1}[U_{0,j}] \oplus T_1^{-1}[U_{1,j+1}] \oplus T_2^{-1}[U_{2,j+2}]$
$$\oplus T_3^{-1}[U_{3,j+3}] \oplus W_{i,j};$$
5. $U \leftarrow X$;
6. FOR $i = 0, 1, 2, 3$ DO
7.   FOR $j = 0, 1, 2, 3$ DO
8. $X_{i,j} \leftarrow S^{-1}[U_{i,j+i}]$;
9. $X \leftarrow X \oplus W_r$;
10. RETURN X.

by c, may be 4, 6, or 8. First we describe the algorithm for constructing W and then discuss some issues.

Algorithm 8.12 RIJNDAEL: ROUND KEY SCHEDULE.

INPUT: Secret key K of c words.
OUTPUT: Round key W of $4(r + 1)$ words.

1. $W \leftarrow K$ (c words);
2. FOR $i = c, c + 1, \ldots, 4(r + 1) - 1$ DO
3. $t \leftarrow w_{i-1}$;
4.   IF $i \bmod c = 0$ THEN
5. $t \leftarrow \text{SubWord}(\text{RotWord}(t)) \oplus \text{Rcon}[i \text{ div } c]$;
6.   ELSE IF $c = 8$ AND $i \bmod c = 4$ THEN
7. $t \leftarrow \text{SubWord}(t)$;
8. $w_i \leftarrow w_{i-c} \oplus t$;
9. RETURN $w_0 \cdots w_{4(r+1)-1}$.

In this algorithm, SubWord(t) is a function applying the S-box of the cipher to each byte of the word t

$$[t_0, t_1, t_2, t_3] \longrightarrow [S[t_1], S[t_2], S[t_3], S[t_0]] .$$

The transformation RotWord(t) is performed by the cyclic shift of word t

left one byte

$$[t_0, t_1, t_2, t_3] \longrightarrow [t_1, t_2, t_3, t_0].$$

The array of round constants Rcon contains the words

$$\text{Rcon}[i] = [y_i, 0, 0, 0]$$

where

$$y_i = x^{i-1} \bmod m(x).$$

The chosen method for round key schedule must facilitate solving the following problems:

(1) to impede the attack to the cipher if the secret key is partially known or related keys (connected by the common rules of construction) are used;

(2) to eliminate any symmetries within the cipher round and between the rounds (the array of round constants Rcon is used for that purpose).

As we have noted when considering the inverse cipher, to produce the round key for decryption one have to apply the transformation MixColumns^{-1} to the blocks of W from the first to the next-to-last.

8.3   Main Modes of Operation of Block Ciphers

The block ciphers are used for solving many problems in cryptography. In this section, we shall consider the main modes of their usage.

In the previous section, the examples of real block ciphers were given. Now we can think of an (idealised) block cipher as a transformation of input block X into output block Y depending on secret key K,

$$Y = E_K(X),$$

the following requirements being fulfilled:

(1) given a known Y, but unknown K, it is practically impossible to recover X;

(2) given arbitrary known X and Y, but unknown K, it is practically impossible to learn K.

First we consider the classical problem of encrypting messages by the use of block ciphers.

8.3.1 ECB Mode

The acronym ECB comes from Electronic Code Book. In this mode, the message X is split into the blocks $X = X_1, X_2, \ldots, X_t$. Each block is encrypted by the block cipher

$$Y_i = E_K(X_i), \quad 1 \le i \le t.$$

We obtain the ciphertext $Y = Y_1, Y_2, \ldots, Y_t$. Decryption is carried out by the scheme

$$X_i = E_K^{-1}(Y_i), \quad 1 \le i \le t.$$

It is easy to see that one can perform decryption by selecting the ciphertext blocks in arbitrary order. This mode is convenient in many cases because it is easy to change or delete some fragments of data independently of the others and to decrypt starting at any point. This is particularly important for database applications.

However, there may be problems in some situations because the similar records will have the similar ciphertexts. We can say that the ECB mode preserves the data pattern. It may provide some information to the adversary. For instance, if the number of *different* records in a database is small then the adversary can make a dictionary of ciphertexts and break the database using the frequency analysis. Note that she will not need to break the cipher.

8.3.2 CBC Mode

The acronym CBC comes from Cipher-Block Chaining. In this mode, the ciphertext is produced by the following rule:

$$Y_i = E_K(X_i \oplus Y_{i-1}), \quad 1 \le i \le t,$$

i.e. each successive plaintext block is covered by the previous ciphertext block prior to encryption. The word Y_0 (often called the *initialisation vector*) must be specified in advance and known to both encrypter and decrypter. The resulting ciphertext can be decrypted by the following way:

$$X_i = Y_{i-1} \oplus E_K^{-1}(Y_i), \quad 1 \le i \le t.$$

With the CBC mode, we obtain the ciphertext in which each successive block depends on all of the previous. This mode destroys any data patterns.

Even if all plaintext blocks are identical, the ciphertext will consist of different blocks. The CBC mode is preferable when encrypting the messages whose length exceeds the blocksize. The drawback, however, is the absence of direct access capability: the message can be decrypted only sequentially, starting at the first block.

Two other block cipher modes will be considered in the context of the stream ciphers.

8.4   Stream Ciphers

In Sec. 7.3, we have considered the Vernam cipher and established its perfect secrecy, i.e. such property that the adversary intercepting the ciphertext obtains no information about the message. In the Vernam cipher, the ciphertext $y_1, y_2, \ldots, y_k$ is produced from the message $x_1, x_2, \ldots, x_k$ under the key $z_1, z_2, \ldots, z_k$ by the following encrypting operation:

$$y_i = x_i \oplus z_i, \quad i = 1, 2, \ldots, k. \tag{8.10}$$

This cipher is perfect only if the key $z_1, z_2, \ldots, z_k$ consists of equiprobable and independent bits and is used only once. This leads to the need of generating random sequences of very large size and transmitting them over secure channels which is highly difficult. Therefore, the idea arose to use instead of truly random sequences the sequences generated by the so-called *pseudo-random number generators*. In this case, one may use the initial state of the generator as the secret key. Of course, the resulting cryptosystem will not be perfect anymore. The maximum of what we may expect is that breaking such cryptosystem will require an enormous amount of time (e.g. it will require the exhaustive search through all possible initial states of the generator). As the compensation for the lost of perfection we obtain the possibility to use short secret keys (say, several hundred bytes) which are significantly easier to maintain and distribute (e.g. they may be created by means of public-key techniques).

The cipher based upon (8.10) where the key sequence $z_1, z_2, \ldots, z_k$ is generated by some deterministic algorithm (e.g. pseudo-random number generator) is called the *stream cipher*. As a rule, the source message and the key sequence are independent streams of bits. Since the encrypting and decrypting transformations are the same for all stream ciphers, the latter differ only in the way of construction of pseudo-random number generators. Indeed, to recover the message $x_1, x_2, \ldots, x_k$ from the ciphertext

$y_1, y_2, \ldots, y_k$ produced by (8.10) one needs to generate the same sequence $z_1, z_2, \ldots, z_k$ as in encryption, and use the formula

$$x_i = y_i \oplus z_i, \quad i = 1, 2, \ldots, k. \tag{8.11}$$

Example 8.1 One of the simplest pseudo-random number generators called the *linear congruential generator* operates according to the recurrence

$$u_{i+1} = (au_i + b) \bmod c \tag{8.12}$$

where a, b, c are some constants and u_i, u_{i+1} the elements of the produced pseudo-random sequence. The initial state is u_0. Take, for instance, $a = 5$, $b = 12$, $c = 23$, and let $u_0 = 4$. Compute several elements of the sequence:

$$
\begin{aligned}
u_1 &= (4 \cdot 5 + 12) \bmod 23 &&= 9, \\
u_2 &= (9 \cdot 5 + 12) \bmod 23 &&= 11, \\
u_3 &= (11 \cdot 5 + 12) \bmod 23 &&= 21, \\
u_4 &= (21 \cdot 5 + 12) \bmod 23 &&= 2, \\
u_5 &= (2 \cdot 5 + 12) \bmod 23 &&= 22, \\
u_6 &= (22 \cdot 5 + 12) \bmod 23 &&= 7, \\
u_7 &= (7 \cdot 5 + 12) \bmod 23 &&= 1.
\end{aligned}
$$

The produced sequence look much like random (it can be converted to a bitstream by using binary representations of numbers, or by extracting particular bits, *etc.*).

For the use in cryptographic applications, the generator must meet the following main requirements:

(1) the period of the generated sequence must be large;
(2) the determination of z_{i+1} given the preceding elements of the sequence must be a hard, infeasible problem;
(3) the sequence generated must be indistinguishable from a truly random sequence by statistical tests.

The above considered linear congruential generator is completely unsuitable for cryptographic purposes since the algorithms are known that allow to recover all the generator's parameters by examining only a few elements of the sequence generated [Plumstead (1982)].

As the examples of cryptographically secure pseudo-random number generators, we shall consider the OFB and CTR block cipher modes and the algorithm RC4.

But first, let's pay attention to one peculiarity which is important for all stream ciphers. For encrypting any other message, one must use different key K and/or initialisation vector Y_0. Otherwise, several messages will be encrypted using the same sequence z and such a cipher can be disclosed. Let's explain the essence of the problem. Let two messages $u_1, u_2, \ldots, u_k$ and $v_1, v_2, \ldots, v_k$ be encrypted using the same sequence z. Then the ciphertexts will be of the form:

$$u_1 \oplus z_1, u_2 \oplus z_2, \ldots, u_k \oplus z_k \quad \text{and}$$
$$v_1 \oplus z_1, v_2 \oplus z_2, \ldots, v_k \oplus z_k \, .$$

Add one ciphertext to the other and, taking into account the equalities $z_i \oplus z_i = 0$, obtain the sequence

$$u_1 \oplus v_1, u_2 \oplus v_2, \ldots, u_k \oplus v_k \, .$$

We have obtained the analogue of the so-called *running-key cipher* in which one text is encrypted using the other text taken from a certain place of a certain book. It is known that this cipher is insecure although it was used in the past [Menezes *et al.* (1996)]. The statistical analysis based on the redundancy of the texts allows in most cases to recover both messages.

8.4.1   *The OFB Block Cipher Mode*

The acronym OFB comes from Output FeedBack. In this mode, the block cipher, parametrised by the secret key K and initialisation vector Y_0, produces a pseudo-random sequence of r-bit numbers $z_1, z_2, \ldots, z_k$ which can be used in (8.10) and (8.11) for encryption and decryption, respectively. We shall assume, as before, that the blocksize of the cipher is n bits.

The pseudo-random sequence is produced by the scheme

$$Y_i = E_K(Y_{i-1}) \, ,$$
$$z_i = r \text{ high-order bits of } Y_i \, , \quad 1 \le i \le k$$

(here r, $1 \le r \le n$, is a parameter of the method).

If a secure block cipher is used, we obtain a secure generator that meets all the above given requirements. More exactly, the average value of the sequence's period (under randomly chosen K and Y_0) is about $r2^{n-1}$ bits (see [Menezes *et al.* (1996)]). Besides, the pseudo-random sequence is unpredictable in the sense that the adversary cannot predict (or compute) z_{i+1} if she has $z_1, \ldots, z_i$. The possibility of such prediction would mean for the block cipher to be insecure with respect to the known-plaintext attack. The prediction of z_{i+1} is an even more difficult problem than breaking the block cipher if $r < n$ [Menezes *et al.* (1996)].

In the OFB mode, the decryption can be carried out only from the beginning since it is not possible to obtain an arbitrary element of the sequence z without having computed the preceding elements. In this sense, the mode is similar to CBC. The advantage of the OFB mode is that the sequence z can be formed in advance in order to encrypt or decrypt data maximally fast when they arrive. It is of importance for the systems processing data in real time.

8.4.2 *The CTR Block Cipher Mode*

The name of this mode comes from the word CounTeR. This mode resembles the OFB. The difference is that not the previous output of the cipher but simply a counter is enciphered. More exactly, the scheme is

$$z_i = r \text{ high-order bits of } E_K(Y_0 + i), \quad i = 1, 2, 3, \ldots$$

where r and Y_0 are parameters.

If the "ideal" block cipher is used, this mode ensures the same security level as the OFB mode. The advantage of the CTR mode is the possibility of direct computation of any element of the sequence z. It allows for encrypting and decrypting any fragments of the message independently of each other.

8.4.3 *The RC4 Algorithm*

The algorithm RC4 suggested by Rivest in 1994 (see [Schneier (1996)]) is a representative of a class of customised methods designed specially for stream ciphers. The pseudo-random generators constructed using such algorithms are usually much faster than the generators based on block ciphers.

The RC4 algorithm operates with n-bit words (usually, $n = 8$). All computations are performed modulo 2^n (the remainder $x \bmod 2^n$ is computed extremely fast by masking all but n low-order bits in x using logical "and" operation) RC4 uses the L-word key $K = K_0 K_1 \ldots K_{L-1}$ and generates the sequence of words $\bar{u} = u_1 u_2 u_3 \ldots$ determined by that K. The state of the generator is defined by the table S of 2^n words and by two variables i and j. At each time instance table S contains all n-bit numbers (from 0 to $2^n - 1$) somehow mixed. Since every element of the table may take on values in the interval $[0,\ 2^n - 1]$, it may be treated in two ways, either as a number or as an index to the other element in the table. The secret key determines only the initial permutation of numbers in the table. This initial permutation is formed by the following algorithm:

$$j \leftarrow 0, \quad S \leftarrow (0, 1, \ldots, 2^n - 1);$$
$$\text{FOR } i = 0, 1, \ldots, 2^n - 1 \text{ DO}$$
$$\quad j \leftarrow (j + S_i + K_{i \bmod L}) \bmod 2^n,$$
$$\quad S_j \leftrightarrow S_i;$$
$$i \leftarrow 0, \quad j \leftarrow 0.$$

After this is done, the generator is ready to work. The generation of a pseudo-random word u_i, $i = 1, 2, 3, \ldots$ is performed by the following algorithm:

$$i \leftarrow (i + 1) \bmod 2^n;$$
$$j \leftarrow (j + S_i) \bmod 2^n;$$
$$S_j \leftrightarrow S_i;$$
$$t \leftarrow (S_i + S_j) \bmod 2^n;$$
$$u_i \leftarrow S_t.$$

Example 8.2   Let $n = 3$, $K = (25)_8$ $(L = 2)$.

Form the initial permutation of numbers in table S (perform all computations modulo 8):

$$
\begin{array}{lll}
 & j = 0, & S = (0, 1, 2, 3, 4, 5, 6, 7), \\
i = 0, & j = 0 + 0 + 2 = 2, & S = (2, 1, 0, 3, 4, 5, 6, 7), \\
i = 1, & j = 2 + 1 + 5 = 0, & S = (1, 2, 0, 3, 4, 5, 6, 7), \\
i = 2, & j = 0 + 0 + 2 = 2, & S = (1, 2, 0, 3, 4, 5, 6, 7), \\
i = 3, & j = 2 + 3 + 5 = 2, & S = (1, 2, 3, 0, 4, 5, 6, 7), \\
i = 4, & j = 2 + 4 + 2 = 0, & S = (4, 2, 3, 0, 1, 5, 6, 7), \\
i = 5, & j = 0 + 5 + 5 = 2, & S = (4, 2, 5, 0, 1, 3, 6, 7), \\
i = 6, & j = 2 + 6 + 2 = 2, & S = (4, 2, 6, 0, 1, 3, 5, 7), \\
i = 7, & j = 2 + 7 + 5 = 6, & S = (4, 2, 6, 0, 1, 3, 7, 5).
\end{array}
$$

Now compute several elements of the pseudo-random sequence $\bar{u}$:

$i = 1,\ j = 0 + 2 = 2,\ S = (4, 6, 2, 0, 1, 3, 7, 5),\ t = 2 + 6 = 0,\ u_1 = 4,$
$i = 2,\ j = 2 + 2 = 4,\ S = (4, 6, 1, 0, 2, 3, 7, 5),\ t = 1 + 2 = 3,\ u_2 = 0,$
$i = 3,\ j = 4 + 0 = 4,\ S = (4, 6, 1, 2, 0, 3, 7, 5),\ t = 2 + 0 = 2,\ u_3 = 1,$
$i = 4,\ j = 4 + 0 = 4,\ S = (4, 6, 1, 2, 0, 3, 7, 5),\ t = 0 + 0 = 0,\ u_4 = 4,$
$i = 5,\ j = 4 + 3 = 7,\ S = (4, 6, 1, 2, 0, 5, 7, 3),\ t = 5 + 3 = 0,\ u_5 = 4,$
$i = 6,\ j = 7 + 7 = 6,\ S = (4, 6, 1, 2, 0, 5, 7, 3),\ t = 7 + 7 = 6,\ u_6 = 7.$

To apply Eq. (8.10) for encrypting write the numbers u_i in binary system. In our example, each number u_i is represented by 3 bits, so we obtain

$$\bar{z} = 1\ 0\ 0\ 0\ 0\ 0\ 0\ 0\ 1\ 1\ 0\ 0\ 1\ 0\ 0\ 1\ 1\ 1\ \ldots$$

8.5 Cryptographic Hash Functions

We have already met the notion of hash function in Chap. 4 where hash functions were parts of digital signature schemes. In those schemes, hash functions were used as the "digests" or "representatives" of the messages to be signed. The signature was actually produced on the hash function value and it was assumed that this value essentially depends on all symbols of the message and one cannot alter the message without affecting the hash function value. In this section, we shall more strictly formulate the requirements and consider one method of construction of cryptographic hash functions.

Definition 8.1 Any function $y = h(x_1 x_2 \ldots x_n)$ which maps the string (message) $x_1 x_2 \ldots x_n$ of *arbitrary* length n into the word (or number) y of a *fixed* length is called the *hash function*.

The example of hash function is the checksum for the message. In this case

$$h(x_1 x_2 \ldots x_n) = (x_1 + x_2 + \ldots + x_n) \bmod 2^w$$

where w is the size of machine word. The length of the number that contains the value of this function is w bits regardless of the length of the message. The checksums are often used for detecting unintentional (random) errors in the message (it is assumed that upon the error the checksum will change with high probability). Nevertheless it is very easy to make an intentional error preserving the checksum value. If such hash function had been used in a digital signature scheme, it would have been possible to alter the signed document. Therefore, the presented checksum hash function is unsuitable for cryptographic use.

Let's formulate the main requirements that any cryptographically secure hash function must meet. Let x be some string (message). Then

(1) for any given x, the computation $h(x)$ must be relatively fast;
(2) given y, it must be computationally infeasible to find a message x such that $y = h(x)$;
(3) given x, it must be computationally infeasible to find any other $x' \neq x$ such that $h(x') = h(x)$;
(4) it must be computationally infeasible to find any pair of distinct messages x and x' for which $h(x') = h(x)$.

Notice that the first requirement must always be fulfilled since, otherwise, the hash function looses any practical meaning. The other requirements are important for various applications. For instance, if the passwords are stored in the form of hash function values then the hash function must meet the second requirement. For the digital signature schemes, the third requirement is important. The fourth requirement is needed in some cryptographic protocols. Notice that the fourth requirement is stronger than the third (i.e. the fulfilment of the fourth implies the fulfilment of the third).

Designing hash functions that would meet all four requirements is not a simple task. Nowadays a number of hash functions are suggested and used (e.g. MD5, SHA-1, RIPEMD-160, see [FIPS 180-1 (1995); Menezes *et al.* (1996)]) that are believed to be secure (but this is not proved). The descriptions of these and the similar functions are rather bulky. So we shall only consider the universal scheme of constructing hash functions based on block ciphers.

Let there be given a block cipher E which maps the input block X into the output block Y under the key K,

$$Y = E_K(X).$$

We present two algorithms for which the length of hash function value equals the blocksize of cipher but note that constructions are known that allow for the length of hash function value to be a multiple to the blocksize.

In the first algorithm, the message is represented as a sequence of blocks $X_1, X_2, \ldots, X_n$. The last block is padded by zeroes, and sometimes the length of the message is written thereto. The value of hash function h results from the following iterative process:

$$h \leftarrow 0;$$
$$\text{FOR } i = 1, 2, \ldots, n \text{ DO}$$
$$h \leftarrow E_h(X_i) \oplus X_i.$$

The initial value of h may be some "magic" number rather than zero, but it is not important. In this algorithm, the value of h obtained in the previous iteration is used as the key to the cipher in the next iteration. Therefore, it is assumed implicitly that the length of key is equal to the blocksize. However, as we have seen in case of RC6, the length of key can be significantly greater than the blocksize (in RC6 the length of key can be as large as 255 bytes). In such cases the second algorithm is more appropriate.

In the second algorithm, the message is represented as a sequence $X_1, X_2, \ldots, X_m$ in which the length of each element equals the length of cipher key. The last element is padded in the same way as in the first algorithm. The value of hash function h is computed as follows:

$$h \leftarrow 0;$$
$$\text{FOR } i = 1, 2, \ldots, m \text{ DO}$$
$$h \leftarrow E_{X_i}(h) \oplus h.$$

Here the message elements play the role of keys for the cipher.

The presented algorithms satisfy all the requirements to cryptographic hash functions provided the underlying block ciphers are secure (see [Goldwasser and Bellare (2001); Menezes *et al.* (1996)]).

Chapter 9

Random Numbers in Cryptography

9.1 Introduction

We have seen in the previous chapters that random and pseudo-random numbers play an important role in cryptography. Actually, all cryptosystems that we have described rely on random choice of the keys and various parameters. Recall also that perfect secrecy of the Vernam cipher is based on the claim that the key sequence consists of equiprobable and independent bits. Finally, we have shown how pseudo-random sequences are used in stream ciphers to encrypt messages. It is natural then that the problem of generating random and pseudo-random numbers is of great interest for the designers of cryptosystems. Moreover, it occurs that many fundamental problems of cryptography are closely connected with generating and testing random numbers. For instance, the theoretical possibility to construct secure pseudo-random generators depends on the existence of one-way functions, and one of the attacks to block ciphers is based on statistical tests designed for detecting deviations from randomness.

In this chapter, we shall consider some problems, ideas, and methods in cryptography connected with generation and testing of random numbers. We begin with the main question: what is the random number or, more generally, the sequence of random numbers? One of the possible definitions is the following. This is a (binary) sequence obtained by fair coin tossing if the sides of the coin are marked by 0 and 1. More formally the random sequence may be defined as a sequence consisting of independent zeroes and ones whose probabilities are equal. Sometimes such sequences are called *completely* random but we shall usually omit the adverb for brevity. Other random numbers, say, random integers from some interval, can easily be produced from binary random sequences and we shall not discuss this issue.

The next question is how to generate random numbers in a computing environment? It is clear that such "manual" methods as coin tossing and drawing cards can hardly be applied. What is really useful is digitising the physical processes that are known to contain randomness. These may be noises in electrical circuits or electronic components (such as diodes), physical particle counters, or computer mouse motions. One of the main problems here is the conversion of physical measurements into completely random sequences of bits. This problem will be addressed in the next section.

Very often we may (and sometimes shall) use pseudo-random numbers instead of random. We have already considered the problem of generating cryptographically secure pseudo-random sequences in Sec. 8.4. We shall recur to this problem in Sec. 9.3 to discuss some extra issues.

The demands to the quality of random and pseudo-random numbers in cryptography are extremely high. First of all, any statistical deviations from the standard must be left out, i.e. zeroes and ones must be equiprobable and independent. For detecting the deviations, special statistical tests are used. The US National Institute of Standards and Technology (NIST) recommends 16 tests for use in cryptography [Rukhin *et al.* (2001)]. In Sec. 9.4 we shall consider some new methods suggested recently that outperform the NIST tests.

As we have noted in the beginning of the chapter, various branches of cryptography are usually connected but this is not always obvious. An example of such connection will be given in the last section where we describe the attack to block ciphers that is closely connected with random numbers and statistical tests.

9.2 Refining Physical Random Number Generators

Assume that we have a physical generator that produces the sequence of random zeroes and ones but the bits of the sequence are not equiprobable and/or exhibit some correlations. Our task is to convert this sequence into completely random. This conversion is often referred to as the *refinement* of the generator. There are two classes of refinement algorithms. The algorithms of the first class are built on the assumption that the source bits are independent but, perhaps, not equiprobable. The second class algorithms assume that bits may also be correlated (more exactly, obey some correlation model). We shall consider only the first class algorithms. The methods of the second class go beyond the scope of the book for two reasons: first, for many physical generators (e.g. based on noise diodes), the measurements made at distant time instances may be considered as independent; second, the methods eliminating dependences, as a rule, can do that only approximately (i.e. the resulting bits are only "almost" independent), their description is complicated and today they are rarely used in practice. But it is worth noting that there exist interesting and elegant methods in this field described in the literature on cryptography and computational complexity (see, e.g. [Nisan and Zuckerman (1996)] and survey [Nisan and Ta-Shma (1999)]).

So, in the rest of the section, we consider the methods refining the sequences of independent but not equiprobable zeroes and ones.

The first algorithm for solving this problem was due to John von Neumann (see [Elias (1987)]). For description of the algorithm, introduce the necessary notation. Let a memoryless source be given generating letters over the alphabet $\{0,1\}$ with probabilities $1 - p$ and p, respectively. The probability p may be unknown. It is required to convert the sequence generated by the source into completely random sequence.

Von Neumann suggested the following method. The source sequence is split into 2-bit blocks that are encoded by the rule

$$00 \to \Lambda, \quad 01 \to 0, \quad 10 \to 1, \quad 11 \to \Lambda \tag{9.1}$$

where Λ denotes an empty word.

Example 9.1 Let the source sequence be $\bar{m} = 1101110110$. We split it into 2-bit blocks (delimited by commas): $\bar{m} = 11, 01, 11, 01, 10$. Now we apply the mapping (9.1) and obtain a completely random sequence $\bar{z} = \Lambda, 0, \Lambda, 0, 1 = 001$. So, we have "extracted" 3 completely random bits from 10-bit source sequence.

For justification of the method, notice that the probabilities of the blocks 01 and 10 are equal since they are $p(1 - p)$ and $(1 - p)p$, respectively. Therefore, the resulting sequence consists of equiprobable zeroes and ones, as required.

The given example demonstrates the disadvantage of the method defined by (9.1): the resulting sequence is much shorter than the source one. More exactly, it is easy to see that given t source symbols we obtain $tp(1 - p)$ output bits on average. For example, if p is close to $1/2$ then we obtain, on average, about $t/4$ output bits.

Peter Elias suggested the conversion method which spends less source bits [Elias (1987)]. This is achieved by encoding the blocks of length n, $n > 2$ (if $n = 2$, the methods of Elias and von Neumann coincide). To measure the effectiveness of the algorithm, Elias introduced the quantity η_n defined as the ratio of the mean length of resulting codeword to the blocklength n. He showed that the natural upper bound for η_n is the source entropy $h(p)$. Recall from Sec. 7.4, Eq. (7.7) that in binary case, $h(p) = -(p \log p + (1 - p) \log(1 - p))$. (It is easy to understand why $h(p)$ is the maximum possible value for the ratio between the lengths of output and input sequences. Informally, on the one hand, the entropy is a measure of uncertainty or randomness of the input sequence. On the other hand, the entropy of the output completely random sequence is equal to its length, since the entropy of one completely random bit is 1.)

In fact, the idea of Elias's approach can be illustrated by one algorithm we have already discussed. Revert to the description of the ideal cipher construction in Sec. 7.6. There is a message generated by a binary memoryless source with unknown statistics (i.e. our input to a refinement algorithm, in terms of the present section) was transformed to the sequence

$$u(\bar{m}_1)v(\bar{m}_1)w(\bar{m}_1)u(\bar{m}_2)v(\bar{m}_2)w(\bar{m}_2)\dots$$

where $\bar{m}_i$, $i = 1, 2, \dots$, denote the input blocks of n bits and $u(\cdot)$, $v(\cdot)$, $w(\cdot)$ some transformations, $w(\bar{m}_i)$ being completely random. Now the output of Elias's algorithm can be obtained by simply discarding the words $u(\bar{m}_i)$ and $v(\bar{m}_i)$, i.e. it will consist of concatenated words $w(\bar{m}_i)$. We may summarise that using this approach we gain the following refinement conversion of the source sequence:

$$\bar{m}_1 \bar{m}_2 \bar{m}_3 \dots \longrightarrow w(\bar{m}_1)w(\bar{m}_2)w(\bar{m}_3)\dots .$$

Example 9.2   Let the same message as in Example 9.1 be generated, $\bar{m} = 1101110110$. Split it into 5-bit blocks: $\bar{m} = 11011, 10110$ where $\bar{m}_1 = 11011$, $\bar{m}_2 = 10110$. Apply to these blocks the coding method described in Sec. 7.6 (with obvious substitution of a_1 for 0 and a_2 for 1). We obtain $w(\bar{m}_1) = (10)_2$ and $w(\bar{m}_2) = (110)_2$, see p. 133. Hence, the source message $\bar{m}$ converts to completely random sequence $w(\bar{m}_1)w(\bar{m}_2)$:

$$1101110110 \longrightarrow 10110 .$$

So, we have extracted 5 completely random bits.

By Proposition 7.5 the average length of each word $w(\bar{m}_i)$ is greater than $nh(p) - 2\log(n+1)$. Hence we obtain the lower bound for η_n,

$$\eta_n > \frac{nh(p) - 2\log(n+1)}{n} = h(p) - \frac{2\log(n+1)}{n}.$$

It is clearly seen that if n increases, η_n approaches $h(p)$.

So, the Elias algorithm allows for the effectiveness η_n to approach the upper bound (Shannon entropy) if the blocksize n increases. But, at the same time, it requires the memory size to grow as 2^n which makes the algorithm intractable for large n. In [Ryabko and Matchikina (2000)], a significantly more efficient method was suggested, with the memory size growing as $n\log^2 n$. We refer the interested reader to the cited paper for more details.

9.3 Pseudo-Random Number Generators

In Sec. 8.4, we have already considered pseudo-random number generators used for constructing stream ciphers and discussed the requirements to cryptographically secure generators. In this section, we shall briefly touch on some additional issues.

First, comment on the last two requirements given on p. 161. They claim that (a) the determination of the next element of the sequence given the preceding elements should be an infeasible problem and (b) the sequence produced by the generator should be indistinguishable from a completely random sequence by any statistical test. It is clear that computational complexity here is crucial. For example, if we are not computationally bounded, then any pseudo-random generator can be predicted. Suppose we have a generated sequence $z_1, z_2, \ldots, z_i$ and wish to predict (to guess) the z_{i+1}. We know that the whole sequence depends on some initial (secret) state of generator which can be represented as an integer s. We can try one value of s after another until such s is found that makes the generator produce exactly $z_1, z_2, \ldots, z_i$. Now knowing s we can easily compute z_{i+1}. If the length of s is $|s|$ bits, this approach requires about $2^{|s|}$ computations and is infeasible if $|s|$ is about 100 bits or greater.

The problem with practical pseudo-random generators, such as RC4, is that computational bounds for their security are not determined mathematically strictly. In case of block-cipher-based generators the computational bound of security is proved to be exponential if the underlying block cipher is "ideal". But, in turn, for practical block ciphers, the correspondence to the "ideality" conditions is not proved. So, many investigators are engaged in searching for new algorithms of statistical testing and prediction in the hope to find some breaches in the generators' constructions, and some recent results in the field will be presented in the following sections.

However, there exists an elegant theory that allows one to connect the above problem with other branches of cryptography and with complexity theory. A detailed exposition of this theory can be found, e.g. in [Goldwasser and Bellare (2001)] but we shall only point out some basic results. First, it is shown that the pseudo-random number generators exist that produce sequences indistinguishable from completely random by any polynomial-time test. This means, in particular, that such sequences can securely substitute for completely random sequences in polynomial-time algorithms. Second, it is shown that both requirements to generated sequences, marked (a) and (b) above, are equivalent if we deal with polynomial-time algorithms. Third, the connection is established between pseudo-random number generators and one-way functions which, in particular, allows to construct "provably secure" generators based on one-way functions. Quotation here means that the proofs are valid under certain conditions typical for complexity theory, e.g. are based on unproved assumptions about one-wayness of certain functions. We shall describe one of such provably secure generators based on RSA.

The parameters of the RSA-based generator are two large primes P and Q ($P \neq Q$), their product $N = PQ$, and a number $e \geq 3$ coprime to $(P-1)(Q-1)$. The initial state x_0 is a randomly chosen number from the interval $(1, N-1)$. The generator produces a sequence of bits $z_1, z_2, \ldots, z_k$ according to the following scheme:

$$x_i \leftarrow x_{i-1}^e \bmod N \,,$$
$$z_i \leftarrow \text{least significant bit of } x_i \,, \quad i = 1, 2, \ldots, k \,.$$

Note that the number e can be 3 which simplifies exponentiation.

The described generator is proved to be cryptographically secure under the assumption that RSA cannot be broken. This generator is significantly slower than the generators described in Sec. 8.4 and is therefore unsuitable for stream ciphers. However, it may be used successfully in other tasks where high security is paramount. For example, it may be used to generate parameters for cryptographic protocols based on a relatively small random number x_0. Other generators that make use of one-way functions may be found in the literature, see, e.g. [Goldwasser and Bellare (2001); Menezes *et al.* (1996)].

9.4 Statistical Tests for Random and Pseudo-Random Number Generators

Random and pseudo-random numbers are widely used not only in cryptography but also in other fields such as computational mathematics, modelling and simulation. This highlights the problem of constructing efficient statistical tests aimed to detecting possible deviations from randomness. Thus the US National Institute of Standards and Technology (NIST) has carried out an investigation of known statistical tests for random and pseudo-random numbers. The results and recommendations for practical usage were published in [Rukhin *et al.* (2001)]. Particularly, 16 methods were recommended for use in cryptography. It is important to note that these tests were selected as a result of a comprehensive theoretical and experimental analysis and may be considered as the state-of-the-art in randomness testing. Recently, in a series of works [Ryabko and Pestunov (2004); Ryabko *et al.* (2004); Ryabko and Monarev (2004)] a number of new tests were suggested whose performance occurred to be significantly greater than that of the NIST tests. In this section, we describe one of these new methods.

In a statistical test for randomness, we consider the main hypothesis H_0 that a bit sequence is generated by the memoryless source with equal probabilities of zeroes and ones. Associated with this null hypothesis is the alternative hypothesis H_1 that the sequence is generated by a stationary ergodic source which differs from the source under H_0, $H_1 = \neg H_0$.

Let's describe the test suggested in [Ryabko and Pestunov (2004)]. In this test, the input sequence $x_1, x_2, \ldots, x_n$ is divided into subwords $x_1, x_2, \ldots, x_s$, $x_{s+1}, x_{s+2}, \ldots, x_{2s}$, $\ldots$, $s \geq 1$, and the hypothesis H_0^* that the subwords obey the uniform distribution (i.e. each subword is generated with the probability 2^{-s}) is tested against $H_1^* = \neg H_0^*$. It is clear that H_1^* is true if H_0 is true. The key idea of the test is as follows. All subwords from the set $\{0,1\}^s$ are ordered and this order changes after processing each subword $x_{js+1}, x_{js+2}, \ldots, x_{js+s}$, $j = 0, 1, \ldots$, in such a way that, loosely speaking, the more frequent subwords have small ordinals. Then the frequencies of different ordinals are estimated (instead of frequencies of the subwords as, say, for chi-square test [Kendall and Stuart (1961);

Knuth (1981)]). The test is based on construction of adaptive code suggested in [Ryabko (1980)] and called *book stack*.

We shall consider the input sequence as generated by a source over the alphabet $A = \{a_1, \ldots, a_S\}$ (in practice, $S = 2^s$ but it is not necessary). Suppose we are given a sample $u_1, u_2, \ldots, u_n$ generated by the source.

In the book stack test, all letters from A are ordered from 1 to S and this order is changed after observing each letter u_t according to the formula

$$\nu^{t+1}(a) = \begin{cases} 1, & \text{if } u_t = a, \\ \nu^t(a) + 1, & \text{if } \nu^t(a) < \nu^t(u_t), \\ \nu^t(a), & \text{if } \nu^t(a) > \nu^t(u_t) \end{cases} \qquad (9.2)$$

where ν^t is the order after observing $u_1, u_2, \ldots, u_t$, $t = 1, \ldots, n$, ν^1 being defined arbitrarily. (For example, we can define $\nu^1 = (a_1, \ldots, a_S)$.)

Let us explain informally (9.2). Suppose that the letters from A are arranged in a stack, like a stack of books, and $\nu^1(a)$ is a position of a in the stack. Let the first letter u_1 of the word $u_1, u_2, \ldots, u_n$ be a. If it occupies the i_1-th position in the stack ($\nu^1(a) = i_1$), then extract a out of the stack and push it to the top. (It means that the order is changed according to (9.2).) Repeat the procedure with the second letter u_2 and the stack obtained, *etc.*

It can help to understand the main idea of the suggested method if we take into account that, if H_1 is true, the frequent letters from A (as frequently used books) will have relatively small ordinals (will spend more time near the top of the stack). On the other hand, if H_0 is true, the probability to find each letter u_i at each position j is equal to $1/S$.

Let's continue the description of the test. The set of all indexes $\{1, \ldots, S\}$ is divided into r, $r \geq 2$, subsets $A_1 = \{1, 2, \ldots, k_1\}$, $A_2 = \{k_1+1, \ldots, k_2\}$, ..., $A_r = \{k_{r-1}+1, \ldots, k_r\}$. Then, using $u_1, u_2, \ldots, u_n$, we calculate how many $\nu^t(x_t)$, $t = 1, \ldots, n$, belong to a subset A_k, $k = 1, \ldots, r$. We denote this number by n_k. More formally,

$$n_k = |\{t : \nu^t(x_t) \in A_k, t = 1, \ldots, n\}|, \quad k = 1, \ldots, r.$$

Obviously, if H_0^* is true, the probability of the event $\nu^t(x_t) \in A_k$ is equal to $|A_j|/S$. Then, using a usual chi-square test, we test the hypothesis

$$\hat{H}_0 = P\{\nu^t(x_t) \in A_k\} = |A_j|/S$$

being based on the empirical frequencies $n_1, \ldots, n_r$, against $\hat{H}_1 = \neg\hat{H}_0$.

Let us recall that the value

$$x^2 = \sum_{i=1}^{r} \frac{(n_i - n(|A_i|/S))^2}{n(|A_i|/S)} \tag{9.3}$$

is computed, when the chi-square test is applied, see, e.g. [Kendall and Stuart (1961); Knuth (1981)]. It is known that x^2 asymptotically follows the chi-square distribution with $(k-1)$ degrees of freedom (χ_{k-1}^2) if $\hat{H}_0$ is true. If the level of significance (or a Type I error) of the chi-square test is α, $0 < \alpha < 1$, the hypothesis $\hat{H}_0$ is accepted when x^2 from (9.3) is less than the $(1-\alpha)$-value of the χ_{k-1}^2 distribution.

We do not describe the exact rule for constructing the subsets A_1, ..., A_r, but recommend to implement some experiments for finding the parameters which make the sample size minimal (or, at least, acceptable). The point is that there are many cryptographic applications where it is possible to implement some experiments for optimising the parameter values and, then, to test the hypothesis based on independent data. For example, in case of testing a pseudo-random number generator it is possible to seek suitable parameters using a part of generated sequence and then to test the generator using a new part of the sequence.

Let us consider an example.

Example 9.3 Let

$$A = \{a_1, \ldots, a_6\}, \quad u_1 \ldots u_8 = a_3 a_6 a_3 a_3 a_6 a_1 a_6 a_1,$$
$$r = 2, \quad A_1 = \{1, 2, 3\}, \quad A_2 = \{4, 5, 6\},$$
$$\nu^1 = (a_1, a_2, a_3, a_4, a_5, a_6).$$

Then

$$
\begin{aligned}
\nu^1 &= (a_1, a_2, a_3, a_4, a_5, a_6), & n_1 &= 0, \, n_2 = 0; \\
\nu^2 &= (a_3, a_1, a_2, a_4, a_5, a_6), & n_1 &= 1; \\
\nu^3 &= (a_6, a_3, a_1, a_2, a_4, a_5), & n_2 &= 1; \\
\nu^4 &= (a_3, a_6, a_1, a_2, a_4, a_5), & n_1 &= 2; \\
\nu^5 &= (a_3, a_6, a_1, a_2, a_4, a_5), & n_1 &= 3; \\
\nu^6 &= (a_6, a_3, a_1, a_2, a_4, a_5), & n_1 &= 4; \\
\nu^7 &= (a_1, a_6, a_3, a_2, a_4, a_5), & n_1 &= 5; \\
\nu^8 &= (a_6, a_1, a_3, a_2, a_4, a_5), & n_1 &= 6; \\
\nu^9 &= (a_1, a_6, a_3, a_2, a_4, a_5), & n_1 &= 7.
\end{aligned}
$$

We can see that the letters a_3 and a_6 are quite frequent and the book stack test indicates this non-uniformity quite well. Indeed, the average values of

n_1 and n_2 are equal to 4, whereas the real values are 7 and 1, respectively.

Let us make two notes here. First, we pay attention to the complexity of this algorithm. The "naive" method of transformation according to (9.2) would take the number of operations proportional to S, but there exist algorithms which can perform all operations in (9.2) in $O(\log S)$ time. Such algorithms can be based on AVL trees, see, e.g. [Aho *et al.* (1976)].

The second comment concerns with the name of the method. The book stack structure is quite popular in information theory and computer science. In information theory, this structure was firstly suggested as a basis of a universal code in [Ryabko (1980)] and then rediscovered in [Bently *et al.* (1986)]. In the literature this code is frequently called "move-to-front" (MTF) scheme as it was suggested in [Bently *et al.* (1986)].

As we have already noted, in [Ryabko and Pestunov (2004); Ryabko and Monarev (2004)], the book stack test was compared to the NIST tests. The power of book stack test was shown to be significantly greater than that of all 16 tests recommended by NIST; see the cited papers for details.

9.5   Statistical Attack to Block Ciphers

Cryptanalysis of block ciphers attracts much research, and new results in the field are always beneficial for improving constructions of the ciphers. Sometimes the complexity of a new attack (measured in the number of memory units and operations required for mounting such an attack) might be quite large. Nevertheless, even if a relatively small decrease in the attack complexity is achieved, in comparison with previously known methods, this can motivate further development of the cipher design. Thus linear cryptanalysis of DES (see [Menezes *et al.* (1996)]) requires 2^{43} known plaintext-ciphertext pairs and is generally considered infeasible in practice. But it has made an important impact on the design principles of modern block ciphers, that are now resistant to this kind of attack. In this section, we described a new attack to block ciphers, referred to as a "gradient statistical attack". This attack connects such different problems as randomness testing and block cipher cryptanalysis.

Consider a block cipher with the blocklength n, key length s, and encryption function $E(x, K)$, where $x \in \{0,1\}^n$ denotes a plaintext block, and $K \in \{0,1\}^s$ a secret key (we need to change the notation slightly as compared to Sec. 8.2). The typical values of n and s for modern block ciphers are $n = 64$ or $n = 128$, $s = 128$ bits (see Sec. 8.2). The majority of block ciphers are iterated, i.e. involve many rounds of transformations usually bracketed by some prologue and epilogue. Either of these, in turn, can sometimes be divided into a number of more simple steps. In respect of this iterated structure, the secret key K is expanded into a sequence of subkeys or round keys $k_1, k_2, \ldots, k_t$, where t is the number of "simple steps" in a block cipher. Denote by x_0 the initial state of block x, and by x_i the state after the i-th step. So the complete encryption is $x_t = E(x_0, K)$ and this can be written as

$$x_1 = E_1(x_0, k_1), \quad \ldots, \quad x_t = E_t(x_{t-1}, k_t), \tag{9.4}$$

where E_i denotes the encrypting transformation at the i-th step.

Example 9.4 Consider the cipher RC5 (see p. 145) with the blocklength 64 and number of rounds r. The encrypting process, with reference to (9.4), is as follows:

input: (a, b)	$x_0 = (a, b)$
prologue:	
$\quad a \leftarrow a + k_1$	$x_1 = E_1(x_0, k_1)$
$\quad b \leftarrow b + k_2$	$x_2 = E_2(x_1, k_2)$
round 1:	
$\quad a \leftarrow ((a \oplus b) \hookleftarrow b) + k_3$	$x_3 = E_3(x_2, k_3)$
$\quad b \leftarrow ((b \oplus a) \hookleftarrow a) + k_4$	$x_4 = E_4(x_3, k_4)$
$\cdots$	$\cdots$
round r:	
$\quad a \leftarrow ((a \oplus b) \hookleftarrow b) + k_{2r+1}$	
$\quad b \leftarrow ((b \oplus a) \hookleftarrow a) + k_{2r+2}$	$x_t = E_t(x_{t-1}, k_t)$
output: (a, b)	$x_t = (a, b)$

Here $t = 2r + 2$, the length of each subkey is 32 bits. Many other ciphers, including RC6 and AES, may also be represented by (9.4) with relatively small, e.g. 32 bits or less, subkeys.

The described attack belongs to a class of chosen-plaintext attacks. Upon that kind of attack, a cryptanalyst is able to input any information to the cipher and observe the corresponding output. Her aim is to recover the secret key or, which is almost the same, the round keys. Such attacks are of practical interest and it is assumed that the block ciphers must be secure against them. We consider a chosen-plaintext attack for the cipher which can be represented by (9.4) with relatively small subkeys. Denote the lengths of the secret key and each subkey by $|K|$ and $|k|$, respectively. The exhaustive key-search requires $O(2^{|K|})$ operations (decrypt with $K = 0, 1, \ldots$ until a known x is obtained). Meanwhile, the described attack requires $O(mt2^{|k|})$ operations, where m is the number of ciphertext blocks sufficient for statistical analysis. The attack succeeds in finding the correct subkeys (instead of K itself), provided the statistical test is able to detect deviations from randomness in a sequence of m blocks. It is essential to use new efficient statistical tests like those presented in Sec. 9.4. As an example, we shall consider experimental implementation of the attack with respect to RC5 block cipher.

As we consider the block ciphers that can be described by (9.4), notice that the sequence corresponding to (9.4) for decryption is

$$x_{t-1} = D_t(x_t, k_t), \quad \ldots, \quad x_0 = D_1(x_1, k_1), \qquad (9.5)$$

where D_i denotes the decrypting transformation inverse to E_i.

One of the requirements to a block cipher is that, given a sequence of different blocks as input, the cipher must output a sequence of bits that looks like completely random (see CTR block cipher mode on p. 163). We shall loosely call bit sequences "more random" or "less random" depending on how much they differ from a completely random sequence. One way to measure randomness is to use some statistic on the sequence with the property that less random sequences have greater statistics (to within some probability of error in decision). This may be a well-known x^2 statistic subjected to χ^2 distribution. Denote such a statistic by $\gamma(x)$, where x is a bit sequence.

Denote by $\alpha_1, \alpha_2, \ldots, \alpha_m$ a sequence of input blocks. Let all the blocks be non-random and pairwise different. A possible example would be $\alpha_1 = 1$, $\alpha_2 = 2, \ldots, \alpha_m = m$, where the numbers are written as n-bit words. For a good block cipher, the encrypted sequence

$$E(\alpha_1, K), \quad E(\alpha_2, K), \quad \ldots, \quad E(\alpha_m, K)$$

must look like random, for any K. Now recall (9.4). Apply only one step of encryption to the input sequence, denoting the result by $\beta_1, \beta_2, \ldots, \beta_m$:

$$\beta_1 = E_1(\alpha_1, k_1), \quad \ldots, \quad \beta_m = E_1(\alpha_m, k_1).$$

We claim that the sequence β is more random than the sequence α, i.e. $\gamma(\beta) < \gamma(\alpha)$. After the second step of encryption, the sequence

$$E_2(\beta_1, k_2), \quad E_2(\beta_2, k_2), \quad \ldots, \quad E_2(\beta_m, k_2)$$

is more random than β, and so on. Each step of encryption increases the degree of randomness.

Notice the obvious consequence: in decryption according to (9.5), the randomness of the data decreases from step to step. For example, the sequence

$$D_1(\beta_1, k_1), \quad D_1(\beta_2, k_1), \quad \ldots, \quad D_1(\beta_m, k_1),$$

which is α, is less random than β. But what is important: this is true only if the decryption is done with the valid key. If the key is not valid, denote it by k_1', then the sequence

$$\alpha_1' = D_1(\beta_1, k_1'), \quad \ldots, \quad \alpha_m' = D_1(\beta_m, k_1')$$

will be *more* random than β, $\gamma(\alpha') < \gamma(\beta)$. This is because decrypting with a different key corresponds to further encrypting with that key, which is the well-known multiple encryption principle [Menezes *et al.* (1996)]. So, generally, decryption with an invalid round key increases randomness, while decryption with the valid round key decreases randomness. This difference can be detected by a statistical test.

The suggested gradient statistical attack is mounted as follows. First encrypt the sequence $\alpha_1, \alpha_2, \ldots, \alpha_m$, defined above. Denote the output sequence by ω,

$$\omega_1 = E(\alpha_1, K), \quad \ldots, \quad \omega_m = E(\alpha_m, K).$$

(Recall that the cipher involves t rounds or steps, and the length of subkey at each step is $|k|$.)

Now begin the main procedure of key search. For all $u \in \{0, 1\}^{|k|}$ compute a sequence

$$\Gamma_t(u) = D_t(\omega_1, u), \quad D_t(\omega_2, u), \quad \ldots, \quad D_t(\omega_m, u)$$

and estimate its randomness, i.e. compute $\gamma(\Gamma_t(u))$. Find such u^* for which $\gamma(\Gamma_t(u^*))$ is maximal. Assume that unknown subkey $k_t = u^*$. Note that the number of operations at this stage is proportional to $m2^{|k|}$.

After that, based upon the sequence $\Gamma_t(k_t)$, repeat the similar computations to find subkey k_{t-1}. Using $\Gamma_{t-1}(k_{t-1})$ find k_{t-2}, and so on down to

k_1. The total number of operations to recover all subkeys is proportional to $mt2^{|k|}$.

We have described the idea of the attack in a pure form. Now let's discuss some implementation variants.

(1) The measure of randomness γ is a parameter. One may apply different measures not only for different ciphers, but also for different rounds of the same cipher. As stated above, any statistical test applicable to checking the main hypothesis H_0 that the binary sequence is truly random versus the opposite hypothesis H_1 that the sequence is not, may be used for that purpose.

(2) The sequence length m was chosen to be constant for simplicity of description. In fact, this length may vary in each round. More lengthy sequences are needed when cipher's output becomes more random, i.e. in the last rounds. The value of m depends on the power of statistical test and the cipher and can usually be determined experimentally.

(3) Some division of encryption process into simple steps may result in a situation where, at a particular step, only part of the block is affected. This may reduce the effective length of the sequence to be tested. Thus the division of RC5 into steps as shown in Example 9.4, assumes that at the odd steps $(1, 3, \ldots, t - 1)$ only the left half of the block, a, changes, and at the even steps $(2, 4, \ldots, t)$ the right half, b. Therefore only one half of the sequence, virtually $m/2$ blocks, is to be subjected to statistical tests.

(3) When searching for a relevant subkey, it is reasonable to keep not a single but several candidate subkeys, say, s different values of $u \in \{0, 1\}^{|k|}$ for which $\gamma(\Gamma_j(u))$ is maximal. Besides, when searching for simple sequences and subkeys, the sequential methods, analogous to sequential criteria in statistics, are appropriate.

(4) The initial non-random sequence $\alpha_1, \alpha_2, \ldots, \alpha_m$ may be constructed in different ways. For example, it seems to make sense to choose the sequence in which consecutive words (α_i, α_{i+1}) not only contain many equal bits but differ in at most one bit (so-called Grey code). Other choices may reflect the peculiarities of a particular cipher.

(5) The last modification may be connected with the fact that many modern ciphers with great number of rounds convert even absolutely non-random input sequence into something "quite random" (at least not distinguishable from a truly random sequence by known tests in acceptable time). Let, for instance, the cipher has r rounds and for some simple initial

sequence α_1^0, α_2^0, ..., α_m^0 the sequences

$$\alpha^1 = E_1(\alpha_1^0, k_1), \quad E_1(\alpha_2^0, k_1), \quad \ldots, \quad E_1(\alpha_m^0, k_1),$$
$$\alpha^2 = E_2(\alpha_1^1, k_2), \quad E_2(\alpha_2^1, k_2), \quad \ldots, \quad E_2(\alpha_m^1, k_2),$$
$$\ldots$$
$$\alpha^d = E_d(\alpha_1^{d-1}, k_d), \quad \ldots, \quad E_d(\alpha_m^{d-1}, k_d)$$

are not random under all subkeys k_1, ..., k_d, $d < r$. Then the suggested attack may be modified in the following manner. For each set of subkeys k_{d+1}, ..., k_r of rounds $d + 1$, ..., r apply the main procedure described above and find unknown subkeys k_1, ..., k_d. In other words, find subkeys k_{d+1}, ..., k_r by exhaustive search, and k_1, ..., k_d by the gradient statistical test. To maintain this combined attack $O(m2^{(r-d)|k|}d2^{|k|})$ operations are required, which, depending on certain parameters, can be smaller than $O(2^{|K|})$ for exhaustive key search.

Let's describe briefly a concrete application of the described attack to one of the most popular ciphers, RC5. The experiments were planned as follows. First, the degree of randomness of encrypted sequences as a function of the number of steps of encryption was analysed. The goal was to find the maximal number of steps at which the tests can tell the encrypted sequence from truly random. Second, the claim the attack is based upon was examined, namely, whether decrypting with a wrong subkey increases randomness in comparison with decrypting using a valid subkey, more exactly, whether these are distinguishable by the tests. Finally, based on the results obtained, the suggested attack started. The experiments were carried out on a multiprocessor system containing 10 1-GHz Alpha processors with 1G bytes of memory per device.

The experiments confirm the assumptions as to principal possibility of the suggested gradient statistical attack. First, the encrypted sequence gets more random as the number of rounds increases. And second, a sequence decrypted with invalid subkey is more random than one decrypted with valid subkey, and the test can detect this. Some additional tricks dependent on the structure of RC5 are used whose description goes beyond the scope of the book. To the date, RC5 with 8 rounds can be broken with 2^{33} chosen plaintext-ciphertext pairs.

Answers to Problems and Exercises

1.1. **a.** $k = 17$. **b.** $k = 23$.

1.2. **a.** PINEAPPLE ($k = 5$). **b.** MANGO ($k = 20$). **2.1.** **a.**
$5 = 5$, $16 = 6$, $27 = 7$, $-4 = 6$, $-13 = -3 = 7$, $3 + 8 = 1$, $3 - 8 = 5$,
$3 \cdot 8 = 4$, $3 \cdot 8 \cdot 5 = 4 \cdot 5 = 0 \pmod{10}$. **b.** $5 = 5$, $16 = 5$, $27 = 5$, $-4 = 7$,
$-13 = -2 = 9$, $3 + 8 = 0$, $3 - 8 = 6$, $3 \cdot 8 = 2$, $3 \cdot 8 \cdot 5 = 2 \cdot 5 = 10 \pmod{11}$.

2.2. $2^8 \bmod 10 = 6$, $3^7 \bmod 10 = 7$, $7^{19} \bmod 100 = 43$, $7^{57} \bmod 100 = 7$.

2.3. $108 = 2 \cdot 2 \cdot 3 \cdot 3 \cdot 3$, $77 = 7 \cdot 11$, $65 = 5 \cdot 13$, $30 = 3 \cdot 3 \cdot 5$, $159 = 3 \cdot 53$.

2.4. Pairs $(25, 12)$ and $(40, 27)$ are coprime, the others are not (numbers $(25, 15)$ are divisible by 5, $(13, 39)$ divisible by 13).

2.5. $\varphi(14) = 6$, $\varphi(20) = 8$.

2.6. $\varphi(53) = 52$, $\varphi(21) = \varphi(7) \cdot \varphi(3) = 6 \cdot 2 = 12$, $\varphi(159) = 2 \cdot 52 = 104$.

2.7. $3^{13} \bmod 13 = 3 \cdot 3^{12} \bmod 13 = 3$, $5^{22} \bmod 11 = 5^2 \cdot 5^{10} \cdot 5^{10} \bmod 11 = 25 \bmod 11 = 3$, $3^{17} \bmod 5 = 3$.

2.8. $3^9 \bmod 20 = 3 \cdot 3^8 \bmod 20 = 3$, $2^{14} \bmod 21 = 2^2 \cdot 2^{12} \bmod 21 = 4$, $2^{107} \bmod 159 = 2^3 \cdot 2^{104} \bmod 159 = 8$.

2.9. $\gcd(21, 12) = 3$, $\gcd(30, 12) = 6$, $\gcd(24, 40) = \gcd(40, 24) = 8$, $\gcd(33, 16) = 1$.

2.10. **a.** $x = -1, y = 2$. **b.** $x = 1, y = -2$. **c.** $x = 2, y = -1$. **d.** $x = 1, y = -2$.

2.11. $3^{-1} \bmod 7 = 5$, $5^{-1} \bmod 8 = 5$, $3^{-1} = 18$, $10^{-1} = 16 \pmod{53}$.

2.12. The primes less than 100 are: 2, 3, 5, 7, 11, 13, 17, 19, 23, 29, 31, 37, 41, 43, 47, 53, 59, 61, 67, 73, 79, 83, 89, 97. Among them, the numbers

5, 7, 11, 23, 47, 59, and 83 correspond to the form $p = 2q + 1$.

2.13. If $p = 11$ then generator g may be either 2, 6, 7, or 8.

2.14.   a. $Y_A = 20$, $Y_B = 17$, $Z_{AB} = 21$.   **b.** $Y_A = 13$, $Y_B = 14$, $Z_{AB} = 10$.   **c.** $Y_A = 21$, $Y_B = 9$, $Z_{AB} = 16$.   **d.** $Y_A = 8$, $Y_B = 5$, $Z_{AB} = 9$.   **e.** $Y_A = 6$, $Y_B = 17$, $Z_{AB} = 16$.

2.15.   a. $d_A = 11$, $d_B = 13$, $x_1 = 17$, $x_2 = 5$, $x_3 = 6$, $x_4 = 4$.   **b.** $d_A = 3$, $d_B = 19$, $x_1 = 8$, $x_2 = 12$, $x_3 = 3$, $x_4 = 6$.   **c.** $d_A = 5$, $d_B = 11$, $x_1 = 14$, $x_2 = 10$, $x_3 = 3$, $x_4 = 10$.   **d.** $d_A = 5$, $d_B = 15$, $x_1 = 7$, $x_2 = 21$, $x_3 = 14$, $x_4 = 17$.   **e.** $d_A = 11$, $d_B = 5$, $x_1 = 15$, $x_2 = 2$, $x_3 = 8$, $x_4 = 9$.

2.16.   a. $d_B = 13$, $r = 14$, $e = 12$, $m' = 5$.   **b.** $d_B = 16$, $r = 9$, $e = 15$, $m' = 10$.   **c.** $d_B = 15$, $r = 16$, $e = 14$, $m' = 10$.   **d.** $d_B = 21$, $r = 14$, $e = 12$, $m' = 5$.   **e.** $d_B = 8$, $r = 5$, $e = 5$, $m' = 10$.

2.17.   a. $N_A = 55$, $\varphi(N_A) = 40$, $c_A = 27$, $e = 23$, $m' = 12$.   **b.** $N_A = 65$, $\varphi(N_A) = 48$, $c_A = 29$, $e = 50$, $m' = 20$.   **c.** $N_A = 77$, $\varphi(N_A) = 60$, $c_A = 43$, $e = 52$, $m' = 17$.   **d.** $N_A = 91$, $\varphi(N_A) = 72$, $c_A = 29$, $e = 88$, $m' = 30$.   **e.** $N_A = 33$, $\varphi(N_A) = 20$, $c_A = 7$, $e = 9$, $m' = 15$.

2.18. $m = 111$.   **3.1.   a.** $x = 17$.   **b.** $x = 10$.   **c.** $x = 28$.   **d.** $x = 14$.   **e.** $x = 30$.

3.2.   a. $x = 20$.   **b.** $x = 45$.   **c.** $x = 34$.   **d.** $x = 53$.   **e.** $x = 25$.

3.3.   a. $x = 10000$.   **b.** $x = 20000$.   **c.** $x = 1000$.   **d.** $x = 12345$.   **e.** $x = 25000$.

4.1.   a. $s = 28$.   **b.** $s = 30$.   **c.** $s = 26$.   **d.** $s = 71$.   **e.** $s = 18$.

4.2.   a. $\langle 7, 28 \rangle$ is authentic, $\langle 22, 15 \rangle$ is not, $\langle 16, 36 \rangle$ is authentic. **b.** $\langle 6, 42 \rangle$ no, $\langle 10, 30 \rangle$ yes, $\langle 6, 41 \rangle$ yes.   **c.** $\langle 13, 41 \rangle$ yes, $\langle 11, 28 \rangle$ no, $\langle 5, 26 \rangle$ yes.   **d.** $\langle 15, 71 \rangle$ yes, $\langle 11, 46 \rangle$ no, $\langle 16, 74 \rangle$ yes.   **e.** $\langle 10, 14 \rangle$ no, $\langle 24, 18 \rangle$ yes, $\langle 17, 8 \rangle$ yes.

4.3.   a. $y = 22$, $r = 10$, $u = 15$, $k^{-1} = 15$, $s = 5$.   **b.** $y = 9$, $r = 19$, $u = 13$, $k^{-1} = 3$, $s = 17$.   **c.** $y = 10$, $r = 21$, $u = 11$, $k^{-1} = 17$, $s = 11$.   **d.** $y = 6$, $r = 17$, $u = 7$, $k^{-1} = 19$, $s = 1$.   **e.** $y = 11$, $r = 7$, $u = 18$, $k^{-1} = 7$, $s = 16$.

4.4.   a. $\langle 15; 20, 3 \rangle$ yes ($y^r = 1$, $r^s = 19$, $g^h = 19$), $\langle 15; 10, 5 \rangle$ yes ($y^r = 1$, $r^s = 19$, $g^h = 19$), $\langle 15; 19, 3 \rangle$ no ($y^r = 22$, $r^s = 5$, $g^h = 19 \neq 18$). **b.** $\langle 5; 19, 17 \rangle$ yes ($y^r = 13$, $r^s = 21$, $g^h = 20$), $\langle 7; 17, 8 \rangle$ no ($y^r = 3$, $r^s = 18$,

$g^h = 17 \neq 8$), $\langle 6; 17, 8 \rangle$ yes ($y^r = 3$, $r^s = 18$, $g^h = 8$). **c.** $\langle 3; 17, 12 \rangle$ yes ($y^r = 17$, $r^s = 6$, $g^h = 10$), $\langle 2; 17, 12 \rangle$ no ($y^r = 17$, $r^s = 6$, $g^h = 2 \neq 10$), $\langle 8; 21, 11 \rangle$ yes ($y^r = 7$, $r^s = 22$, $g^h = 16$). **d.** $\langle 5; 17, 1 \rangle$ yes ($y^r = 12$, $r^s = 17$, $g^h = 20$), $\langle 5; 11, 3 \rangle$ yes ($y^r = 1$, $r^s = 20$, $g^h = 20$), $\langle 5; 17, 10 \rangle$ no ($y^r = 12$, $r^s = 4$, $g^h = 20 \neq 2$). **e.** $\langle 15; 7, 1 \rangle$ no ($y^r = 7$, $r^s = 7$, $g^h = 19 \neq 3$), $\langle 10; 15, 3 \rangle$ yes ($y^r = 10$, $r^s = 17$, $g^h = 9$), $\langle 15; 7, 16 \rangle$ yes ($y^r = 7$, $r^s = 6$, $g^h = 19$).

4.5. **a.** $y = 14$, $r = 3$, $s = 8$. **b.** $y = 24$, $r = 3$, $s = 1$. **c.** $y = 40$, $r = 9$, $s = 8$. **d.** $y = 22$, $r = 9$, $s = 5$. **e.** $y = 64$, $r = 7$, $s = 3$.

4.6. **a.** $\langle 10; 4, 5 \rangle$ no ($s^{-1} = 9$, $u_1 = 2$, $u_2 = 3$, $a^{u_1} = 40$, $y^{u_2} = 64$, $v = 3 \neq 4$), $\langle 10; 7, 4 \rangle$ yes ($s^{-1} = 3$, $u_1 = 8$, $u_2 = 10$, $a^{u_1} = 24$, $y^{u_2} = 24$, $v = 7$), $\langle 10; 3, 8 \rangle$ yes ($s^{-1} = 7$, $u_1 = 4$, $u_2 = 10$, $a^{u_1} = 15$, $y^{u_2} = 24$, $v = 3$). **b.** $\langle 1; 3, 1 \rangle$ yes ($s^{-1} = 1$, $u_1 = 1$, $u_2 = 3$, $a^{u_1} = 25$, $y^{u_2} = 22$, $v = 3$), $\langle 1; 9, 1 \rangle$ yes ($s^{-1} = 1$, $u_1 = 1$, $u_2 = 9$, $a^{u_1} = 25$, $y^{u_2} = 62$, $v = 9$), $\langle 1; 4, 5 \rangle$ no ($s^{-1} = 9$, $u_1 = 9$, $u_2 = 3$, $a^{u_1} = 64$, $y^{u_2} = 22$, $v = 1 \neq 4$). **c.** $\langle 7; 7, 4 \rangle$ yes ($s^{-1} = 3$, $u_1 = 10$, $u_2 = 10$, $a^{u_1} = 59$, $y^{u_2} = 62$, $v = 7$), $\langle 7; 9, 2 \rangle$ no ($s^{-1} = 6$, $u_1 = 9$, $u_2 = 10$, $a^{u_1} = 64$, $y^{u_2} = 62$, $v = 4 \neq 9$), $\langle 5; 9, 8 \rangle$ yes ($s^{-1} = 7$, $u_1 = 2$, $u_2 = 8$, $a^{u_1} = 22$, $y^{u_2} = 9$, $v = 9$). **d.** $\langle 6; 9, 5 \rangle$ yes ($s^{-1} = 9$, $u_1 = 10$, $u_2 = 4$, $a^{u_1} = 59$, $y^{u_2} = 24$, $v = 9$), $\langle 8; 8, 3 \rangle$ no ($s^{-1} = 4$, $u_1 = 10$, $u_2 = 10$, $a^{u_1} = 59$, $y^{u_2} = 64$, $v = 2 \neq 8$), $\langle 7; 4, 7 \rangle$ yes ($s^{-1} = 8$, $u_1 = 1$, $u_2 = 10$, $a^{u_1} = 25$, $y^{u_2} = 64$, $v = 4$). **e.** $\langle 10; 7, 8 \rangle$ yes ($s^{-1} = 7$, $u_1 = 4$, $u_2 = 5$, $a^{u_1} = 15$, $y^{u_2} = 25$, $v = 7$), $\langle 7; 7, 3 \rangle$ yes ($s^{-1} = 4$, $u_1 = 6$, $u_2 = 6$, $a^{u_1} = 62$, $y^{u_2} = 59$, $v = 7$), $\langle 8; 7, 5 \rangle$ no ($s^{-1} = 9$, $u_1 = 6$, $u_2 = 8$, $a^{u_1} = 62$, $y^{u_2} = 62$, $v = 3 \neq 7$).

5.1. **a.** $d_A = 17$, $d_B = 9$, Alice's hand is γ, Bob's is β; transmitted over the channel are the numbers (11, 20, 21), (11), (14, 10), (17). **b.** $d_A = 19$, $d_B = 3$, Alice's hand is γ, Bob's is α; transmitted over the channel are the numbers (17, 19, 5), (19), (15, 19), (19). **c.** $d_A = 7$, $d_B = 15$, Alice's hand is α, Bob's is β; transmitted over the channel are the numbers (11, 7, 10), (7), (11, 20), (21). **d.** $d_A = 5$, $d_B = 19$, Alice's hand is α, Bob's is β; transmitted over the channel are the numbers (21, 15, 11), (11), (10, 11), (5). **e.** $d_A = 3$, $d_B = 9$, Alice's hand is α, Bob's is γ; transmitted over the channel are the numbers (19, 14, 17), (19), (21, 15), (15).

5.2. **a.** $\hat{n} = 103$, $\hat{s} = 52$, $r^{-1} = 24$, bank note is $\langle 11, 58 \rangle$. **b.** $\hat{n} = 13$, $\hat{s} = 13$, $r^{-1} = 20$, bank note is $\langle 99, 22 \rangle$. **c.** $\hat{n} = 58$, $\hat{s} = 74$, $r^{-1} = 12$, bank note is $\langle 55, 55 \rangle$. **d.** $\hat{n} = 37$, $\hat{s} = 46$, $r^{-1} = 8$, bank note is $\langle 44, 11 \rangle$. **e.** $\hat{n} = 49$, $\hat{s} = 70$, $r^{-1} = 4$, bank note is $\langle 77, 42 \rangle$.

6.1. Only the following points from the list are on the curve: $(1,1)$, $(2,1)$, and $(5,8)$.

6.2. $[2](2,2) = (3,5)$, $[2](4,6) = (1,3)$, $(1,3) + (1,4) = \mathcal{O}$, $(2,2) + (3,2) = (2,5)$, $(3,5) + (5,1) = (3,2)$.   **7.1.**   **a.** $\bar{e} = 1111001110.$ **b.** $\bar{e} = 1111110101.$ **c.** $\bar{e} = 0001000110.$ **d.** $\bar{e} = 0101011011.$ **e.** $\bar{e} = 0001010001.$

7.2.   **a.** $P_1 \approx 0.002$, $P_2 \approx 0.006$, $P_3 \approx 0.623$, $P_4 \approx 0.051$, $P_5 \approx 0.311$, $P_6 \approx 0.007$.   **b.** $P_1 \approx 0.000$, $P_2 \approx 0.009$, $P_3 \approx 0.000$, $P_4 \approx 0.000$, $P_5 \approx 0.892$, $P_6 \approx 0.099$.   **c.** $P_1 \approx 0.000$, $P_2 \approx 0.697$, $P_3 \approx 0.000$, $P_4 \approx 0.004$, $P_5 \approx 0.299$, $P_6 \approx 0.000$.   **d.** $P_1 \approx 0.003$, $P_2 \approx 0.000$, $P_3 \approx 0.036$, $P_4 \approx 0.000$, $P_5 \approx 0.801$, $P_6 \approx 0.160$.   **e.** $P_1 \approx 0.196$, $P_2 \approx 0.000$, $P_3 \approx 0.001$, $P_4 \approx 0.000$, $P_5 \approx 0.018$, $P_6 \approx 0.785$.

7.3.   **a.** $H \approx 1.16$, $n \approx 6.04$.   **b.** $H \approx 0.52$, $n \approx 2.42$.   **c.** $H \approx 0.9$, $n \approx 3.76$.   **d.** $H \approx 1.08$, $n \approx 5.08$.   **e.** $H \approx 1.16$, $n \approx 6.04$.

7.4.   **a.** $P_1 \approx 0.7$ ($\bar{m} = bcacbcacc$), $P_2 = 0$, $P_3 \approx 0.3$ ($\bar{m} = acbcacbcc$), $P_4 = 0$, $P_5 = 0$, $P_6 = 0$.   **b.** $P_1 = 0$, $P_2 = 0$, $P_3 = 0$, $P_4 \approx 0.21$ ($\bar{m} = bcccaccac$), $P_5 \approx 0.20$ ($\bar{m} = abbbcbbcb$), $P_6 \approx 0.59$ ($\bar{m} = acccbccbc$). **c.** $P_1 = 0$, $P_2 = 0$, $P_3 = 0$, $P_4 = 1$ ($\bar{m} = ccbcabccb$), $P_5 = 0$, $P_6 = 0$. **d.** $P_1 = 0$, $P_2 = 0$, $P_3 \approx 0.000$ ($\bar{m} = acbbbbcbb$), $P_4 \approx 1.000$ ($\bar{m} = abcccbcc$), $P_5 = 0$, $P_6 = 0$.   **e.** $P_1 = 0$, $P_2 = 0$, $P_3 \approx 0.009$ ($\bar{m} = bbbcbbbcb$), $P_4 \approx 0.970$ ($\bar{m} = cccbcccbc$), $P_5 = 0$, $P_6 \approx 0.021$ ($\bar{m} = cccacccac$).

Bibliography

Adleman, L. M. (1979). A subexponential algorithm for the discrete logarithm problem with applications to crypotgraphy, *Proc. IEEE 20th Ann. Symp. on Foundations of Comput. Sci.*, pp. 55–60.

Agrawal, M., Kayal, N. and Saxena N. (2002). *PRIMES is in P*, available on-line: http://www.cse.iitk.ac.in/users/manindra.

Aho, A. V., Hopcroft, J. E. and Ulman, J. D. (1976). *The Design and Analysis of Computer Algorithms*, Addison–Wesley, Reading MA.

Alexi, W., Chor, B., Goldreich, O. and Schnorr, C. P. (1988). RSA and Rabin functions: Certain parts are as hard as the whole, *SIAM J. on Comput.*, **17**, pp. 194–209.

Bellare, M. and Rogaway, P. (2004). *Introduction to Modern Cryptography*, http://www-cse.ucsd.edu/users/mihir/crypto-lecnotes.html.

Bently, J. L., Sleator, D. D., Tarjan, R. E. and Wei, V. K. (1986). A locally adaptive data compression scheme, *Comm. ACM*, **29**, pp. 320–330.

Billingsley, P. (1965). *Ergodic Theory and Information*, John Wiley & Sons, New York.

Blahut, R. E. (1987). *Principles and Practice of Information Theory*, Addison–Wesley, Reading, MA.

Blake, I., Seroussi, G. and Smart, N. (1999). *Elliptic Curves in Cryptography*, Cambridge University Press.

Blum, M. (1986). How to prove a theorem so no one else can claim it, *Proc. Int. Congress of Mathematicians*, Berkeley, CA, pp. 1444–1451.

Chaum, D. (1983). Blind signatures for untraceable payments, *Advances in Cryptology — Proc. Crypto 82*, pp. 199–203.

Chaum, D. (1985). Security without identification: transaction systems to make big brother obsolete, *Comm ACM*, **28**, pp. 1030–1044.

Cormen, T. H., Leiserson, C. E. and Rivest, R. L. (1990). *Introduction to Algorithms*, MIT Press, Cambridge, MA.

Daemen, J. and Rijmen, V. (2002) *The Design of Rijndael*, Springer. (see also http://csrc.nist.gov/CryptoToolkit/aes/rijndael/).

Diffie, W. and Hellman, M. E. (1976). New directions in cryptography, *IEEE Trans. Inform. Theory*, **22**, pp. 644–654.

ElGamal, T. (1985). A public key cryptosystem and a signature scheme based on discrete logarithms, *IEEE Trans. Inform. Theory*, **31**, pp. 469–472.

Elias, P. (1987). Interval and recency rank source coding: two on-line adaptive variable-length schemes, *IEEE Trans. Inform. Theory*, **33**, 1, pp. 3–10.

Feistel, H. (1973). Cryptography and computer privacy, *Scientific American*, **228**, pp. 15–23.

Feller, W. (1968). *An Introduction to Probability Theory and its Applications*, John Wiley & Sons, New York, 3rd edition.

FIPS 180-1. (1995). *Secure Hash Standard*, Federal Information Processing Standards Publication 180-1, U.S. Department of Commerce/N.I.S.T., National Technical Information Service, Springfield, Virginia.

FIPS 186-2. (2000). *Digital Signature Standard*, Federal Information Processing Standards Publication 186-2, U.S. Department of Commerce/N.I.S.T., National Technical Information Service, Springfield, Virginia.

FIPS 197. (2001) *Advanced Encryption Standard*, Federal Information Processing Standards Publication 197, U.S. Department of Commerce/N.I.S.T., National Technical Information Service, Springfield, Virginia.

Gallager, R. G. (1968). *Information Theory and Reliable Communication*, John Wiley & Sons, New York.

Goldreich, O., Micali, S. and Wigderson A. (1987). How to prove all NP statements in zero knowledge and a methodology of cryptographic protocol design, *Advances in Cryptology — CRYPTO 86*, SpringerVerlag, pp. 171–185.

Goldwasser, S. and Bellare, M. (2001). *Lecture Notes on Cryptography*, http://www-cse.ucsd.edu/users/mihir/crypto-lecnotes.html.

Kahn, D. (1967). *The Codebreakers*, Macmillan Publishing Company, New York.

Kendall, M. G. and Stuart, A. (1961) *The Advanced Theory of Statistics*, **2** — *Inference and Relationship*, London.

Kerckhoffs, A. (1883). La cryptographie militaire, *J. des Sciences Militaires*, **9**, pp. 161–191.

Knuth, D. E. (1973). *The Art of Computer Programming*, **3** — *Sorting and Searching*, Addison–Wesley, Reading, MA.

Knuth, D. E. (1981). *The Art of Computer Programming*, **2** — *Semi-numerical Algorithms*, Addison–Wesley, Reading, MA, 2nd edition.

Koblitz, N. (1987). Elliptic curve cryptosystems, *Math. of Comp.*, **48**, pp. 203–209.

Krichevsky, R. (1993). *Universal Compression and Retrival*, Kluver Academic Publishers.

Lenstra, A. K. and Lenstra, H. W., editors. (1993). *The Development of the Number Field Sieve*, Springer-Verlag, LNM, **1554**.

McEliece, R. J. (1984). *The Theory of Information and Coding: A Mathematical Framework for Communication*, Cambridge University Press, Cambridge.

Menezes, A. (1993) *Elliptic Curve Public Key Cryptosystems*, Kluwer Academic Publishers.

Menezes, A., van Oorschot, P. and Vanstone, S. (1996) *Handbook of Applied Cryptography*, CRC Press.

Mercle, R. C. (1979). *Secrecy, Authentication, and Public Key Systems*, UMI

Research Press, Ann Arbor, Michigan.

Miller, V. S. (1986). Use of elliptic curves in cryptography, *Advances in cryptology — CRYPTO'85*, LNCS, **218**, pp. 417–426.

Montgomery, P. L. (1985). Modular multiplication without trial division, *Math. Comp.*, **44**, pp. 519–521.

Needham, R. M. and Schroeder, M. D. (1978). Using encryption for authentication in large networks of computers, *Comm. ACM*, **21**, pp. 993–999.

Nisan, N. and Ta-Shma, A. (1999). Extracting randomness: a survey and new constructions, *J. Comp. and System Sci.*, **58**, 1, pp. 148–173.

Nisan, N. and Zuckerman, D. (1996). Randomness is linear in space, *J. Comp. and System Sci.*, **52**, 1, pp. 43-52.

Papadimitriou, C. H. (1994). *Computational Complexity*, Addison–Wesley, Reading, MA.

Plumstead, J. B. (1982). Inferring a sequence produced by a linear congruence, *Advances in Cryptology - Proc. Crypto 82*, pp. 317–319.

Pohlig, S. C. and Hellman, M. E. (1978). An improved algorithm for computing logarithms over $GF(p)$ and its cryptographic significance, *IEEE Trans. Inform. Theory*, **24**, pp. 106–110.

Rivest, R. L., Shamir, A. and Adleman, L. M. (1978). A method for obtaining digital signatures and public-key cryptosystems, *Comm. ACM*, **21**, pp. 120–126.

Rivest, R. L., Robshaw, M. J. B., Sidney, R. and Yin, Y. L. (1998) *The RC6 Block Cipher*, http://www.rsasecurity.com/rsalabs/.

Rosen, K. H. (1992). *Elementary Number Theory and its Applications*, Addison–Wesley, Reading, MA.

Rukhin, A. *et al.* (2001). *A Statistical Test Suite for Random and Pseudorandom Number Generators for Cryptographic Applications*, NIST Special Publication 800-22 (rev. May, 15, 2001).

Ryabko, B. Ya. (1980). Information compression by a book stack, *Probl. Inform. Transmission*, **16**, 4, pp. 16–21.

Ryabko, B. Ya. (1998). The fast enumeration of combinatorial objects, *Discrete Math. and Applications*, **10**, 2, pp. 101–119.

Ryabko, B. Ya. (2000). Simply realizable ideal cryptographic system, *Probl. Inform. Transmission*, **36**, 1, pp. 90–95.

Ryabko, B. Ya., Stognienko, V. S. and Shokin, Yu. I. (2004). A new test for randomness and its application to some cryptographic problems, *J. Statistical Planning and Inference*, **123**, 2, pp. 365–376.

Ryabko, B. and Fionov, A. (1997). The fast method of randomization, *Probl. Inform. Transmission*, **33**, 3, pp. 3–14.

Ryabko, B. and Fionov, A. (1999a). Efficient homophonic coding, *IEEE Trans. Inform. Theory*, **45**, 6, pp. 2083–2091.

Ryabko, B. and Fionov, A. (1999b) Fast and space-efficient adaptive arithmetic coding, *Cryptography and Coding*, Springer, LNCS, **1746**, pp. 270–279.

Ryabko, B. and Matchikina, E. (2000). Fast and efficient construction of an unbiased random sequence, *IEEE Trans. Inform. Theory*, **46**, 3, pp. 1090–1093.

Ryabko, B. Ya. and Monarev, V. A. (2004). Using information theory approach to randomness testing, *J. Statistical Planning and Inference*, in press.

Ryabko, B. and Pestunov, A. (2004). "Book stack" as a new statistical test for random numbers, *Probl. Inform. Transmission*, **40**, 1, pp. 66–71.

Schneier, B. (1996). *Applied Cryptography, Second Edition: Protocols, Algorthms, and Source Code in C*, John Wiley & Sons, New York.

Schneier, B. (2000). Self-study course in block cipher cryptanalysis, *Cryptologia*, **24**, 1, pp. 18–34.

Schoof, R. (1995). Counting points on elliptic curves over finite fields, *J. Théorie des Nombres de Bordeaux*, **7**, pp. 219–254.

Shannon, C. E. (1948). A mathematical theory of communication, *Bell System Technical J.*, **27**, pp. 379–423, 623–656.

Shannon, C. E. (1949). Communication theory of secrecy systems, *Bell System Technical J.*, **28**, pp. 656–715.

Silverman, J., H. (1986). *The Arithmetic of Elliptic Curves*, Springer-Verlag, GTM 106.

Vernam, G. S. (1926). Cipher printing telegraph systems for secret wire and radio telegraphic communications, *J. American Inst. Electrical Eng.*, **55**, pp. 109–115.

Welsh, D. (1988). *Codes and Cryptography*, Claredon Press, Oxford.

Author Index

Adleman, L. M.   27, 37, 39, 43

Blum, M.   63

Chaum, D.   71

Daemen, J.   141, 148
Diffie, W.   6, 12, 13

ElGamal, T.   24, 46
Elias, P.   172

Feistel, H.   142
Fionov, A. N.   130

Hasse, H.   102
Hellman, M. E.   6, 12–14, 92

Kahn, D.   6
Kerckhoffs, A.   3
Koblitz, N.   83

Matchikina, E.   173
Menezes, A.   93
Mercle, R. C.   6
Miller, V. S.   83
Monarev, V. A.   175
Montgomery, P. L.   102

Needham, R. M.   79
Neumann, J. von   171
Nisan, N.   171

Okamoto, T.   93

Pestunov, A.   175
Plumstead, J. B.   161
Pohlig, S. C.   14, 92

Rijmen, V.   141, 148
Rivest, R. L.   27, 43, 144, 163
Ryabko, B. Ya.   130–132, 173, 175, 176

Schoof, R.   102
Schroeder, M. D.   79
Shamir, A.   22, 27, 43
Shannon, C. E.   5, 115, 118, 119, 130
Shokin, Yu. I.   175
Stognienko, V. S.   176

Ta-Shma, A.   171

Vanstone, S.   93
Vernam, G. S.   118

Zuckerman, D.   171

193

Subject Index

AES block cipher, 92, 141, 148
asymmetric-key, *see* public key
attack, 3, 76

baby-step giant-step algorithm, 9,
  35–37, 91
blind signature, 72, 73
block cipher, 140, 166
book stack test, 176
brute-force attack, 3

Caesar cipher, 2, 137
CBC block cipher mode, 159
challenge–response protocol, 12
chi-square test, 176
Chinese remainder theorem, 104, 109
chosen-plaintext attack, 5, 140, 179
cipher key, *see* secret key
ciphertext, 2
ciphertext-only attack, 5, 139
computationally secure cipher, 137
coprime numbers, 15
cryptogram, 116
cryptographic protocol, 55
cryptosystem, 3
CTR block cipher mode, 163, 180

DES block cipher, 141
differential cryptanalysis, 140, 148
Diffie–Hellman key agreement, *see*
  Diffie–Hellman system
Diffie–Hellman system, 12–15, 24, 41,

76, 77, 115
digital cash protocol, 70–75
digital signature, 30, 43, 72, 77, 165
digital signature algorithm, *see* DSA
discrete logarithm, 8
discrete logarithm problem, 14, 24,
  26, 33–41, 46, 58
DSA, 49–52, 95

ECB block cipher mode, 159
ElGamal cipher, *see* ElGamal
  encryption
ElGamal digital signature, 46–49
ElGamal encryption, 24–26, 41, 46,
  80, 94
elliptic curve, 83, 84
  affine representation, 97
  anomalous, 93
  discrete logarithm problem, 91, 94
  division polynomial, 103
  mixed addition, 99
  point addition, *see* point
    composition
  point at infinity, 86
  point composition, 85, 96, 97, 100,
    101
  point doubling, *see* point
    composition
  point multiplication, 91, 96
  projective representation, 98
  singular, 85
  supersingular, 93

torsion point, 103
entropy, *see* Shannon entropy
Euclidean algorithm, 17, 109
Euler (totient) function, 16
Euler theorem, 16
exhaustive key search, 4, 140
exponentiation, 8, 9, 21
extended Euclidean algorithm, 18, 20, 98

Feistel structure, 142
Fermat theorem, 16
frequency cryptanalysis, 138

gcd, *see* greatest common divisor
GOST 28147-89 block cipher, 141–144
gradient statistical attack, 178
graph colouring problem, 60–63
greatest common divisor, 17

Hamiltonian cycle problem, 63, 64
hash function, 8, 44, 46, 50, 74, 112, 165

ideal cryptosystem, *see* strongly ideal cryptosystem
identification, 77
index calculus algorithm, 37–41
initialisation vector, 159
integer factorisation problem, 29, 41, 46
inverse cipher, 2, 139, 140
inverse number, 19
inverse polynomial, 151

Kerckhoffs assumptions, 3
key agreement, 13
key distribution scheme, 12
key establishment, *see also* key agreement, 77–80
key source, 3
known-plaintext attack, 5, 139, 149, 163

linear congruential generator, 161

linear cryptanalysis, 140, 148

Markov source, 128
memoryless source, 124, 125
mental poker, 55–59
mutual identification, 76, 78–80

Needham–Schroeder protocol, 79, 80, 115
NP-complete problem, 60, 64
number field sieve, 41

OFB block cipher mode, 162
one-time pad, *see* Vernam cipher
one-way function, 7, 27, 29, 73, 174

password, 7, 10–12
perfect secrecy, *see* perfectly secure cryptosystem
perfectly secure cryptosystem, 116–118, 131
plaintext, 2
Pohlig–Hellman algorithm, 14, 92
prime number, 15
private key, 13, 25, 27, 44, 46, 49, 94
pseudo-random number generator, 160, 173
pseudo-random sequence, 145
public key, 6, 13, 25, 27, 44, 46, 49, 77, 94
public key certification, 76
public-key cipher, 77, 137

random number, 169
random number generator, 13, 170
randomised cipher, 66
randomness testing, 175, 178
RC4 stream cipher, 163–165
RC5 block cipher, 144–146, 179
RC6 block cipher, 144, 146–148
redundancy, 5, 74, 79, 124
relatively prime numbers, *see* coprime numbers
Rijndael block cipher, 144, 148–158
round key, 142
round key schedule, 145

round of cipher, 140
RSA cipher, *see* RSA encryption
RSA digital signature, 30, 43–46, 71
RSA encryption, 27–30, 41, 46, 62,
    65, 68, 77, 93, 174
RSA multiplicative property, 73, 74
RSA-based generator, 174
running-key cipher, 162

S-box, 142, 152
Schoof's algorithm, 102–110
secret key, 2, 76, 94
secret-key cryptosystem, 125
secure channel, 2, 115
secured channel, 115
Shamir cipher, 22–24, 41
Shannon entropy, 120, 172, 173
smooth number, 37
statistical test, 170
stream cipher, 160
strongly ideal cipher, 130
strongly ideal cryptosystem, 119

theoretically secure ciphers, 137
trace of Frobenius, 102
trapdoor function, 27, 29

unicity distance, 127, 128

Vernam cipher, 118–119, 130, 160

zero-knowledge proof, 59–70

Printed in the United States
By Bookmasters